Which would you want to carry to the client's site?

FIPS PUB 140-2

CHANGE NOTICES (12-03-2002)

FEDERAL INFORMATION PROCESSING STANDARDS PUBLICATION
(Supercedes FIPS PUB 140-1, 1994 January 11)

SECURITY REQUIREMENTS FOR CRYPTOGRAPHIC MODULES

CATEGORY: COMPUTER SECURITY   SUBCATEGORY: CRYPTOGRAPHY

Information Technology Laboratory
National Institute of Standards and Technology
Gaithersburg, MD 20899-8900

Issued May 25, 2001

U.S. Department of Commerce
Donald L. Evans, Secretary

Technology Administration
Phillip J. Bond, Under Secretary for Technology

National Institute of Standards and Technology
Arden L. Bement, Jr., Director

Foreword

The Federal Information Processing Standards Publication Series of the National Institute of Standards and Technology (NIST) is the official series of publications relating to standards and guidelines adopted and promulgated under the provisions of Section 5131 of the Information Technology Management Reform Act of 1996 (Public Law 104-106) and the Computer Security Act of 1987 (Public Law 100-235). These mandates have given the Secretary of Commerce and NIST important responsibilities for improving the utilization and management of computer and related telecommunications systems in the Federal government. The NIST, through its Information Technology Laboratory, provides leadership, technical guidance, and coordination of government efforts in the development of standards and guidelines in these areas.

Comments concerning Federal Information Processing Standards Publications are welcomed and should be addressed to the Director, Information Technology Laboratory, National Institute of Standards and Technology, 100 Bureau Drive, Stop 8900, Gaithersburg, MD 20899-8900.

William Mehuron, Director
Information Technology Laboratory

Abstract

The selective application of technological and related procedural safeguards is an important responsibility of every Federal organization in providing adequate security in its computer and telecommunication systems. This publication provides a standard that will be used by Federal organizations when these organizations specify that cryptographic-based security systems are to be used to provide protection for sensitive or valuable data. Protection of a cryptographic module within a security system is necessary to maintain the confidentiality and integrity of the information protected by the module. This standard specifies the security requirements that will be satisfied by a cryptographic module. The standard provides four increasing, qualitative levels of security intended to cover a wide range of potential applications and environments. The security requirements cover areas related to the secure design and implementation of a cryptographic module. These areas include cryptographic module specification; cryptographic module ports and interfaces; roles, services, and authentication; finite state model; physical security; operational environment; cryptographic key management; electromagnetic interference/electromagnetic compatibility (EMI/EMC); self-tests; design assurance; and mitigation of other attacks.

Key words: computer security, telecommunication security, cryptography, cryptographic modules, Federal Information Processing Standard (FIPS).

National Institute of Standards and Technology
FIPS PUB 140-2
64 pages (May 25, 2001)

U.S. Government Printing Office
Washington: 2001

For Sale by the National
Technical Information
Service
U.S. Department of Commerce

**Federal Information
Processing Standards Publication 140-2**

May 25, 2001

Announcing the Standard for

SECURITY REQUIREMENTS FOR CRYPTOGRAPHIC MODULES

Federal Information Processing Standards Publications (FIPS PUBS) are issued by the National Institute of Standards and Technology (NIST) after approval by the Secretary of Commerce pursuant to Section 5131 of the Information Technology Management Reform Act of 1996 (Public Law 104-106) and the Computer Security Act of 1987 (Public Law 100-235).

1. **Name of Standard.** Security Requirements for Cryptographic Modules (FIPS PUB 140-2).

2. **Category of Standard.** Computer Security Standard, Cryptography.

3. **Explanation.** This standard specifies the security requirements that will be satisfied by a cryptographic module utilized within a security system protecting sensitive but unclassified information (hereafter referred to as sensitive information). The standard provides four increasing, qualitative levels of security: Level 1, Level 2, Level 3, and Level 4. These levels are intended to cover the wide range of potential applications and environments in which cryptographic modules may be employed. The security requirements cover areas related to the secure design and implementation of a cryptographic module. These areas include cryptographic module specification, cryptographic module ports and interfaces; roles, services, and authentication; finite state model; physical security; operational environment; cryptographic key management; electromagnetic interference/electromagnetic compatibility (EMI/EMC); self-tests; design assurance; and mitigation of other attacks. This standard supersedes FIPS 140-1, *Security Requirements for Cryptographic Modules*, in its entirety.

The Cryptographic Module Validation Program (CMVP) validates cryptographic modules to Federal Information Processing Standard (FIPS) 140-2 and other cryptography based standards. The CMVP is a joint effort between NIST and the Communications Security Establishment (CSE) of the Government of Canada. Products validated as conforming to FIPS 140-2 are accepted by the Federal agencies of both countries for the protection of sensitive information (United States) or Designated Information (Canada). The goal of the CMVP is to promote the use of validated cryptographic modules and provide Federal agencies with a security metric to use in procuring equipment containing validated cryptographic modules.

In the CMVP, vendors of cryptographic modules use independent, accredited testing laboratories to have their modules tested. National Voluntary Laboratory Accreditation Program (NVLAP) accredited laboratories perform cryptographic module compliance/conformance testing.

4. **Approving Authority.** Secretary of Commerce.

5. **Maintenance Agency.** Department of Commerce, National Institute of Standards and Technology, Information Technology Laboratory (ITL).

6. **Cross Index.**

    a. FIPS PUB 46-3, Data Encryption Standard.
    b. FIPS PUB 74, Guidelines for Implementing and Using the NBS Data Encryption Standard.
    c. FIPS PUB 81, DES Modes of Operation.
    d. FIPS PUB 113, Computer Data Authentication.

e. FIPS PUB 171, Key Management Using ANSI X9.17.
f. FIPS PUB 180-1, Secure Hash Standard.
g. FIPS PUB 186-2, Digital Signature Standard.
h. Special Publication 800-2, Public Key Cryptography.
i. Special Publication 800-20, Modes of Operation Validation System for the Triple Data Encryption Algorithm (TMOVS): Requirements and Procedures

These documents may be found at the CMVP URL http://www.nist.gov/cmvp. Other NIST publications may be applicable to the implementation and use of this standard. A list (NIST Publications List 91) of currently available computer security publications, including ordering information, can be obtained from NIST.

7. Applicability. This standard is applicable to all Federal agencies that use cryptographic-based security systems to protect sensitive information in computer and telecommunication systems (including voice systems) as defined in Section 5131 of the Information Technology Management Reform Act of 1996, Public Law 104-106. This standard shall be used in designing and implementing cryptographic modules that Federal departments and agencies operate or are operated for them under contract. Cryptographic modules that have been approved for classified use may be used in lieu of modules that have been validated against this standard. The adoption and use of this standard is available to private and commercial organizations.

8. Applications. Cryptographic-based security systems may be utilized in various computer and telecommunication applications (e.g., data storage, access control and personal identification, network communications, radio, facsimile, and video) and in various environments (e.g., centralized computer facilities, office environments, and hostile environments). The cryptographic services (e.g., encryption, authentication, digital signature, and key management) provided by a cryptographic module are based on many factors that are specific to the application and environment. The security level to which a cryptographic module is validated must be chosen to provide a level of security appropriate for the security requirements of the application and environment in which the module will be utilized and the security services that the module will provide. The security requirements for a particular security level include both the security requirements specific to that level and the security requirements that apply to all modules regardless of the level.

9. Specifications. Federal Information Processing Standard (FIPS) 140-2, Security Requirements for Cryptographic Modules (affixed).

10. Implementations. This standard covers implementations of cryptographic modules including, but not limited to, hardware components or modules, software/firmware programs or modules or any combination thereof. Cryptographic modules that are validated under the CMVP will be considered as conforming to this standard. Information about the CMVP can be obtained from the

a. National Institute of Standards and Technology, Information Technology Laboratory, 100 Bureau Drive, Stop 8900, Gaithersburg, MD 20899-8900.
b. Communications Security Establishment, ITS Client Services, 1500 Bronson Ave., Ottawa, ON K1G 3Z4.
c. CMVP URL http://www.nist.gov/cmvp.

11. Approved Security Functions. Cryptographic modules that conform to this standard shall employ Approved security functions such as cryptographic algorithms, cryptographic key management techniques, and authentication techniques that have been approved for protecting Federal government sensitive information. Approved security functions include those that are either:

a. specified in a Federal Information Processing Standard (FIPS),
b. adopted in a FIPS and specified either in an appendix to the FIPS or in a document referenced by the FIPS, or
c. specified in the list of Approved security functions.

12. Interpretation. Questions concerning the content and specifications of this standard should be addressed to: Director, Information Technology Laboratory, ATTN: FIPS 140-2 Interpretation, National Institute of Standards and Technology, 100 Bureau Drive, Stop 8900, Gaithersburg, MD 20899-8900. Resolution of questions regarding this standard will be provided by the validation authorities at NIST and CSE.

13. Export Control. Certain cryptographic devices and technical data regarding them are subject to Federal export controls and exports of cryptographic modules implementing this standard and technical data regarding them must comply with these Federal regulations and be licensed by the Bureau of Export Administration of the U.S. Department of Commerce. Applicable Federal government export controls are specified in Title 15, Code of Federal Regulations (CFR) Part 740.17; Title 15, CFR Part 742; and Title 15, CFR Part 774, Category 5, Part 2.

14. Implementation Schedule. This standard becomes effective six months after approval by the Secretary of Commerce. A transition period from November 25, 2001 until six months after the effective date is provided to enable all agencies to develop plans for the acquisition of products that are compliant with FIPS 140-2. Agencies may retain and use FIPS 140-1 validated products that have been purchased before the end of the transition period. After the transition period, modules will no longer be tested against the FIPS 140-1 requirements. After the transition period, all previous validations against FIPS 140-1 will still be recognized. Figure 1 summarizes the FIPS 140-2 implementation schedule.

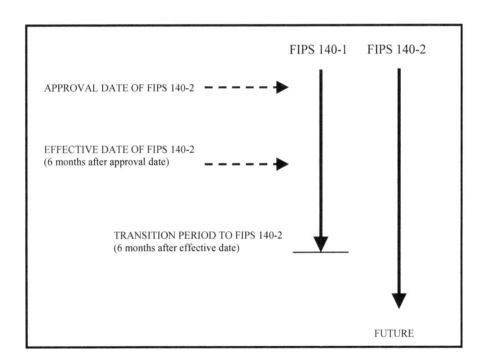

Figure 1. *FIPS 140-2 Implementation Schedule*

15. Qualifications. The security requirements specified in this standard are based upon information provided by many sources within the Federal government and private industry. The requirements are designed to protect against adversaries mounting cost-effective attacks on sensitive government or commercial data (e.g., hackers, organized crime, and economic competitors). The primary goal in designing an effective security system is to make the cost of any attack greater than the possible payoff.

While the security requirements specified in this standard are intended to maintain the security provided by a cryptographic module, conformance to this standard is not sufficient to ensure that a particular module is secure. The operator of a cryptographic module is responsible for ensuring that the security provided by a module is sufficient and acceptable to the owner of the information that is being protected and that any residual risk is acknowledged and accepted.

Similarly, the use of a validated cryptographic module in a computer or telecommunications system does not guarantee the security of the overall system. The responsible authority in each agency shall ensure that the security of the system is sufficient and acceptable.

Since a standard of this nature must be flexible enough to adapt to advancements and innovations in science and technology, this standard will be reviewed every five years in order to consider new or revised requirements that may be needed to meet technological and economic changes.

16. Waiver Procedure. Under certain exceptional circumstances, the heads of Federal agencies, or their delegates, may approve waivers to Federal Information Processing Standards (FIPS), for their agency. The heads of such agencies may redelegate such authority only to a senior official designated pursuant to Section 3506(b) of Title 44, U.S. Code. Waivers shall be granted only when compliance with a standard would

    a. adversely affect the accomplishment of the mission of an operator of Federal computer system or

    b. cause a major adverse financial impact on the operator that is not offset by government-wide savings.

Agency heads may act upon a written waiver request containing the information detailed above. Agency heads may also act without a written waiver request when they determine which conditions for meeting the standard cannot be met. Agency heads may approve waivers only by a written decision that explains the basis on which the agency head made the required finding(s). A copy of each such decision, with procurement sensitive or classified portions clearly identified, shall be sent to: National Institute of Standards and Technology; ATTN: FIPS Waiver Decision, Information Technology Laboratory, 100 Bureau Drive, Stop 8900, Gaithersburg, MD 20899-8900.

In addition, notice of each waiver granted and each delegation of authority to approve waivers shall be sent promptly to the Committee on Government Operations of the House of Representatives and the Committee on Government Affairs of the Senate and shall be published promptly in the Federal Register.

When the determination on a waiver applies to the procurement of equipment and/or services, a notice of the waiver determination must be published in the Commerce Business Daily as a part of the notice of solicitation for offers of an acquisition or, if the waiver determination is made after that notice is published, by amendment to such notice.

A copy of the waiver, any supporting documents, the document approving the waiver and any supporting and accompanying documents, with such deletions as the agency is authorized and decides to make under Section 552(b) of Title 5, U.S. Code, shall be part of the procurement documentation and retained by the agency.

17. Where to obtain copies. Copies of this publication are available from the URL: http://csrc.nist.gov/publications. Copies are available for sale by the National Technical Information Service, U.S. Department of Commerce, Springfield, VA 22161. When ordering, refer to Federal Information Processing Standards Publication 140-2 (FIPSPUB1402) and identify the title. When microfiche is desired, this should be specified. Prices are published by NTIS in current catalogs and other issuances. Payment may be made by check, money order, deposit account, or charged to a credit card accepted by NTIS.

18. CHANGE NOTICE. See important change notice at the end of this document.

TABLE OF CONTENTS

1. OVERVIEW

This standard specifies the security requirements for a cryptographic module utilized within a security system protecting sensitive information in computer and telecommunication systems (including voice systems) as defined in Section 5131 of the Information Technology Management Reform Act of 1996, Public Law 104-106.

FIPS 140-1 was developed by a government and industry working group composed of both operators and vendors. The working group identified requirements for four security levels for cryptographic modules to provide for a wide spectrum of data sensitivity (e.g., low value administrative data, million dollar funds transfers, and life protecting data) and a diversity of application environments (e.g., a guarded facility, an office, and a completely unprotected location). Four security levels are specified for each of 11 requirement areas. Each security level offers an increase in security over the preceding level. These four increasing levels of security allow cost-effective solutions that are appropriate for different degrees of data sensitivity and different application environments. FIPS 140-2 incorporates changes in applicable standards and technology since the development of FIPS 140-1 as well as changes that are based on comments received from the vendor, laboratory, and user communities.

While the security requirements specified in this standard are intended to maintain the security provided by a cryptographic module, conformance to this standard is not sufficient to ensure that a particular module is secure. The operator of a cryptographic module is responsible for ensuring that the security provided by the module is sufficient and acceptable to the owner of the information that is being protected, and that any residual risk is acknowledged and accepted.

Similarly, the use of a validated cryptographic module in a computer or telecommunications system is not sufficient to ensure the security of the overall system. The overall security level of a cryptographic module must be chosen to provide a level of security appropriate for the security requirements of the application and environment in which the module is to be utilized and for the security services that the module is to provide. The responsible authority in each organization should ensure that their computer and telecommunication systems that utilize cryptographic modules provide an acceptable level of security for the given application and environment.

The importance of security awareness and of making information security a management priority should be communicated to all users. Since information security requirements vary for different applications, organizations should identify their information resources and determine the sensitivity to and the potential impact of losses. Controls should be based on the potential risks and should be selected from available controls, including administrative policies and procedures, physical and environmental controls, information and data controls, software development and acquisition controls, and backup and contingency planning.

The following sections provide an overview of the four security levels. Common examples, given to illustrate how the requirements might be met, are not intended to be restrictive or exhaustive.

The location of Annexes A, B, C, and D can be found in APPENDIX D: SELECTED BIBLIOGRAPHY.

1.1   Security Level 1

Security Level 1 provides the lowest level of security. Basic security requirements are specified for a cryptographic module (e.g., at least one Approved algorithm or Approved security function shall be used). No specific physical security mechanisms are required in a Security Level 1 cryptographic module beyond the basic requirement for production-grade components. An example of a Security Level 1 cryptographic module is a personal computer (PC) encryption board.

Security Level 1 allows the software and firmware components of a cryptographic module to be executed on a general purpose computing system using an unevaluated operating system. Such implementations may be appropriate for some low-level security applications when other controls, such as physical security, network security, and administrative procedures are limited or nonexistent. The implementation of cryptographic software may be more cost-effective than corresponding hardware-based mechanisms, enabling organizations to select from alternative cryptographic solutions to meet lower-level security requirements.

1.2   Security Level 2

Security Level 2 enhances the physical security mechanisms of a Security Level 1 cryptographic module by adding the requirement for tamper-evidence, which includes the use of tamper-evident coatings or seals or for pick-resistant locks on removable covers or doors of the module. Tamper-evident coatings or seals are placed on a cryptographic module so that the coating or seal must be broken to attain physical access to the plaintext cryptographic keys and critical security parameters (CSPs) within the module. Tamper-evident seals or pick-resistant locks are placed on covers or doors to protect against unauthorized physical access.

Security Level 2 requires, at a minimum, role-based authentication in which a cryptographic module authenticates the authorization of an operator to assume a specific role and perform a corresponding set of services.

Security Level 2 allows the software and firmware components of a cryptographic module to be executed on a general purpose computing system using an operating system that

- meets the functional requirements specified in the Common Criteria (CC) Protection Profiles (PPs) listed in Annex B and

- is evaluated at the CC evaluation assurance level EAL2 (or higher).

An equivalent evaluated trusted operating system may be used. A trusted operating system provides a level of trust so that cryptographic modules executing on general purpose computing platforms are comparable to cryptographic modules implemented using dedicated hardware systems.

1.3   Security Level 3

In addition to the tamper-evident physical security mechanisms required at Security Level 2, Security Level 3 attempts to prevent the intruder from gaining access to CSPs held within the cryptographic module. Physical security mechanisms required at Security Level 3 are intended to have a high probability of detecting and responding to attempts at physical access, use or modification of the cryptographic module. The physical security mechanisms may include the use of strong enclosures and tamper detection/response circuitry that zeroizes all plaintext CSPs when the removable covers/doors of the cryptographic module are opened.

Security Level 3 requires identity-based authentication mechanisms, enhancing the security provided by the role-based authentication mechanisms specified for Security Level 2. A cryptographic module authenticates the identity of an operator and verifies that the identified operator is authorized to assume a specific role and perform a corresponding set of services.

Security Level 3 requires the entry or output of plaintext CSPs (including the entry or output of plaintext CSPs using split knowledge procedures) be performed using ports that are physically separated from other ports, or interfaces that are logically separated using a trusted path from other interfaces. Plaintext CSPs may be entered into or output from the cryptographic module in encrypted form (in which case they may travel through enclosing or intervening systems).

Security Level 3 allows the software and firmware components of a cryptographic module to be executed on a general purpose computing system using an operating system that

- meets the functional requirements specified in the PPs listed in Annex B with the additional functional requirement of a Trusted Path (FTP_TRP.1) and

- is evaluated at the CC evaluation assurance level EAL3 (or higher) with the additional assurance requirement of an Informal Target of Evaluation (TOE) Security Policy Model (ADV_SPM.1).

An equivalent evaluated trusted operating system may be used. The implementation of a trusted path protects plaintext CSPs and the software and firmware components of the cryptographic module from other untrusted software or firmware that may be executing on the system.

1.4   Security Level 4

Security Level 4 provides the highest level of security defined in this standard. At this security level, the physical security mechanisms provide a complete envelope of protection around the cryptographic module with the intent of detecting and responding to all unauthorized attempts at physical access. Penetration of the cryptographic module enclosure from any direction has a very high probability of being detected, resulting in the immediate zeroization of all plaintext CSPs. Security Level 4 cryptographic modules are useful for operation in physically unprotected environments.

Security Level 4 also protects a cryptographic module against a security compromise due to environmental conditions or fluctuations outside of the module's normal operating ranges for voltage and temperature. Intentional excursions beyond the normal operating ranges may be used by an attacker to thwart a cryptographic module's defenses. A cryptographic module is required to either include special environmental protection features designed to detect fluctuations and zeroize CSPs, or to undergo rigorous environmental failure testing to provide a reasonable assurance that the module will not be affected by fluctuations outside of the normal operating range in a manner that can compromise the security of the module.

Security Level 4 allows the software and firmware components of a cryptographic module to be executed on a general purpose computing system using an operating system that

- meets the functional requirements specified for Security Level 3 and

- is evaluated at the CC evaluation assurance level EAL4 (or higher).

An equivalent evaluated trusted operating system may be used.

2. GLOSSARY OF TERMS AND ACRONYMS

2.1 Glossary of Terms

The following definitions are tailored for use in this standard:

Approved: FIPS-Approved and/or NIST-recommended.

Approved mode of operation: a mode of the cryptographic module that employs only Approved security functions (not to be confused with a specific mode of an Approved security function, e.g., DES CBC mode).

Approved security function: for this standard, a security function (e.g., cryptographic algorithm, cryptographic key management technique, or authentication technique) that is either

    a) specified in an Approved standard,
    b) adopted in an Approved standard and specified either in an appendix of the Approved standard or in a document referenced by the Approved standard, or
    c) specified in the list of Approved security functions.

Authentication code: a cryptographic checksum based on an Approved security function (also known as a Message Authentication Code).

Automated key transport: the transport of cryptographic keys, usually in encrypted form, using electronic means such as a computer network (e.g., key transport/agreement protocols).

Compromise: the unauthorized disclosure, modification, substitution, or use of sensitive data (including plaintext cryptographic keys and other CSPs).

Confidentiality: the property that sensitive information is not disclosed to unauthorized individuals, entities, or processes.

Control information: information that is entered into a cryptographic module for the purposes of directing the operation of the module.

Critical security parameter (CSP): security-related information (e.g., secret and private cryptographic keys, and authentication data such as passwords and PINs) whose disclosure or modification can compromise the security of a cryptographic module.

Cryptographic boundary: an explicitly defined continuous perimeter that establishes the physical bounds of a cryptographic module and contains all the hardware, software, and/or firmware components of a cryptographic module.

Cryptographic key (key): a parameter used in conjunction with a cryptographic algorithm that determines

- the transformation of plaintext data into ciphertext data,
- the transformation of ciphertext data into plaintext data,
- a digital signature computed from data,
- the verification of a digital signature computed from data,
- an authentication code computed from data, or
- an exchange agreement of a shared secret.

Cryptographic key component (key component): a parameter used in conjunction with other key components in an Approved security function to form a plaintext cryptographic key or perform a cryptographic function.

Cryptographic module: the set of hardware, software, and/or firmware that implements Approved security functions (including cryptographic algorithms and key generation) and is contained within the cryptographic boundary.

Cryptographic module security policy: a precise specification of the security rules under which a cryptographic module will operate, including the rules derived from the requirements of this standard and additional rules imposed by the vendor. (See Appendix C.)

Crypto officer: an operator or process (subject), acting on behalf of the operator, performing cryptographic initialization or management functions.

Data path: the physical or logical route over which data passes; a physical data path may be shared by multiple logical data paths.

Differential power analysis (DPA): an analysis of the variations of the electrical power consumption of a cryptographic module, using advanced statistical methods and/or other techniques, for the purpose of extracting information correlated to cryptographic keys used in a cryptographic algorithm.

Digital signature: the result of a cryptographic transformation of data which, when properly implemented, provides the services of:
   1.   origin authentication
   2.   data integrity, and
   3.   signer non-repudiation.

Electromagnetic compatibility (EMC): the ability of electronic devices to function satisfactorily in an electromagnetic environment without introducing intolerable electromagnetic disturbances to other devices in that environment.

Electromagnetic interference (EMI): electromagnetic emissions from a device, equipment, or system that interfere with the normal operation of another device, equipment, or system.

Electronic key entry: the entry of cryptographic keys into a cryptographic module using electronic methods such as a smart card or a key-loading device. (The operator of the key may have no knowledge of the value of the key being entered.)

Encrypted key: a cryptographic key that has been encrypted using an Approved security function with a key encrypting key, a PIN, or a password in order to disguise the value of the underlying plaintext key.

Environmental failure protection (EFP): the use of features to protect against a compromise of the security of a cryptographic module due to environmental conditions or fluctuations outside of the module's normal operating range.

Environmental failure testing (EFT): the use of testing to provide a reasonable assurance that the security of a cryptographic module will not be compromised by environmental conditions or fluctuations outside of the module's normal operating range.

Error detection code (EDC): a code computed from data and comprised of redundant bits of information designed to detect, but not correct, unintentional changes in the data.

Finite state model: a mathematical model of a sequential machine that is comprised of a finite set of input events, a finite set of output events, a finite set of states, a function that maps states and input to output, a function that maps states and inputs to states (a state transition function), and a specification that describes the initial state.

Firmware: the programs and data components of a cryptographic module that are stored in hardware (e.g., ROM, PROM, EPROM, EEPROM or FLASH) within the cryptographic boundary and cannot be dynamically written or modified during execution.

Hardware: the physical equipment within the cryptographic boundary used to process programs and data.

Hash-based message authentication code (HMAC): a message authentication code that utilizes a keyed hash.

Initialization vector (IV): a vector used in defining the starting point of an encryption process within a cryptographic algorithm.

Input data: information that is entered into a cryptographic module for the purposes of transformation or computation using an Approved security function.

Integrity: the property that sensitive data has not been modified or deleted in an unauthorized and undetected manner.

Interface: a logical entry or exit point of a cryptographic module that provides access to the module for logical information flows representing physical signals.

Key encrypting key: a cryptographic key that is used for the encryption or decryption of other keys.

Key establishment: the process by which cryptographic keys are securely distributed among cryptographic modules using manual transport methods (e.g., key loaders), automated methods (e.g., key transport and/or key agreement protocols), or a combination of automated and manual methods (consists of key transport plus key agreement).

Key loader: a self-contained unit that is capable of storing at least one plaintext or encrypted cryptographic key or key component that can be transferred, upon request, into a cryptographic module.

Key management: the activities involving the handling of cryptographic keys and other related security parameters (e.g., IVs and passwords) during the entire life cycle of the keys, including their generation, storage, establishment, entry and output, and zeroization.

Key transport: secure transport of cryptographic keys from one cryptographic module to another module.

Manual key transport: a non-electronic means of transporting cryptographic keys.

Manual key entry: the entry of cryptographic keys into a cryptographic module, using devices such as a keyboard.

Microcode: the elementary processor instructions that correspond to an executable program instruction.

Operator: an individual accessing a cryptographic module or a process (subject) operating on behalf of the individual, regardless of the assumed role.

Output data: information that is produced from a cryptographic module.

Password: a string of characters (letters, numbers, and other symbols) used to authenticate an identity or to verify access authorization.

Personal identification number (PIN): an alphanumeric code or password used to authenticate an identity.

Physical protection: the safeguarding of a cryptographic module, cryptographic keys, or CSPs using physical means.

Plaintext key: an unencrypted cryptographic key.

Port: a physical entry or exit point of a cryptographic module that provides access to the module for physical signals, represented by logical information flows (physically separated ports do not share the same physical pin or wire).

Private key: a cryptographic key, used with a public key cryptographic algorithm, that is uniquely associated with an entity and is not made public.

Protection Profile: an implementation-independent set of security requirements for a category of Targets of Evaluation (TOEs) that meet specific consumer needs.

Public key: a cryptographic key used with a public key cryptographic algorithm that is uniquely associated with an entity and that may be made public. (Public keys are not considered CSPs.)

Public key certificate: a set of data that uniquely identifies an entity, contains the entity's public key, and is digitally signed by a trusted party, thereby binding the public key to the entity.

Public key (asymmetric) cryptographic algorithm: a cryptographic algorithm that uses two related keys, a public key and a private key. The two keys have the property that deriving the private key from the public key is computationally infeasible.

Random Number Generator: Random Number Generators (RNGs) used for cryptographic applications typically produce a sequence of zero and one bits that may be combined into sub-sequences or blocks of random numbers. There are two basic classes: deterministic and nondeterministic. A deterministic RNG consists of an algorithm that produces a sequence of bits from an initial value called a seed. A nondeterministic RNG produces output that is dependent on some unpredictable physical source that is outside human control.

Removable cover: a cover designed to permit physical access to the contents of a cryptographic module.

Secret key: a cryptographic key, used with a secret key cryptographic algorithm, that is uniquely associated with one or more entities and should not be made public.

Secret key (symmetric) cryptographic algorithm: a cryptographic algorithm that uses a single secret key for both encryption and decryption.

Security policy: see Cryptographic module security policy.

Seed key: a secret value used to initialize a cryptographic function or operation.

Simple power analysis (SPA): a direct (primarily visual) analysis of patterns of instruction execution (or execution of individual instructions), obtained through monitoring the variations in electrical power consumption of a cryptographic module, for the purpose of revealing the features and implementations of cryptographic algorithms and subsequently the values of cryptographic keys.

Software: the programs and data components within the cryptographic boundary, usually stored on erasable media (e.g., disk), that can be dynamically written and modified during execution.

Split knowledge: a process by which a cryptographic key is split into multiple key components, individually sharing no knowledge of the original key, that can be subsequently input into, or output from, a cryptographic module by separate entities and combined to recreate the original cryptographic key.

Status information: information that is output from a cryptographic module for the purposes of indicating certain operational characteristics or states of the module.

System software: the special software within the cryptographic boundary (e.g., operating system, compilers or utility programs) designed for a specific computer system or family of computer systems to facilitate the operation and maintenance of the computer system, and associated programs, and data.

Tamper detection: the automatic determination by a cryptographic module that an attempt has been made to compromise the physical security of the module.

Tamper evidence: the external indication that an attempt has been made to compromise the physical security of a cryptographic module. (The evidence of the tamper attempt should be observable by an operator subsequent to the attempt.)

Tamper response: the automatic action taken by a cryptographic module when a tamper detection has occurred (the minimum response action is the zeroization of plaintext keys and CSPs).

Target of Evaluation (TOE): an information technology product or system and associated administrator and user guidance documentation that is the subject of an evaluation.

TEMPEST: a name referring to the investigation, study, and control of unintentional compromising emanations from telecommunications and automated information systems equipment.

TOE Security Functions (TSF): used in the Common Criteria, a set of the TOE consisting of all hardware, software, and firmware that must be relied upon for the correct enforcement of the TOE Security Policy.

TOE Security Policy (TSP): used in the Common Criteria, a set of rules that regulate how assets are managed, protected, and distributed within a Target of Evaluation.

Trusted path: a means by which an operator and a TOE Security Function can communicate with the necessary confidence to support the TOE Security Policy.

User: an individual or a process (subject) acting on behalf of the individual that accesses a cryptographic module in order to obtain cryptographic services.

Validation authorities: NIST and CSE.

Zeroization: a method of erasing electronically stored data, cryptographic keys, and CSPs by altering or deleting the contents of the data storage to prevent recovery of the data.

2.2   Acronyms

The following acronyms and abbreviations are used throughout this standard:

ANSI   American National Standards Institute

API   Application Program Interface

CAPP	Controlled Access Protection Profile
CBC	Cipher Block Chaining
CC	Common Criteria
CMVP	Cryptographic Module Validation Program
CSE	Communications Security Establishment of the Government of Canada
CSP	Critical Security Parameter
DES	Data Encryption Standard
DOD	Department of Defense
DPA	Differential Power Analysis
DTR	Derived Test Requirements
EAL	Common Criteria Evaluation Assurance Level
EDC	Error Detection Code
EEPROM	Electronically-Erasable Programmable Read-Only Memory
EFP	Environmental Failure Protection
EFT	Environmental Failure Testing
EMC	Electromagnetic Compatibility
EMI	Electromagnetic Interference
EPROM	Erasable Programmable Read-Only Memory
FCC	Federal Communications Commission
FIPS	Federal Information Processing Standard
FIPS PUB	FIPS Publication
HDL	Hardware Description Language
HMAC	Hash-Based Message Authentication Code
IC	Integrated Circuit
IG	Implementation Guidance
ISO	International Organization for Standardization
ITSEC	Information Technology Security Evaluation Criteria
IV	Initialization Vector

NIST	National Institute of Standards and Technology
NTIS	National Technical Information Service
PIN	Personal Identification Number
PROM	Programmable Read-Only Memory
RAM	Random Access Memory
RNG	Random Number Generator
ROM	Read-Only Memory
SPA	Simple Power Analysis
TOE	Target of Evaluation
TSF	Target of Evaluation Security Functions
TSP	Target of Evaluation Security Policy
URL	Uniform Resource Locator

3. FUNCTIONAL SECURITY OBJECTIVES

The security requirements specified in this standard relate to the secure design and implementation of a cryptographic module. The requirements are derived from the following high-level functional security objectives for a cryptographic module:

- To employ and correctly implement the Approved security functions for the protection of sensitive information.

- To protect a cryptographic module from unauthorized operation or use.

- To prevent the unauthorized disclosure of the contents of the cryptographic module, including plaintext cryptographic keys and CSPs.

- To prevent the unauthorized and undetected modification of the cryptographic module and cryptographic algorithms, including the unauthorized modification, substitution, insertion, and deletion of cryptographic keys and CSPs.

- To provide indications of the operational state of the cryptographic module.

- To ensure that the cryptographic module performs properly when operating in an Approved mode of operation.

- To detect errors in the operation of the cryptographic module and to prevent the compromise of sensitive data and CSPs resulting from these errors.

4.   SECURITY REQUIREMENTS

This section specifies the security requirements that shall be satisfied by cryptographic modules conforming to this standard.   The security requirements cover areas related to the design and implementation of a cryptographic module.   These areas include cryptographic module specification; module ports and interfaces; roles, services, and authentication; finite state model; physical security; operational environment; cryptographic key management; electromagnetic interference/electromagnetic compatibility (EMI/EMC); self-tests; and design assurance.   An additional area concerned with the mitigation of other attacks is currently not tested but the vendor is required to document implemented controls (e.g., differential power analysis, and TEMPEST).   Table 1 summarizes the security requirements in each of these areas.

	Security Level 1	*Security Level 2*	*Security Level 3*	*Security Level 4*
Cryptographic Module Specification	Specification of cryptographic module, cryptographic boundary, Approved algorithms, and Approved modes of operation. Description of cryptographic module, including all hardware, software, and firmware components. Statement of module security policy.			
Cryptographic Module Ports and Interfaces	Required and optional interfaces. Specification of all interfaces and of all input and output data paths.		Data ports for unprotected critical security parameters logically or physically separated from other data ports.	
Roles, Services, and Authentication	Logical separation of required and optional roles and services.	Role-based or identity-based operator authentication.	Identity-based operator authentication.	
Finite State Model	Specification of finite state model. Required states and optional states. State transition diagram and specification of state transitions.			
Physical Security	Production grade equipment.	Locks or tamper evidence.	Tamper detection and response for covers and doors.	Tamper detection and response envelope. EFP or EFT.
Operational Environment	Single operator. Executable code. Approved integrity technique.	Referenced PPs evaluated at EAL2 with specified discretionary access control mechanisms and auditing.	Referenced PPs plus trusted path evaluated at EAL3 plus security policy modeling.	Referenced PPs plus trusted path evaluated at EAL4.
Cryptographic Key Management	Key management mechanisms: random number and key generation, key establishment, key distribution, key entry/output, key storage, and key zeroization.			
	Secret and private keys established using manual methods may be entered or output in plaintext form.		Secret and private keys established using manual methods shall be entered or output encrypted or with split knowledge procedures.	
EMI/EMC	47 CFR FCC Part 15. Subpart B, Class A (Business use). Applicable FCC requirements (for radio).		47 CFR FCC Part 15. Subpart B, Class B (Home use).	
Self-Tests	Power-up tests: cryptographic algorithm tests, software/firmware integrity tests, critical functions tests. Conditional tests.			
Design Assurance	Configuration management (CM). Secure installation and generation. Design and policy correspondence. Guidance documents.	CM system. Secure distribution. Functional specification.	High-level language implementation.	Formal model. Detailed explanations (informal proofs). Preconditions and postconditions.
Mitigation of Other Attacks	Specification of mitigation of attacks for which no testable requirements are currently available.			

Table 1: *Summary of security requirements*

A cryptographic module shall be tested against the requirements of each area addressed in this section.   The cryptographic module shall be independently rated in each area.   Several areas provide for increasing levels of security with cumulative security requirements for each security level.   In these areas, the cryptographic module will receive a rating that reflects the maximum security level for which the module fulfills all of the requirements of that area. In areas that do not provide for different levels of security (i.e., standard set of requirements), the cryptographic module will receive a rating commensurate with the overall level of security.

In addition to receiving independent ratings for each of the security areas, a cryptographic module will also receive an overall rating. The overall rating will indicate the minimum of the independent ratings received in the areas.

Many of the security requirements of this standard include specific documentation requirements that are summarized in Appendices A and C. All documentation, including copies of the user and installation manuals, shall be provided to the testing laboratory by the vendor.

4.1   Cryptographic Module Specification

A cryptographic module shall be a set of hardware, software, firmware, or some combination thereof that implements cryptographic functions or processes, including cryptographic algorithms and, optionally, key generation, and is contained within a defined cryptographic boundary. A cryptographic module shall implement at least one Approved security function used in an Approved mode of operation. Non-Approved security functions may also be included for use in non-Approved modes of operation. The operator shall be able to determine when an Approved mode of operation is selected. For Security Levels 1 and 2, the cryptographic module security policy may specify when a cryptographic module is performing in an Approved mode of operation. For Security Levels 3 and 4, a cryptographic module shall indicate when an Approved mode of operation is selected. (Approved security functions are listed in Annex A to this standard.)

A cryptographic boundary shall consist of an explicitly defined perimeter that establishes the physical bounds of a cryptographic module. If a cryptographic module consists of software or firmware components, the cryptographic boundary shall contain the processor(s) and other hardware components that store and protect the software and firmware components. Hardware, software, and firmware components of a cryptographic module can be excluded from the requirements of this standard if shown that these components do not affect the security of the module.

The following documentation requirements shall apply to all security-specific hardware, software, and firmware contained within a cryptographic module. These requirements do not apply to microcode or system software whose source code is not available to the vendor or to any hardware, software, or firmware components that can be shown not to affect the security of the cryptographic module.

- Documentation shall specify the hardware, software, and firmware components of a cryptographic module, specify the cryptographic boundary surrounding these components, and describe the physical configuration of the module (see Section 4.5).

- Documentation shall specify any hardware, software, or firmware components of a cryptographic module that are excluded from the security requirements of this standard and explain the rationale for the exclusion.

- Documentation shall specify the physical ports and logical interfaces and all defined input and output data paths of a cryptographic module.

- Documentation shall specify the manual or logical controls of a cryptographic module, physical or logical status indicators, and applicable physical, logical, and electrical characteristics.

- Documentation shall list all security functions, both Approved and non-Approved, that are employed by a cryptographic module and shall specify all modes of operation, both Approved and non-Approved.

- Documentation shall specify:

  ❑ a block diagram depicting all of the major hardware components of a cryptographic module and component interconnections, including any microprocessors, input/output buffers, plaintext/ciphertext buffers, control buffers, key storage, working memory, and program memory, and

  ❑ the design of the hardware, software, and firmware components of a cryptographic module. High-level specification languages for software/firmware or schematics for hardware shall be used to document the design.

- Documentation shall specify all security-related information, including secret and private cryptographic keys (both plaintext and encrypted), authentication data (e.g., passwords, PINs), CSPs, and other protected information (e.g., audited events, audit data) whose disclosure or modification can compromise the security of the cryptographic module.

- Documentation shall specify a cryptographic module security policy. The security policy shall include the rules derived from the requirements of this standard and the rules derived from any additional requirements imposed by the vendor (see Appendix C).

4.2   Cryptographic Module Ports and Interfaces

A cryptographic module shall restrict all information flow and physical access points to physical ports and logical interfaces that define all entry and exit points to and from the module. The cryptographic module interfaces shall be logically distinct from each other although they may share one physical port (e.g., input data may enter and output data may exit via the same port) or may be distributed over one or more physical ports (e.g., input data may enter via both a serial and a parallel port). An Application Program Interface (API) of a software component of a cryptographic module may be defined as one or more logical interfaces(s).

A cryptographic module shall have the following four logical interfaces ("input" and "output" are indicated from the perspective of the module):

Data input interface. All data (except control data entered via the control input interface) that is input to and processed by a cryptographic module (including plaintext data, ciphertext data, cryptographic keys and CSPs, authentication data, and status information from another module) shall enter via the "data input" interface.

Data output interface. All data (except status data output via the status output interface) that is output from a cryptographic module (including plaintext data, ciphertext data, cryptographic keys and CSPs, authentication data, and control information for another module) shall exit via the "data output" interface. All data output via the data output interface shall be inhibited when an error state exists and during self-tests (see Section 4.9).

Control input interface. All input commands, signals, and control data (including function calls and manual controls such as switches, buttons, and keyboards) used to control the operation of a cryptographic module shall enter via the "control input" interface.

Status output interface. All output signals, indicators, and status data (including return codes and physical indicators such as Light Emitting Diodes and displays) used to indicate the status of a cryptographic module shall exit via the "status output" interface.

All external electrical power that is input to a cryptographic module (including power from an external power source or batteries) shall enter via a power port. A power port is not required when all power is provided or maintained internally to the cryptographic boundary of the cryptographic module (e.g., an internal battery).

The cryptographic module shall distinguish between data and control for input and data and status for output. All input data entering the cryptographic module via the "data input" interface shall only pass through the input data path. All output data exiting the cryptographic module via the "data output" interface shall only pass through the output data path. The output data path shall be logically disconnected from the circuitry and processes while performing key generation, manual key entry, or key zeroization. To prevent the inadvertent output of sensitive information, two independent internal actions shall be required to output data via any output interface through which plaintext cryptographic keys or CSPs or sensitive data are output (e.g., two different software flags are set, one of which may be user initiated; or two hardware gates are set serially from two separate actions).

SECURITY LEVELS 1 AND 2

For Security Levels 1 and 2, the physical port(s) and logical interface(s) used for the input and output of plaintext cryptographic keys, cryptographic key components, authentication data, and CSPs may be shared physically and logically with other ports and interfaces of the cryptographic module.

SECURITY LEVELS 3 AND 4

For Security Levels 3 and 4,

- the physical port(s) used for the input and output of plaintext cryptographic key components, authentication data, and CSPs shall be physically separated from all other ports of the cryptographic module

or

- the logical interfaces used for the input and output of plaintext cryptographic key components, authentication data, and CSPs shall be logically separated from all other interfaces using a trusted path,

and

- plaintext cryptographic key components, authentication data, and other CSPs shall be directly entered into the cryptographic module (e.g., via a trusted path or directly attached cable). (See Section 4.7.4.)

4.3   Roles, Services, and Authentication

A cryptographic module shall support authorized roles for operators and corresponding services within each role. Multiple roles may be assumed by a single operator. If a cryptographic module supports concurrent operators, then the module shall internally maintain the separation of the roles assumed by each operator and the corresponding services. An operator is not required to assume an authorized role to perform services where cryptographic keys and CSPs are not modified, disclosed, or substituted (e.g., *show status, self-tests,* or other services that do not affect the security of the module).

Authentication mechanisms may be required within a cryptographic module to authenticate an operator accessing the module, and to verify that the operator is authorized to assume the requested role and perform the services within the role.

4.3.1 Roles

A cryptographic module shall support the following authorized roles for operators:

User Role. The role assumed to perform general security services, including cryptographic operations and other Approved security functions.

Crypto Officer Role: The role assumed to perform cryptographic initialization or management functions (e.g., module initialization, input/output of cryptographic keys and CSPs, and audit functions).

If the cryptographic module allows operators to perform maintenance services, then the module shall support the following authorized role:

Maintenance Role: The role assumed to perform physical maintenance and/or logical maintenance services (e.g., hardware/software diagnostics). All plaintext secret and private keys and unprotected CSPs shall be zeroized when entering or exiting the maintenance role.

A cryptographic module may support other roles or sub-roles in addition to the roles specified above.

Documentation shall specify all authorized roles supported by the cryptographic module.

4.3.2 Services

Services shall refer to all of the services, operations, or functions that can be performed by a cryptographic module. *Service inputs* shall consist of all data or control inputs to the cryptographic module that initiate or obtain specific services, operations, or functions. *Service outputs* shall consist of all data and status outputs that result from services, operations, or functions initiated or obtained by service inputs. Each service input shall result in a service output.

A cryptographic module shall provide the following services to operators:

Show Status. Output the current status of the cryptographic module.

Perform Self-Tests. Initiate and run the self-tests as specified in Section 4.9.

Perform Approved Security Function. Perform at least one Approved security function used in an Approved mode of operation, as specified in Section 4.1.

A cryptographic module may provide other services, operations, or functions, both Approved and non-Approved, in addition to the services specified above. Specific services may be provided in more than one role (e.g., key entry services may be provided in the user role and the crypto officer role).

If a cryptographic module implements a *bypass* capability, where services are provided without cryptographic processing (e.g., transferring plaintext through the module without encryption), then

- two independent internal actions shall be required to activate the capability to prevent the inadvertent bypass of plaintext data due to a single error (e.g., two different software or hardware flags are set, one of which may be user-initiated), and

- the module shall show status to indicate whether

1) the bypass capability *is not* activated, and the module is exclusively providing services *with* cryptographic processing (e.g., plaintext data *is* encrypted),

2) the bypass capability *is* activated and the module is exclusively providing services *without* cryptographic processing (e.g., plaintext data *is not* encrypted), or

3) the bypass capability *is alternately* activated and deactivated and the module is providing some services *with* cryptographic processing and some services *without* cryptographic processing (e.g., for modules with multiple communication channels, plaintext data *is* or *is not* encrypted depending on each channel configuration).

Documentation shall specify:

- the services, operations, or functions provided by the cryptographic module, both Approved and non-Approved,

- for each service provided by the module, the service inputs, corresponding service outputs, and the authorized role(s) in which the service can be performed, and

- any services provided by the cryptographic module for which the operator is not required to assume an authorized role, and how these services do not modify, disclose, or substitute cryptographic keys and CSPs, or otherwise affect the security of the module.

4.3.3 Operator Authentication

Authentication mechanisms may be required within a cryptographic module to authenticate an operator accessing the module and to verify that the operator is authorized to assume the requested role and perform services within that role. Depending on the security level, a cryptographic module shall support at least one of the following mechanisms to control access to the module:

Role-Based Authentication: If role-based authentication mechanisms are supported by a cryptographic module, the module shall require that one or more roles either be implicitly or explicitly selected by the operator and shall authenticate the assumption of the selected role (or set of roles). The cryptographic module is not required to authenticate the individual identity of the operator. The selection of roles and the authentication of the assumption of selected roles may be combined. If a cryptographic module permits an operator to change roles, then the module shall authenticate the assumption of any role that was not previously authenticated.

Identity-Based Authentication: If identity-based authentication mechanisms are supported by a cryptographic module, the module shall require that the operator be individually identified, shall require that one or more roles either be implicitly or explicitly selected by the operator, and shall authenticate the identity of the operator and the authorization of the operator to assume the selected role (or set of roles). The authentication of the identity of the operator, selection of roles, and the authorization of the assumption of the selected roles may be combined. If a cryptographic module permits an operator to change roles, then the module shall verify the authorization of the identified operator to assume any role that was not previously authorized.

A cryptographic module may permit an authenticated operator to perform all of the services allowed within an authorized role, or may require separate authentication for each service or for different sets of services. When a cryptographic module is powered off and subsequently powered on, the results of previous authentications shall not be retained and the module shall require the operator to be re-authenticated.

Various types of authentication data may be required by a cryptographic module to implement the supported authentication mechanisms, including (but not limited to) the knowledge or possession of a password, PIN, cryptographic key, or equivalent; possession of a physical key, token, or equivalent; or verification of personal characteristics (e.g., biometrics). Authentication data within a cryptographic module shall be protected against unauthorized disclosure, modification, and substitution.

The initialization of authentication mechanisms may warrant special treatment. If a cryptographic module does not contain the authentication data required to authenticate the operator for the first time the module is accessed, then other authorized methods (e.g., procedural controls or use of factory-set or default authentication data) shall be used to control access to the module and initialize the authentication mechanisms.

The strength of the authentication mechanism shall conform to the following specifications:

- For each attempt to use the authentication mechanism, the probability shall be less than one in 1,000,000 that a random attempt will succeed or a false acceptance will occur (e.g., guessing a password or PIN, false acceptance error rate of a biometric device, or some combination of authentication methods).

- For multiple attempts to use the authentication mechanism during a one-minute period, the probability shall be less than one in 100,000 that a random attempt will succeed or a false acceptance will occur.

- Feedback of authentication data to an operator shall be obscured during authentication (e.g., no visible display of characters when entering a password).

- Feedback provided to an operator during an attempted authentication shall not weaken the strength of the authentication mechanism.

Documentation shall specify:

- the authentication mechanisms supported by a cryptographic module,

- the types of authentication data required by the module to implement the supported authentication mechanisms,

- the authorized methods used to control access to the module for the first time and initialize the authentication mechanisms, and

- the strength of the authentication mechanisms supported by the module.

SECURITY LEVEL 1

For Security Level 1, a cryptographic module is not required to employ authentication mechanisms to control access to the module. If authentication mechanisms are not supported by a cryptographic module, the module shall require that one or more roles either be implicitly or explicitly selected by the operator.

SECURITY LEVEL 2

For Security Level 2, a cryptographic module shall employ *role-based* authentication to control access to the module.

SECURITY LEVELS 3 AND 4

For Security Levels 3 and 4, a cryptographic module shall employ *identity-based* authentication mechanisms to control access to the module.

4.4   Finite State Model

The operation of a cryptographic module shall be specified using a finite state model (or equivalent) represented by a state transition diagram and/or a state transition table.

The state transition diagram and/or state transition table includes:

- all operational and error states of a cryptographic module,

- the corresponding transitions from one state to another,

- the input events that cause transitions from one state to another, and

- the output events resulting from transitions from one state to another.

A cryptographic module shall include the following operational and error states:

Power on/off states. States for primary, secondary, or backup power. These states may distinguish between power sources being applied to a cryptographic module.

Crypto officer states. States in which the crypto officer services are performed (e.g., cryptographic initialization and key management).

Key/CSP entry states. States for entering cryptographic keys and CSPs into the cryptographic module.

User states. States in which authorized users obtain security services, perform cryptographic operations, or perform other Approved or non-Approved functions.

Self-test states. States in which the cryptographic module is performing self-tests.

Error states. States when the cryptographic module has encountered an error (e.g., failed a self-test or attempted to encrypt when missing operational keys or CSPs). Error states may include "hard" errors that indicate an equipment malfunction and that may require maintenance, service or repair of the cryptographic module, or recoverable "soft" errors that may require initialization or resetting of the module. Recovery from error states shall be possible except for those caused by hard errors that require maintenance, service, or repair of the cryptographic module.

A cryptographic module may contain other states including, but not limited to, the following:

Bypass states. States in which a bypass capability is activated and services are provided without cryptographic processing (e.g., transferring plaintext through the cryptographic module).

Maintenance states. States for maintaining and servicing a cryptographic module, including physical and logical maintenance testing. If a cryptographic module contains a maintenance role, then a maintenance state shall be included.

Documentation shall include a representation of the finite state model (or equivalent) using a state transition diagram and/or state transition table that shall specify:

- all operational and error states of a cryptographic module,

- the corresponding transitions from one state to another,

- the input events, including data inputs and control inputs, that cause transitions from one state to another, and

- the output events, including internal module conditions, data outputs, and status outputs resulting from transitions from one state to another.

4.5   Physical Security

A cryptographic module shall employ physical security mechanisms in order to restrict unauthorized physical access to the contents of the module and to deter unauthorized use or modification of the module (including substitution of the entire module) when installed. All hardware, software, firmware, and data components within the cryptographic boundary shall be protected.

A cryptographic module that is implemented completely in software such that the physical security is provided solely by the host platform is not subject to the physical security requirements of this standard.

Physical security requirements are specified for three defined physical embodiments of a cryptographic module:

- *Single-chip cryptographic modules* are physical embodiments in which a single integrated circuit (IC) chip may be used as a standalone device or may be embedded within an enclosure or a product that may not be physically protected. Examples of single-chip cryptographic modules include single IC chips or smart cards with a single IC chip.

- *Multiple-chip embedded cryptographic modules* are physical embodiments in which two or more IC chips are interconnected and are embedded within an enclosure or a product that may not be physically protected. Examples of multiple-chip embedded cryptographic modules include adapters and expansion boards.

- *Multiple-chip standalone cryptographic modules* are physical embodiments in which two or more IC chips are interconnected and the entire enclosure is physically protected. Examples of multiple-chip, standalone cryptographic modules include encrypting routers or secure radios.

Depending on the physical security mechanisms of a cryptographic module, unauthorized attempts at physical access, use, or modification will have a high probability of being detected

- subsequent to an attempt by leaving visible signs (i.e., tamper evidence)

and/or

- during an attempt so that appropriate actions can be taken by the cryptographic module to protect plaintext secret and private keys and CSPs (i.e., tamper response).

Table 2 summarizes the physical security requirements, both general and embodiment-specific, for each of the four security levels. The general physical security requirements at each security level are all three distinct physical embodiments of a cryptographic module. The embodiment-specific physical security requirements at each security level enhance the general requirements at the same level, and the embodiment-specific requirements of the previous level.

	General Requirements for all Embodiments	Single-Chip Cryptographic Modules	Multiple-Chip Embedded Cryptographic Modules	Multiple-Chip Standalone Cryptographic Modules
Security Level 1	Production-grade components (with standard passivation).	No additional requirements.	If applicable, production-grade enclosure or removable cover.	Production-grade enclosure.
Security Level 2	Evidence of tampering (e.g., cover, enclosure, or seal).	Opaque tamper-evident coating on chip or enclosure.	Opaque tamper-evident encapsulating material or enclosure with tamper-evident seals or pick-resistant locks for doors or removable covers.	Opaque enclosure with tamper-evident seals or pick-resistant locks for doors or removable covers.
Security Level 3	Automatic zeroization when accessing the maintenance access interface. Tamper response and zeroization circuitry. Protected vents.	Hard opaque tamper-evident coating on chip or strong removal-resistant and penetration resistant enclosure.	Hard opaque potting material encapsulation of multiple chip circuitry embodiment or applicable Multiple-Chip Standalone Security Level 3 requirements.	Hard opaque potting material encapsulation of multiple chip circuitry embodiment or strong enclosure with removal/penetration attempts causing serious damage.
Security Level 4	EFP or EFT for temperature and voltage.	Hard opaque removal-resistant coating on chip.	Tamper detection envelope with tamper response and zeroization circuitry.	Tamper detection/ response envelope with tamper response and zeroization circuitry.

Table 2: *Summary of physical security requirements*

In general, Security Level 1 requires minimal physical protection. Security Level 2 requires the addition of tamper-evident mechanisms. Security Level 3 adds requirements for the use of strong enclosures with tamper detection and response mechanisms for removable covers and doors. Security Level 4 adds requirements for the use of strong enclosures with tamper detection and response mechanisms for the entire enclosure. Environmental failure protection (EFP) or environmental failure testing (EFT) is required at Security Level 4. Tamper detection and tamper response are not substitutes for tamper evidence.

Security requirements are specified for a maintenance access interface when a cryptographic module is designed to permit physical access (e.g., by the module vendor or other authorized individuals).

4.5.1   General Physical Security Requirements

The following requirements shall apply to all physical embodiments.

- Documentation shall specify the physical embodiment and the security level for which the physical security mechanisms of a cryptographic module are implemented.

- Documentation shall specify the physical security mechanisms of a cryptographic module.

- If a cryptographic module includes a maintenance role that requires physical access to the contents of the module or if the module is designed to permit physical access (e.g., by the module vendor or other authorized individual), then:

  ❑ a maintenance access interface shall be defined,

- the maintenance access interface shall include all physical access paths to the contents of the cryptographic module, including any removable covers or doors,

- any removable covers or doors included within the maintenance access interface shall be safeguarded using the appropriate physical security mechanisms,

- all plaintext secret and private keys and CSPs shall be zeroized when the maintenance access interface is accessed, and

- documentation shall specify the maintenance access interface and how plaintext secret and private keys and CSPs are zeroized when the maintenance access interface is accessed.

SECURITY LEVEL 1

The following requirements shall apply to all cryptographic modules for Security Level 1.

- The cryptographic module shall consist of production-grade components that shall include standard passivation techniques (e.g., a conformal coating or a sealing coat applied over the module's circuitry to protect against environmental or other physical damage).

- When performing physical maintenance, all plaintext secret and private keys and other unprotected CSPs contained in the cryptographic module shall be zeroized. Zeroization shall either be performed procedurally by the operator or automatically by the cryptographic module.

SECURITY LEVEL 2

In addition to the general requirements for Security Level 1, the following requirement shall apply to all cryptographic modules for Security Level 2.

- The cryptographic module shall provide evidence of tampering (e.g., on the cover, enclosure, and seal) when physical access to the module is attempted.

SECURITY LEVEL 3

In addition to the general requirements for Security Levels 1 and 2, the following requirements shall apply to all cryptographic modules for Security Level 3.

- If the cryptographic module contains any doors or removable covers or if a maintenance access interface is defined, then the module shall contain tamper response and zeroization circuitry. The tamper response and zeroization circuitry shall immediately zeroize all plaintext secret and private keys and CSPs when a door is opened, a cover is removed, or when the maintenance access interface is accessed. The tamper response and zeroization circuitry shall remain operational when plaintext secret and private cryptographic keys or CSPs are contained within the cryptographic module.

- If the cryptographic module contains ventilation holes or slits, then the holes or slits shall be constructed in a manner that prevents undetected physical probing inside the enclosure (e.g., require at least one 90 degree bend or obstruction with a substantial blocking material).

SECURITY LEVEL 4

In addition to the general requirements for Security Levels 1, 2, and 3, the following requirement shall apply to all cryptographic modules for Security Level 4.

- The cryptographic module shall either include environmental failure protection (EFP) features or undergo environmental failure testing (EFT) as specified in Section 4.5.5.

4.5.2 Single-Chip Cryptographic Modules

In addition to the general security requirements specified in Section 4.5.1, the following requirements are specific to single-chip cryptographic modules.

SECURITY LEVEL 1

There are no additional Security Level 1 requirements for single-chip cryptographic modules.

SECURITY LEVEL 2

In addition to the requirements for Security Level 1, the following requirements shall apply to single-chip cryptographic modules for Security Level 2.

- The cryptographic module shall be covered with a tamper-evident coating (e.g., a tamper-evident passivation material or a tamper-evident material covering the passivation) or contained in a tamper-evident enclosure to deter direct observation, probing, or manipulation of the module and to provide evidence of attempts to tamper with or remove the module.

- The tamper-evident coating or tamper-evident enclosure shall be opaque within the visible spectrum.

SECURITY LEVEL 3

In addition to the requirements for Security Levels 1 and 2, the following requirements shall apply to single-chip cryptographic modules for Security Level 3.

Either

- the cryptographic module shall be covered with a hard opaque tamper-evident coating (e.g., a hard opaque epoxy covering the passivation)

or

- the enclosure shall be implemented so that attempts at removal or penetration of the enclosure shall have a high probability of causing serious damage to the cryptographic module (i.e., the module will not function).

SECURITY LEVEL 4

In addition to the requirements for Security Levels 1, 2, and 3, the following requirements shall apply to single-chip cryptographic modules for Security Level 4.

- The cryptographic module shall be covered with a hard, opaque removal-resistant coating with hardness and adhesion characteristics such that attempting to peel or pry the coating from the module will have a high probability of resulting in serious damage to the module (i.e., the module will not function).

- The removal-resistant coating shall have solvency characteristics such that dissolving the coating will have a high probability of dissolving or seriously damaging the module (i.e., the module will not function).

4.5.3 Multiple-Chip Embedded Cryptographic Modules

In addition to the general security requirements specified in Section 4.5.1, the following requirements are specific to multiple-chip embedded cryptographic modules.

SECURITY LEVEL 1

The following requirement shall apply to multiple-chip embedded cryptographic modules for Security Level 1.

- If the cryptographic module is contained within an enclosure or removable cover, a production-grade enclosure or removable cover shall be used.

SECURITY LEVEL 2

In addition to the requirement for Security Level 1, the following requirements shall apply to multiple-chip embedded cryptographic modules for Security Level 2.

Either

- the cryptographic module components shall be covered with a tamper-evident coating or potting material (e.g., etch-resistant coating or bleeding paint) or contained in a tamper-evident enclosure to deter direct observation, probing, or manipulation of module components and to provide evidence of attempts to tamper with or remove module components, and

- the tamper-evident coating or tamper-evident enclosure shall be opaque within the visible spectrum,

or

- the cryptographic module shall be entirely contained within a metal or hard plastic production-grade enclosure that may include doors or removable covers,

- the enclosure shall be opaque within the visible spectrum, and

- if the enclosure includes any doors or removable covers, then the doors or covers shall be locked with pick-resistant mechanical locks employing physical or logical keys or shall be protected with tamper-evident seals (e.g., evidence tape or holographic seals).

SECURITY LEVEL 3

In addition to the requirements for Security Levels 1 and 2, the following requirements shall apply to multiple-chip embedded cryptographic modules for Security Level 3.

Either

- the multiple-chip embodiment of the circuitry within the cryptographic module shall be covered with a hard coating or potting material (e.g., a hard epoxy material) that is opaque within the visible spectrum

or

- the applicable Security Level 3 requirements for multiple-chip standalone cryptographic modules shall apply. (Section 4.5.4)

SECURITY LEVEL 4

In addition to the requirements for Security Levels 1, 2, and 3, the following requirements shall apply to multiple-chip embedded cryptographic modules for Security Level 4.

- The cryptographic module components shall be covered by potting material or contained within an enclosure encapsulated by a tamper detection envelope (e.g., a flexible mylar printed circuit with a serpentine geometric pattern of conductors or a wire-wound package or a non-flexible, brittle circuit or a strong enclosure) that shall detect tampering by means such as cutting, drilling, milling, grinding, or dissolving of the potting material or enclosure to an extent sufficient for accessing plaintext secret and private keys cryptographic keys or CSPs.

- The cryptographic module shall contain tamper response and zeroization circuitry that shall continuously monitor the tamper detection envelope and, upon the detection of tampering, shall immediately zeroize all plaintext secret and private cryptographic keys and CSPs. The tamper response and zeroization circuitry shall remain operational when plaintext secret and private cryptographic keys or CSPs are contained within the cryptographic module.

4.5.4 Multiple-Chip Standalone Cryptographic Modules

In addition to the general security requirements specified in Section 4.5.1, the following requirements are specific to multiple-chip standalone cryptographic modules.

SECURITY LEVEL 1

The following requirement shall apply to multiple-chip standalone cryptographic modules for Security Level 1.

- The cryptographic module shall be entirely contained within a metal or hard plastic production-grade enclosure that may include doors or removable covers.

SECURITY LEVEL 2

In addition to the requirements for Security Level 1, the following requirements shall apply to multiple-chip standalone cryptographic modules for Security Level 2.

- The enclosure of the cryptographic module shall be opaque within the visible spectrum.

- If the enclosure of the cryptographic module includes any doors or removable covers, then the doors or covers shall be locked with pick-resistant mechanical locks employing physical or logical keys or shall be protected with tamper-evident seals (e.g., evidence tape or holographic seals).

SECURITY LEVEL 3

In addition to the requirements for Security Levels 1 and 2, the following requirements shall apply to multiple-chip standalone cryptographic modules for Security Level 3.

Either

- the multiple-chip embodiment of the circuitry within the cryptographic module shall be covered with a hard potting material (e.g., a hard epoxy material) that is opaque within the visible spectrum

or

- the cryptographic module shall be contained within a strong enclosure such that attempts at removal or penetration of the enclosure will have a high probability of causing serious damage to the module (i.e., the module will not function).

SECURITY LEVEL 4

In addition to the requirements for Security Levels 1, 2, and 3, the following requirements shall apply to multiple-chip standalone cryptographic modules for Security Level 4.

- The potting material or enclosure of the cryptographic module shall be encapsulated by a tamper detection envelope, by the use of tamper detection mechanisms such as cover switches (e.g., microswitches, magnetic Hall effect switches, permanent magnetic actuators, etc.), motion detectors (e.g., ultrasonic, infrared, or microwave), or other tamper detection mechanisms as described above for multiple-chip embedded cryptographic modules. The tamper detection mechanisms shall detect tampering by means such as cutting, drilling, milling, grinding, or dissolving of the potting material or enclosure, to an extent sufficient for accessing plaintext secret and private cryptographic keys and CSPs.

- The cryptographic module shall contain tamper response and zeroization circuitry that shall continuously monitor the tamper detection envelope and, upon the detection of tampering, shall immediately zeroize all plaintext secret and private cryptographic keys and CSPs. The tamper response and zeroization circuitry shall remain operational when plaintext cryptographic keys and CSPs are contained within the cryptographic module.

4.5.5   Environmental Failure Protection/Testing

The electronic devices and circuitry are designed to operate within a particular range of environmental conditions. Deliberate or accidental excursions outside the specified normal operating ranges of voltage and temperature can cause erratic operation or failure of the electronic devices or circuitry that can compromise the security of the cryptographic module. Reasonable assurance that the security of a cryptographic module cannot be compromised by extreme environmental conditions can be provided by having the module employ environmental failure protection (EFP) features or undergo environmental failure testing (EFT).

For Security Levels 1, 2, and 3, a cryptographic module is not required to employ environmental failure protection (EFP) features or undergo environmental failure testing (EFT). At Security Level 4, a cryptographic module shall either employ environmental failure protection (EFP) features or undergo environmental failure testing (EFT).

4.5.5.1 Environmental Failure Protection Features (Alternative 1)

Environmental failure protection (EFP) features shall protect a cryptographic module against unusual environmental conditions or fluctuations (accidental or induced) outside of the module's normal operating range that can compromise the security of the module. In particular, the cryptographic module shall monitor and correctly respond to fluctuations in the operating *temperature* and *voltage* outside of the specified normal operating ranges.

The EFP features shall involve electronic circuitry or devices that continuously measure the operating temperature and voltage of a cryptographic module. If the temperature or voltage fall outside of the cryptographic module's normal operating range, the protection circuitry shall either (1) shutdown the module to prevent further operation or (2) immediately zeroize all plaintext secret and private cryptographic keys and CSPs.

Documentation shall specify the normal operating ranges of a cryptographic module and the environmental failure protection features employed by the module.

4.5.5.2 Environmental Failure Testing Procedures (Alternative 2)

Environmental failure testing (EFT) shall involve a combination of analysis, simulation, and testing of a cryptographic module to provide reasonable assurance that environmental conditions or fluctuations (accidental or induced) outside the module's normal operating ranges for temperature and voltage will not compromise the security of the module.

EFT shall demonstrate that, if the operating temperature or voltage falls outside the normal operating range of the cryptographic module resulting in a failure of the electronic devices or circuitry within the module, at no time shall the security of the cryptographic module be compromised.

The temperature range to be tested shall be from -100° to +200° Celsius (-150° to +400° Fahrenheit). The voltage range to be tested shall be from the smallest negative voltage (with respect to ground) that causes the zeroization of the electronic devices or circuitry to the smallest positive voltage (with respect to ground) that causes the zeroization of the electronic devices or circuitry, including reversing the polarity of the voltages.

Documentation shall specify the normal operating ranges of the cryptographic module and the environmental failure tests performed.

4.6 Operational Environment

The *operational environment* of a cryptographic module refers to the management of the software, firmware, and/or hardware components required for the module to operate. The operational environment can be non-modifiable (e.g., firmware contained in ROM, or software contained in a computer with I/O devices disabled), or modifiable (e.g., firmware contained in RAM or software executed by a general purpose computer). An operating system is an important component of the operating environment of a cryptographic module.

A *general purpose operational environment* refers to the use of a commercially-available general purpose operating system (i.e., resource manager) that manages the software and firmware components within the cryptographic boundary, and also manages system and operator(s) processes/thread(s), including general-purpose application software such as word processors.

A *limited operational environment* refers to a static non-modifiable virtual operational environment (e.g., JAVA virtual machine on a non-programmable PC card) with no underlying general purpose operating system upon which the operational environment uniquely resides.

A *modifiable operational environment* refers to an operating environment that *may* be reconfigured to add/delete/modify functionality, and/or *may* include general purpose operating system capabilities (e.g., use of a computer O/S, configurable smart card O/S, or programmable firmware). Operating systems are considered to be modifiable operational environments if software/firmware components can be modified by the operator and/or the operator can load and execute software or firmware (e.g., a word processor) that was not included as part of the validation of the module.

If the operational environment is a modifiable operational environment, the operating system requirements in Section 4.6.1 shall apply. If the operational environment is a limited operational environment, the operating system requirements in Section 4.6.1 do not apply.

Documentation shall specify the operational environment for a cryptographic module, including, if applicable, the operating system employed by the module, and for Security Levels 2, 3, and 4, the Protection Profile and the CC assurance level.

4.6.1 Operating System Requirements

SECURITY LEVEL 1

The following requirements shall apply to operating systems for Security Level 1.

- For Security Level 1 only, the operating system shall be restricted to a single operator mode of operation (i.e., concurrent operators are explicitly excluded).

- For Security Level 1 only, the cryptographic module shall prevent access by other processes to plaintext private and secret keys, CSPs, and intermediate key generation values during the time the cryptographic module is executing/operational. Processes that are spawned by the cryptographic module are owned by the module and are not owned by external processes/operators. Non-cryptographic processes shall not interrupt a cryptographic module during execution.

- All cryptographic software and firmware shall be installed in a form that protects the software and firmware source and executable code from unauthorized disclosure and modification.

- A cryptographic mechanism using an Approved integrity technique (e.g., an Approved message authentication code or digital signature algorithm) shall be applied to all cryptographic software and firmware components within the cryptographic module. This cryptographic mechanism requirement may be incorporated as part of the Software/Firmware Integrity Test (Section 4.9.1) if an Approved authentication technique is employed for that test.

SECURITY LEVEL 2

In addition to the applicable requirements for Security Level 1, the following requirements shall also apply for Security Level 2.

- All cryptographic software and firmware, cryptographic keys and CSPs, and control and status information shall be under the control of

  - an operating system that meets the functional requirements specified in the Protection Profiles listed in Annex B and is evaluated at the CC evaluation assurance level EAL2, or

  - an equivalent evaluated trusted operating system.

- To protect plaintext data, cryptographic software and firmware, cryptographic keys and CSPs, and authentication data, the discretionary access control mechanisms of the operating system shall be configured to:

  - Specify the set of roles that can *execute* stored cryptographic software and firmware.

  - Specify the set of roles that can *modify* (i.e., write, replace, and delete) the following cryptographic module software or firmware components stored within the cryptographic boundary: cryptographic programs, cryptographic data (e.g., cryptographic keys and audit data), CSPs, and plaintext data.

  - Specify the set of roles that can *read* the following cryptographic software components stored within the cryptographic boundary: cryptographic data (e.g., cryptographic keys and audit data), CSPs, and plaintext data.

  - Specify the set of roles that can *enter* cryptographic keys and CSPs.

- The operating system shall prevent all operators and executing processes from modifying executing cryptographic processes (i.e., loaded and executing cryptographic program images). In this case, executing processes refer to all non-operating system processes (i.e., operator-initiated), cryptographic or not.

- The operating system shall prevent operators and executing processes from reading cryptographic software stored within the cryptographic boundary.

- The operating system shall provide an audit mechanism to record modifications, accesses, deletions, and additions of cryptographic data and CSPs.

  ❑ The following events shall be recorded by the audit mechanism:

    – attempts to provide invalid input for crypto officer functions, and
    – the addition or deletion of an operator to/from a crypto officer role.

  ❑ The audit mechanism shall be capable of auditing the following events:

    – operations to process audit data stored in the audit trail,
    – requests to use authentication data management mechanisms,
    – use of a security-relevant crypto officer function,
    – requests to access user authentication data associated with the cryptographic module,
    – use of an authentication mechanism (e.g., login) associated with the cryptographic module,
    – explicit requests to assume a crypto officer role, and
    – the allocation of a function to a crypto officer role.

SECURITY LEVEL 3

In addition to the applicable requirements for Security Levels 1 and 2, the following requirements shall apply for Security Level 3.

- All cryptographic software and firmware, cryptographic keys and CSPs, and control and status information shall be under the control of

  ❑ an operating system that meets the functional requirements specified in the Protection Profiles listed in Annex B. The operating system shall be evaluated at the CC evaluation assurance level EAL3 and include the following additional requirements: Trusted Path (FTP_TRP.1) and Informal TOE Security Policy Model (ADV_SPM.1), or

  ❑ an equivalent evaluated trusted operating system.

- All cryptographic keys and CSPs, authentication data, control inputs, and status outputs shall be communicated via a trusted mechanism (e.g., a dedicated I/O physical port or a trusted path). If a trusted path is used, the Target of Evaluation Security Functions (TSF) shall support the trusted path between the TSF and the operator when a positive TSF-to-operator connection is required. Communications via this trusted path shall be activated exclusively by an operator or the TSF and shall be logically isolated from other paths.

- In addition to the audit requirements of Security Level 2, the following events shall be recorded by the audit mechanism:

  ❑ attempts to use the trusted path function, and

  ❑ identification of the initiator and target of a trusted path.

SECURITY LEVEL 4

In addition to the applicable requirements for Security Levels 1, 2, and 3, the following requirements shall also apply to operating systems for Security Level 4.

- All cryptographic software, cryptographic keys and CSPs, and control and status information shall be under the control of

  ❑ an operating system that meets the functional requirements specified in the Protection Profiles listed in Annex B. The operating system shall be evaluated at the CC evaluation assurance level EAL4, or

  ❑ an equivalent evaluated trusted operating system.

4.7 Cryptographic Key Management

The security requirements for cryptographic key management encompass the entire lifecycle of cryptographic keys, cryptographic key components, and CSPs employed by the cryptographic module. Key management includes random number and key generation, key establishment, key distribution, key entry/output, key storage, and key zeroization. A cryptographic module may also employ the key management mechanisms of another cryptographic module. Encrypted cryptographic keys and CSPs refer to keys and CSPs that are encrypted using an Approved algorithm or Approved security function. Cryptographic keys and CSPs encrypted using a non-Approved algorithm or proprietary algorithm or method are considered in plaintext form, within the scope of this standard

Secret keys, private keys, and CSPs shall be protected within the cryptographic module from unauthorized disclosure, modification, and substitution. Public keys shall be protected within the cryptographic module against unauthorized modification and substitution.

Documentation shall specify all cryptographic keys, cryptographic key components, and CSPs employed by a cryptographic module.

4.7.1 Random Number Generators (RNGs)

A cryptographic module may employ random number generators (RNGs). If a cryptographic module employs Approved or non-Approved RNGs in an Approved mode of operation, the data output from the RNG shall pass the continuous random number generator test as specified in Section 4.9.2. Approved RNGs shall be subject to the cryptographic algorithm test in Section 4.9.1. Approved RNGs are listed in Annex C to this standard.

Until such time as an Approved nondeterministic RNG standard exists, nondeterministic RNGs approved for use in classified applications may be used for key generation or to seed Approved deterministic RNGs used in key generation. Commercially available nondeterministic RNGs may be used for the purpose of generating seeds for Approved deterministic RNGs. Nondeterministic RNGs shall comply with all applicable RNG requirements of this standard.

An Approved RNG shall be used for the generation of cryptographic keys used by an Approved security function. The output from a non-Approved RNG may be used 1) as input (e.g., seed, and seed key) to an Approved deterministic RNG or 2) to generate initialization vectors (IVs) for Approved security function(s). The seed and seed key shall not have the same value.

Documentation shall specify each RNG (Approved and non-Approved) employed by a cryptographic module.

4.7.2   Key Generation

A cryptographic module may generate cryptographic keys internally. Cryptographic keys generated by the cryptographic module for use by an Approved algorithm or security function shall be generated using an Approved key generation method. Approved key generation methods are listed in Annex C to this standard. If an Approved key generation method requires input from a RNG, then an Approved RNG that meets the requirements specified in Section 4.7.1 shall be used.

Compromising the security of the key generation method (e.g., guessing the seed value to initialize the deterministic RNG) shall require as least as many operations as determining the value of the generated key.

If a seed key is entered during the key generation process, entry of the key shall meet the key entry requirements specified in Section 4.7.4. If intermediate key generation values are output from the cryptographic module, the values shall be output either 1) in encrypted form or 2) under split knowledge procedures.

Documentation shall specify each of the key generation methods (Approved and non-Approved) employed by a cryptographic module.

4.7.3   Key Establishment

Key establishment may be performed by automated methods (e.g., use of a public key algorithm), manual methods (use of a manually-transported key loading device), or a combination of automated and manual methods. If key establishment methods are employed by a cryptographic module, only Approved key establishment methods shall be used.   Approved key establishment methods are listed in Annex D to this standard.

If, in lieu of an Approved key establishment method, a radio communications cryptographic module implements Over-The-Air-Rekeying (OTAR), it shall be implemented as specified in the TIA/EIA Telecommunications Systems Bulletin, APCO Project 25, *Over-The-Air-Rekeying (OTAR) Protocol*, New Technology Standards Project, Digital Radio Technical Standards, TSB102.AACA, January, 1996, Telecommunications Industry Association.

Compromising the security of the key establishment method (e.g., compromising the security of the algorithm used for key establishment) shall require at least as many operations as determining the value of the cryptographic key being transported or agreed upon.

If a *key transport* method is used, the cryptographic key being transported shall meet the key entry/output requirements of Section 4.7.4. If a *key agreement* method is used (e.g., a cryptographic key is derived from shared intermediate values), the shared values are not required to meet the key entry/output requirements of Section 4.7.4.

Documentation shall specify the key establishment methods employed by a cryptographic module.

4.7.4   Key Entry and Output

Cryptographic keys may be entered into or output from a cryptographic module. If cryptographic keys are entered into or output from a cryptographic module, the entry or output of keys shall be performed using either manual (e.g., via a keyboard) or electronic methods (e.g., smart cards/tokens, PC cards, or other electronic key loading devices).

A seed key, if entered during key generation, shall be entered in the same manner as cryptographic keys.

All encrypted secret and private keys, entered into or output from a cryptographic module and used in an Approved mode of operation, shall be encrypted using an Approved algorithm. Public keys may be entered into or output from a cryptographic module in plaintext form. A cryptographic module shall associate a key (secret, private, or public) entered into or output from the module with the correct entity (i.e., person, group, or process) to which the key is assigned.

Manually-entered cryptographic keys (keys entered using manual methods) shall be verified during entry into a cryptographic module for accuracy using the manual key entry test specified in Section 4.9.2. During key entry, the manually entered values may be temporarily displayed to allow visual verification and to improve accuracy. If encrypted cryptographic keys or key components are manually entered into the cryptographic module, then the plaintext values of the cryptographic keys or key components shall not be displayed.

Documentation shall specify the key entry and output methods employed by a cryptographic module.

SECURITY LEVELS 1 AND 2

For Security Levels 1 and 2, secret and private keys established using *automated methods* shall be entered into and output from a cryptographic module in encrypted form. Secret and private keys established using *manual methods* may be entered into or output from a cryptographic module in plaintext form.

SECURITY LEVELS 3 AND 4

For Security Levels 3 and 4:

- Secret and private keys established using *automated methods* shall be entered into and output from a cryptographic module in encrypted form.

- Secret and private keys established using *manual methods* shall be entered into or output from a cryptographic module either (1) in encrypted form or (2) using split knowledge procedures (i.e., as two or more plaintext cryptographic key components).

  If split knowledge procedures are used:

  ❑ the cryptographic module shall separately authenticate the operator entering or outputting each key component,

  ❑ plaintext cryptographic key components shall be directly entered into or output from the cryptographic module (e.g., via a trusted path or directly attached cable) without traveling through any enclosing or intervening systems where the key components may inadvertently be stored, combined, or otherwise processed (see Section 4.2),

  ❑ at least two key components shall be required to reconstruct the original cryptographic key,

  ❑ documentation shall prove that if knowledge of n key components is required to reconstruct the original key, then knowledge of any n-1 key components provides no information about the original key other than the length, and

  ❑ documentation shall specify the procedures employed by a cryptographic module.

4.7.5 Key Storage

Cryptographic keys stored within a cryptographic module shall be stored either in plaintext form or encrypted form. Plaintext secret and private keys shall not be accessible from outside the cryptographic module to unauthorized operators.

A cryptographic module shall associate a cryptographic key (secret, private, or public) stored within the module with the correct entity (e.g., person, group, or process) to which the key is assigned.

Documentation shall specify the key storage methods employed by a cryptographic module.

4.7.6 Key Zeroization

A cryptographic module shall provide methods to zeroize all plaintext secret and private cryptographic keys and CSPs within the module. Zeroization of encrypted cryptographic keys and CSPs or keys otherwise physically or logically protected within an additional embedded validated module (meeting the requirements of this standard) is not required.

Documentation shall specify the key zeroization methods employed by a cryptographic module.

4.8 Electromagnetic Interference/Electromagnetic Compatibility (EMI/EMC)

Cryptographic modules shall meet the following requirements for EMI/EMC. Radios are explicitly excluded from these requirements but shall meet all applicable FCC requirements.

Documentation shall include proof of conformance to EMI/EMC requirements.

SECURITY LEVELS 1 AND 2

For Security Levels 1 and 2, a cryptographic module shall (at a minimum) conform to the EMI/EMC requirements specified by 47 Code of Federal Regulations, Part 15, Subpart B, Unintentional Radiators, Digital Devices, Class A (i.e., for business use).

SECURITY LEVELS 3 AND 4

For Security Levels 3 and 4, a cryptographic module shall (at a minimum) conform to the EMI/EMC requirements specified by 47 Code of Federal Regulations, Part 15, Subpart B, Unintentional Radiators, Digital Devices, Class B (i.e., for home use).

4.9 Self-Tests

A cryptographic module shall perform power-up self-tests and conditional self-tests to ensure that the module is functioning properly. *Power-up self-tests* shall be performed when the cryptographic module is powered up. *Conditional self-tests* shall be performed when an applicable security function or operation is invoked (i.e., security functions for which self-tests are required). A cryptographic module may perform other power-up or conditional self-tests in addition to the tests specified in this standard.

If a cryptographic module fails a self-test, the module shall enter an error state and output an error indicator via the status output interface. The cryptographic module shall not perform any cryptographic operations while in an error state. All data output via the data output interface shall be inhibited when an error state exists.

Documentation shall specify:

- the self-tests performed by a cryptographic module, including power-up and conditional tests,

- the error states that a cryptographic module can enter when a self-test fails, and

- the conditions and actions necessary to exit the error states and resume normal operation of a cryptographic module (i.e., this may include maintenance of the module, or returning the module to the vendor for servicing.)

4.9.1 Power-Up Tests

Power-up tests shall be performed by a cryptographic module when the module is powered up (after being powered off, reset, rebooted, etc.). The power-up tests shall be initiated automatically and shall not require operator intervention. When the power-up tests are completed, the results (i.e., indications of success or failure) shall be output via the "status output" interface. All data output via the data output interface shall be inhibited when the power-up tests are performed.

In addition to performing the power-up tests when powered up, a cryptographic module shall permit operators to initiate the tests on demand for periodic testing of the module. Resetting, rebooting, and power cycling are acceptable means for the on-demand initiation of power-up tests.

A cryptographic module shall perform the following power-up tests: cryptographic algorithm test, software/firmware integrity test, and critical functions test.

Cryptographic algorithm test. A cryptographic algorithm test using a known answer shall be conducted for all cryptographic functions (e.g., encryption, decryption, authentication, and random number generation) of each Approved cryptographic algorithm implemented by a cryptographic module. A known-answer test involves operating the cryptographic algorithm on data for which the correct output is already known and comparing the calculated output with the previously generated output (the known answer). If the calculated output does not equal the known answer, the known-answer test shall fail.

Cryptographic algorithms whose outputs vary for a given set of inputs (e.g., the Digital Signature Algorithm) shall be tested using a known-answer test or shall be tested using a pair-wise consistency test (specified below). Message digest algorithms shall have an independent known-answer test or the known-answer test shall be included with the associated cryptographic algorithm test (e.g., the Digital Signature Standard).

If a cryptographic module includes two independent implementations of the same cryptographic algorithm, then:

- the known-answer test may be omitted,

- the outputs of two implementations shall be continuously compared, and

- if the outputs of two implementations are not equal, the cryptographic algorithm test shall fail.

Software/firmware integrity test. A software/firmware integrity test using an error detection code (EDC) or Approved authentication technique (e.g., an Approved message authentication code or digital signature algorithm) shall be applied to all validated software and firmware components within a cryptographic module when the module is powered up. The software/firmware integrity test is not required for any software and firmware components excluded from the security requirements of this standard (refer to

34

Section 4.1). If the calculated result does not equal the previously generated result, the software/firmware test shall fail.

If an EDC is used, the EDC shall be at least 16 bits in length.

Critical functions test. Other security functions critical to the secure operation of a cryptographic module shall be tested when the module is powered up as part of the power-up tests. Other critical security functions performed under specific conditions shall be tested as conditional tests.

Documentation shall specify all security functions critical to the secure operation of a cryptographic module and shall identify the applicable power-up tests and conditional tests performed by the module.

4.9.2 Conditional Tests

Conditional tests shall be performed by a cryptographic module when the conditions specified for the following tests occur: pair-wise consistency test, software/firmware load test, manual key entry test, continuous random number generator test, and bypass test.

Pair-wise consistency test (for public and private keys). If a cryptographic module generates public or private keys, then the following pair-wise consistency tests for public and private keys shall be performed:

1. If the keys are used to perform an approved key transport method, then the public key shall encrypt a plaintext value. The resulting ciphertext value shall be compared to the original plaintext value. If the two values are equal, then the test shall fail. If the two values differ, then the private key shall be used to decrypt the ciphertext and the resulting value shall be compared to the original plaintext value. If the two values are not equal, the test shall fail.

2. If the keys are used to perform the calculation and verification of digital signatures, then the consistency of the keys shall be tested by the calculation and verification of a digital signature. If the digital signature cannot be verified, the test shall fail.

Software/firmware load test. If software or firmware components can be externally loaded into a cryptographic module, then the following software/firmware load tests shall be performed:

1. An Approved authentication technique (e.g., an Approved message authentication code, digital signature algorithm, or HMAC) shall be applied to all validated software and firmware components when the components are externally loaded into a cryptographic module. The software/firmware load test is not required for any software and firmware components excluded from the security requirements of this standard (refer to Section 4.1).

2. The calculated result shall be compared with a previously generated result. If the calculated result does not equal the previously generated result, the software/firmware load test shall fail.

Manual key entry test. If cryptographic keys or key components are manually entered into a cryptographic module, then the following manual key entry tests shall be performed:

1. The cryptographic key or key components shall have an EDC applied, or shall be entered using duplicate entries.

2. If an EDC is used, the EDC shall be at least 16 bits in length.

3. If the EDC cannot be verified, or the duplicate entries do not match, the test shall fail.

Continuous random number generator test. If a cryptographic module employs   Approved or non-Approved RNGs in an Approved mode of operation, the module shall perform the following continuous random number generator test on each RNG that tests for failure to a constant value.

1. If each call to a RNG produces blocks of n bits (where $n > 15$), the first n-bit block generated after power-up, initialization, or reset shall not be used, but shall be saved for comparison with the next n-bit block to be generated. Each subsequent generation of an n-bit block shall be compared with the previously generated block. The test shall fail if any two compared n-bit blocks are equal.

2. If each call to a RNG produces fewer than 16 bits, the first n bits generated after power-up, initialization, or reset (for some $n > 15$) shall not be used, but shall be saved for comparison with the next n generated bits. Each subsequent generation of n bits shall be compared with the previously generated n bits. The test fails if any two compared n-bit sequences are equal.

Bypass test. If a cryptographic module implements a *bypass* capability where the services may be provided without cryptographic processing (e.g., transferring plaintext through the module), then the following bypass tests shall be performed to ensure that a single point of failure of module components will not result in the unintentional output of plaintext:

1. A cryptographic module shall test for the correct operation of the services providing cryptographic processing when a switch takes place between an exclusive bypass service and an exclusive cryptographic service.

2. If a cryptographic module can automatically alternate between a bypass service and a cryptographic service, providing some services *with* cryptographic processing and some services *without* cryptographic processing, then the module shall test for the correct operation of the services providing cryptographic processing when the mechanism governing the switching procedure is modified (e.g., an IP address source/destination table).

Documentation shall specify the mechanism or logic governing the switching procedure.

4.10   Design Assurance

Design assurance refers to the use of best practices by the vendor of a cryptographic module during the design, deployment, and operation of a cryptographic module, providing assurance that the module is properly tested, configured, delivered, installed, and developed, and that the proper operator guidance documentation is provided. Security requirements are specified for configuration management, delivery and operation, development, and guidance documents.

4.10.1 Configuration Management

Configuration management specifies the security requirements for a configuration management system implemented by a cryptographic module vendor, providing assurance that the functional requirements and specifications are realized in the implementation.

A configuration management system shall be implemented for a cryptographic module and module components within the cryptographic boundary, and for associated module documentation. Each version of each configuration item (e.g., cryptographic module, module components, user guidance, security policy, and operating system) that comprises the module and associated documentation shall be assigned and labeled with a unique identification number.

4.10.2 Delivery and Operation

Delivery and operation specifies the security requirements for the secure delivery, installation, and startup of a cryptographic module, providing assurance that the module is securely delivered to authorized operators, and is installed and initialized in a correct and secure manner.

SECURITY LEVEL 1

For Security Level 1, documentation shall specify the procedures for secure installation, initialization, and startup of a cryptographic module.

SECURITY LEVELS 2, 3, AND 4

For Security Levels 2, 3, and 4, in addition to the requirements of Security Level 1, documentation shall specify the procedures required for maintaining security while distributing and delivering versions of a cryptographic module to authorized operators.

4.10.3 Development

Development specifies the security requirements for the representation of a cryptographic module security functionality at various levels of abstraction from the functional interface to the implementation representation. Development provides assurance that the implementation of a cryptographic module corresponds to the module security policy and functional specification.

Functional specification refers to a high-level description of the ports and interfaces visible to the operator and a high-level description of the behavior of the cryptographic module.

SECURITY LEVEL 1

The following requirements shall apply to cryptographic modules for Security Level 1.

- Documentation shall specify the correspondence between the design of the hardware, software, and firmware components of a cryptographic module and the cryptographic module security policy (see Section 4.1).

- If a cryptographic module contains software or firmware components, documentation shall specify the source code for the software and firmware components, annotated with comments that clearly depict the correspondence of the components to the design of the module.

- If a cryptographic module contains hardware components, documentation shall specify the schematics and/or Hardware Description Language (HDL) listings for the hardware components.

SECURITY LEVEL 2

In addition to the requirements for Security Level 1, the following requirement shall apply to cryptographic modules for Security Level 2.

- Documentation shall specify a functional specification that informally describes a cryptographic module, the external ports and interfaces of the module, and the purpose of the interfaces.

SECURITY LEVEL 3

In addition to the requirements for Security Levels 1 and 2, the following requirements shall apply to cryptographic modules for Security Level 3.

- All software and firmware components within a cryptographic module shall be implemented using a high-level language, except that the limited use of a low-level language (e.g., assembly language or microcode) is allowed if essential to the performance of the module or when a high-level language is not available.

- If HDL is used, all hardware components within a cryptographic module shall be implemented using a high-level specification language.

SECURITY LEVEL 4

In addition to the requirements for Security Levels 1, 2, and 3, the following requirements shall apply to cryptographic modules for Security Level 4.

- Documentation shall specify a formal model that describes the rules and characteristics of the cryptographic module security policy. The formal model shall be specified using a formal specification language that is a rigorous notation based on established mathematics, such as first order logic or set theory.

- Documentation shall specify a rationale that demonstrates the consistency and completeness of the formal model with respect to the cryptographic module security policy.

- Documentation shall specify an informal proof of the correspondence between the formal model and the functional specification.

- For each cryptographic module hardware, software, and firmware component, the source code shall be annotated with comments that specify (1) the preconditions required upon entry into the module component, function, or procedure in order to execute correctly and (2) the postconditions expected to be true when execution of the module component, function, or procedure is complete. The preconditions and postconditions may be specified using any notation that is sufficiently detailed to completely and unambiguously explain the behavior of the cryptographic module component, function, or procedure.

- Documentation shall specify an informal proof of the correspondence between the design of the cryptographic module (as reflected by the precondition and postcondition annotations) and the functional specification.

RECOMMENDED SOFTWARE DEVELOPMENT PRACTICES FOR ALL LEVELS

Implementation of software and firmware components within a cryptographic module using recommended development practices listed in Appendix B will facilitate the analysis of the components for conformance to the requirements in this standard and will reduce the chance of design errors.

4.10.4 Guidance Documents

Crypto officer guidance is concerned with the correct configuration, maintenance, and administration of the cryptographic module. *User guidance* describes the security functions of the cryptographic module along with instructions, guidelines, and warnings for the secure use of the module. If a cryptographic module supports a maintenance role, user/crypto officer guidance describes the physical and/or logical maintenance services for operators assuming the maintenance role.

Crypto officer guidance shall specify:

- the administrative functions, security events, security parameters (and parameter values, as appropriate), physical ports, and logical interfaces of the cryptographic module available to the crypto officer,

- procedures on how to administer the cryptographic module in a secure manner, and

- assumptions regarding user behavior that are relevant to the secure operation of the cryptographic module.

User guidance shall specify:

- the Approved security functions, physical ports, and logical interfaces available to the users of a cryptographic module, and

- all user responsibilities necessary for the secure operation of a cryptographic module.

4. 11 Mitigation of Other Attacks

Cryptographic modules may be susceptible to other attacks for which testable security requirements were not available at the time this version of the standard was issued (e.g., power analysis, timing analysis, and/or fault induction) or the attacks were outside of the scope of the standard (e.g., TEMPEST). Susceptibility of a cryptographic module to such attacks depends on module type, implementation, and implementation environment. Such attacks may be of particular concern for cryptographic modules implemented in hostile environments (e.g., where the attackers may be the authorized operators of the module). Such types of attacks generally rely on the analysis of information obtained from sources physically external to the module. In all cases, the attacks attempt to determine some knowledge about the cryptographic keys and CSPs within the cryptographic module. Brief summaries of currently known attacks are provided below.

Power Analysis: Attacks based on the analysis of power consumption can be divided into two general categories, Simple Power Analysis (SPA) and Differential Power Analysis (DPA). SPA involves a direct (primarily visual) analysis of electrical power consumption patterns and timings derived from the execution of individual instructions carried out by a cryptographic module during a cryptographic process. The patterns are obtained through monitoring the variations in electrical power consumption of a cryptographic module for the purpose of revealing the features and implementations of cryptographic algorithms and subsequently values of cryptographic keys. DPA has the same goals but utilizes advanced statistical methods and/or other techniques to analyze the variations of the electrical power consumption of a cryptographic module. Cryptographic modules that utilize external power (direct current) sources appear to be at greatest risk. Methods that may reduce the overall risk of Power Analysis attacks include the use of capacitors to level the power consumption, the use of internal power sources, and the manipulation of the individual operations of the algorithms or processes to level the rate of power consumption during cryptographic processing.

Timing Analysis: Timing Analysis attacks rely on precisely measuring the time required by a cryptographic module to perform specific mathematical operations associated with a cryptographic algorithm or process. The timing information collected is analyzed to determine the relationship between the inputs to the module and the cryptographic keys used by the underlying algorithms or processes. The analysis of the relationship may be used to exploit the timing measurements to reveal the cryptographic key or CSPs. Timing Analysis attacks assume that the attacker has knowledge of the design of the cryptographic module. Manipulation of the individual operations of the algorithms or processes to reduce timing fluctuations during processing is one method to reduce the risk of this attack.

Fault Induction: Fault Induction attacks utilize external forces such as microwaves, temperature extremes, and voltage manipulation to cause processing errors within the cryptographic module. An analysis of these errors and their patterns can be used in an attempt to reverse engineer the cryptographic module, revealing certain features and implementations of cryptographic algorithms and subsequently revealing the values of cryptographic keys. Cryptographic modules with limited physical security appear to be at greatest risk. Proper selection of physical security features may be used to reduce the risk of this attack.

TEMPEST: TEMPEST attacks involve the remote or external detection and collection of the electromagnetic signals emitted from a cryptographic module and associated equipment during processing. Such an attack can be used to obtain keystroke information, messages displayed on a video screen, and other forms of critical security information (e.g., cryptographic keys). Special shielding of all components, including network cabling, is the mechanism used to reduce the risk of such an attack. Shielding reduces and, in some cases, prevents the emission of electromagnetic signals.

If a cryptographic module is designed to mitigate one or more specific attacks, then the module's security policy shall specify the security mechanisms employed by the module to mitigate the attack(s). The existence and proper functioning of the security mechanisms will be validated when requirements and associated tests are developed.

APPENDIX A: SUMMARY OF DOCUMENTATION REQUIREMENTS

The following check list summarizes the documentation requirements of this standard. All documentation shall be provided to the validation facility by the vendor of a cryptographic module.

CRYPTOGRAPHIC MODULE SPECIFICATION

- Specification of the hardware, software, and firmware components of a cryptographic module, specification of the cryptographic boundary surrounding these components, and description of the physical configuration of the module. *(Security Levels 1, 2, 3, and 4)*

- Specification of any hardware, software, or firmware components of a cryptographic module that are excluded from the security requirements of this standard and an explanation of the rationale for the exclusion. *(Security Levels 1, 2, 3, and 4)*

- Specification of the physical ports and logical interfaces of a cryptographic module. *(Security Levels 1, 2, 3, and 4)*

- Specification of the manual or logical controls of a cryptographic module, physical or logical status indicators, and applicable physical, logical, and electrical characteristics. *(Security Levels 1, 2, 3, and 4)*

- List of all security functions, both Approved and non-Approved, that are employed by a cryptographic module and specification of all modes of operation, both Approved and non-Approved. *(Security Levels 1, 2, 3, and 4)*

- Block diagram depicting all of the major hardware components of a cryptographic module and component interconnections, including any microprocessors, input/output buffers, plaintext/ciphertext buffers, control buffers, key storage, working memory, and program memory. *(Security Levels 1, 2, 3, and 4)*

- Specification of the design of the hardware, software, and firmware components of a cryptographic module. *(Security Levels 1, 2, 3, and 4)*

- Specification of all security-related information, including secret and private cryptographic keys (both plaintext and encrypted), authentication data (e.g., passwords, PINs), CSPs, and other protected information (e.g., audited events, audit data) whose disclosure or modification can compromise the security of the cryptographic module.

- Specification of a cryptographic module security policy including the rules derived from the requirements of this standard and the rules derived from any additional requirements imposed by the vendor). *(Security Levels 1, 2, 3, and 4)*

CRYPTOGRAPHIC MODULE PORTS AND INTERFACES

- Specification of the physical ports and logical interfaces of a cryptographic module and all defined input and output data paths. *(Security Levels 1, 2, 3, and 4)*

ROLES, SERVICES, AND AUTHENTICATION

- Specification of all authorized roles supported by a cryptographic module. *(Security Levels 1, 2, 3, and 4)*

- Specification of the services, operations, or functions provided by a cryptographic module, both Approved and non-Approved. For each service, specification of the service inputs, corresponding service outputs, and the authorized role(s) in which the service can be performed. *(Security Levels 1, 2, 3, and 4)*

- Specification of any services provided by a cryptographic module for which the operator is not required to assume an authorized role, and how these services do not modify, disclose, or substitute cryptographic keys and CSPs, or otherwise affect the security of the module.

- Specification of the authentication mechanisms supported by a cryptographic module, the types of authentication data required to implement supported authentication mechanisms, the authorized methods used to control access to the module for the first time and initialize the authentication mechanism, and the corresponding strength of the mechanisms supported by the module. *(Security Levels 2, 3, and 4)*

FINITE STATE MODEL

- Representation of a finite state model (or equivalent) using the state transition diagram and/or state transition table that specifies all operational and error states, corresponding transitions from one state to another, input events (including data inputs and control outputs) that cause transitions from one state to another, and output events (including internal module conditions, data outputs, and status outputs) resulting from transitions from one state to another. *(Security Levels 1, 2, 3, and 4)*

PHYSICAL SECURITY

- Specification of the physical embodiment and security level for which the physical security mechanisms of a cryptographic module are implemented. Specification of the physical security mechanisms that are employed by a module. *(Security Levels 1, 2, 3, and 4)*

- If a cryptographic module includes a maintenance role that requires physical access to the contents of the module or if the module is designed to permit physical access, specification of the maintenance access interface and how plaintext secret and private keys and CSPs are to be zeroized when the maintenance access interface is accessed. *(Security Levels 1, 2, 3, and 4)*

- Specification of the normal operating ranges of a cryptographic module. Specification of the environmental failure protection features employed by a cryptographic module or specification of the environmental failure tests performed. *(Security Level 4)*

OPERATIONAL ENVIRONMENT

- Specification of the operational environment for the cryptographic module. *(Security Levels 1, 2, 3, and 4)*

- Identification of the operating system employed by a cryptographic module, the applicable Protection Profile, and the CC assurance level. *(Security Levels 2, 3, and 4)*

CRYPTOGRAPHIC KEY MANAGEMENT

- Specification of all cryptographic keys, cryptographic key components, and CSPs employed by a cryptographic module.

- Specification of each RNG (Approved and non-Approved) employed by a cryptographic module. *(Security Levels 1, 2, 3, and 4)*

- Specification of each of the key generation methods (Approved and non-Approved) employed by a cryptographic module. *(Security Levels 1, 2, 3, and 4)*

- Specification of the key establishment methods employed by a cryptographic module. *(Security Levels 1, 2, 3, and 4)*

- Specification of the key entry and output methods employed by a cryptographic module. *(Security Levels 1, 2, 3, and 4)*

- If split knowledge procedures are used, proof that if knowledge of *n* key components is required to reconstruct the original key, then knowledge that any *n*-1 key components provides no information about the original key other than length, and specification of the split-knowledge procedures employed by a cryptographic module. *(Security Levels 3 and 4)*

- Specification of the key storage methods employed by a cryptographic module. *(Security Levels 1, 2, 3, and 4)*

- Specification of the key zeroization methods employed by a cryptographic module. *(Security Levels 1, 2, 3, and 4)*

ELECTROMAGNETIC INTERFERENCE/ELECTROMAGNETIC COMPATIBILITY

- Proof of conformance to EMI/EMC requirements. *(Security Levels 1, 2, 3, and 4)*

SELF-TESTS

- Specification of the self-tests performed by a cryptographic module including power-up and conditional tests. *(Security Levels 1, 2, 3, and 4)*

- Specification of the error states that a cryptographic module can enter when a self-test fails, and the conditions and actions necessary to exit the error states and resume normal operation of a module. *(Security Levels 1, 2, 3, and 4)*

- Specification of all security functions critical to the secure operation of a cryptographic module and identification of the applicable power-up tests and conditional tests performed by the module. *(Security Levels 1, 2, 3, and 4)*

- If a cryptographic module implements a bypass capability, specification of the mechanism or logic governing the switching procedure. *(Security Levels 1, 2, 3, and 4)*

DESIGN ASSURANCE

- Specification of procedures for secure installation, generation, and start-up of a cryptographic module. *(Security Levels 1, 2, 3, and 4)*

- Specification of the procedures for maintaining security while distributing and delivering versions of a cryptographic module to authorized operators. *(Security Level 2, 3, and 4)*

- Specification of the correspondence between the design of the hardware, software, and firmware components of a cryptographic module and the cryptographic module security policy (i.e., the rules of operation). *(Security Levels 1, 2, 3, and 4)*

- If a cryptographic module contains software or firmware components, specification of the source code for the software and firmware components, annotated with comments that clearly depict the correspondence of the components to the design of the module. *(Security Levels 1, 2, 3, and 4)*

- If a cryptographic module contains hardware components, specification of the schematics and/or Hardware Description Language (HDL) listings for the hardware components. *(Security Levels 1, 2, 3, and 4)*

- Functional specification that informally describes a cryptographic module, the external ports and interfaces of the module, and the purpose of the interfaces. *(Security Levels 2, 3, and 4)*

- Specification of a formal model that describes the rules and characteristics of the cryptographic module security policy, using a formal specification language that is a rigorous notation based on established mathematics, such as first order logic or set theory. *(Security Level 4)*

- Specification of a rationale that demonstrates the consistency and completeness of the formal model with respect to the cryptographic module security policy. *(Security Level 4)*

- Specification of an informal proof of the correspondence between the formal model and the functional specification. *(Security Level 4)*

- For each hardware, software, and firmware component, source code annotation with comments that specify (1) the preconditions required upon entry into the module component, function or procedure in order to execute correctly and (2) the postconditions expected to be true when execution of the module component, function, or procedure is complete. *(Security Level 4)*

- Specification of an informal proof of the correspondence between the design of the cryptographic module (as reflected by the precondition and postcondition annotations) and the functional specification. *(Security Level 4)*

- For crypto officer guidance, specification of:

  - the administrative functions, security events, security parameters (and parameter values, as appropriate), physical ports, and logical interfaces of the cryptographic module available to the crypto officer *(Security Levels 1, 2, 3, and 4)*,

  - procedures on how to administer the cryptographic module in a secure manner *(Security Levels 1, 2, 3, and 4)*, and

  - assumptions regarding user behavior that is relevant to the secure operation of the cryptographic module. *(Security Levels 1, 2, 3, and 4)*

- For user guidance, specification of

  - the Approved security functions, physical ports, and logical interfaces available to the users of the cryptographic module *(Security Levels 1, 2, 3, and 4)*, and

  - all user responsibilities necessary for the secure operation of the module. *(Security Levels 1, 2, 3, and 4)*

MITIGATION OF OTHER ATTACKS

- If a cryptographic module is designed to mitigate one or more specific attacks, specification in the module's security policy of the security mechanisms employed by the cryptographic module to mitigate the attack(s). *(Security Levels 1, 2, 3, and 4)*

SECURITY POLICY

- See Appendix C. *(Security Levels 1, 2, 3, and 4)*

APPENDIX B: RECOMMENDED SOFTWARE DEVELOPMENT PRACTICES

This Appendix is provided for informational purposes only and does not contain security requirements applicable to cryptographic modules within the scope of the standard.

Life-cycle software engineering recommendations (dealing with the specification, construction, verification, testing, maintenance, and documentation of software) should be followed. Software engineering practices may include documented unit testing, code reviews, explicit high-level and low-level design documents, explicit requirements and functional specifications, structure charts and data flow diagrams, function-point analysis, defect and resolution tracking, configuration management, and a documented software development process.

For all software development, both large and small, the following programming techniques are consistent with current practices and should be used to facilitate analysis of software components of a cryptographic module and to reduce chances of programming errors.

MODULAR DESIGN

- A modular design is recommended, especially for moderate to large-scale software development efforts. Each software module should have well-defined and readily understood logical interfaces.

- Software components should be constructed using the principles of data abstraction. If available, an object-oriented, high-level language that supports the construction of abstract data types should be used.

- The software should be hierarchically structured as a series of layers.

SOFTWARE MODULE/PROCEDURE INTERFACES

- Entries to a software module or procedure should be through external calls on explicitly defined interfaces.

- Each procedure should have only one entry point and at most two exit points, one for normal exits and one for error exits.

- Data should be communicated between software modules and between procedures through the use of argument lists and/or explicit return values. Global variables should not be used among procedures except where necessary for the implementation of abstract data types. Input values should be checked for range errors using assertion statements (if provided by the programming language in use).

INTERNAL CONSTRUCTION

- Each procedure should perform only a single, well-defined function.

- Control flow within a single thread of execution should be defined using only sequencing, structured programming constructs for conditionals (e.g., if-then-else or case), and structured constructs for loops (e.g., while-do or repeat-until).

- If concurrent execution is employed (e.g., via multiple threads, tasks, or processes), the software components should enforce limits on the maximum allowable degree of concurrency and should use structured synchronization constructs to control access to shared data.

- Equivalence of variables should not be used to permit multiple memory usage for conflicting purposes.

- Robust command parsing and range checking mechanisms should be implemented to guard against malformed requests, out-of-range parameters, and I/O buffer overflows.

IN-LINE DOCUMENTATION

- Each software module, procedure, and major programming construct should be documented specifying the functions performed along with a (formal or informal) specification of preconditions and postconditions.

- Each loop should be preceded by a convincing argument (as a comment) that termination is guaranteed.

- Variable names should be used in only one context within the same procedure.

- Each variable should have an associated comment identifying the purpose of the variable and noting the range of allowable values, including if the range is unrestricted.

- If concurrency is employed, the documentation should specify how limits are enforced on the maximum allowable degree of concurrency and how accesses to shared data are synchronized in order to avoid (possibly undetected) run-time errors.

ASSEMBLY LANGUAGE

The following additional programming practices should be used when the implementation is in assembly language.

- All code should be position independent except where appropriate security concerns, efficiency, or hardware constraints require position dependency.

- All register references should use symbolic register names.

- Self-modifying code should not be used.

- All procedures should be responsible for saving and restoring the contents of any register that is used within the procedure.

- Control transfer instructions should not use numeric literals.

- Each unit should contain comments describing register use in the unit.

APPENDIX C: CRYPTOGRAPHIC MODULE SECURITY POLICY

A cryptographic module security policy shall be included in the documentation provided by the vendor. The following paragraphs outline the required contents of the security policy.

C.1 Definition of Cryptographic Module Security Policy

A cryptographic module security policy shall consist of:

- a specification of the security rules, under which a cryptographic module shall operate, including the security rules derived from the requirements of the standard and the additional security rules imposed by the vendor.

The specification shall be sufficiently detailed to answer the following questions:

- What access does operator X, performing service Y while in role Z, have to security-relevant data item W for every role, service, and security-relevant data item contained in the cryptographic module?

- What physical security mechanisms are implemented to protect a cryptographic module and what actions are required to ensure that the physical security of a module is maintained?

- What security mechanisms are implemented in a cryptographic module to mitigate against attacks for which testable requirements are not defined in the standard?

C.2 Purpose of Cryptographic Module Security Policy

There are two major reasons for developing and following a precise cryptographic module security policy:

- To provide a specification of the cryptographic security that will allow individuals and organizations to determine whether a cryptographic module, as implemented, satisfies a stated security policy.

- To describe to individuals and organizations the capabilities, protection, and access rights provided by the cryptographic module, thereby allowing an assessment of whether the module will adequately serve the individual or organizational security requirements.

C.3 Specification of a Cryptographic Module Security Policy

A cryptographic module security policy shall be expressed in terms of roles, services, and cryptographic keys and CSPs. At a minimum, the following shall be specified:

- an identification and authentication (I&A) policy,

- an access control policy,

- a physical security policy, and

- a security policy for mitigation of other attacks.

C.3.1 Identification and Authentication Policy

The cryptographic module security policy shall specify an identification and authentication policy, including

- all roles (e.g., user, crypto officer, and maintenance) and associated type of authentication (e.g., identity-based, role-based, or none) and

- the authentication data required of each role or operator (e.g., password or biometric data) and the corresponding strength of the authentication mechanism.

C.3.2 Access Control Policy

The cryptographic module security policy shall specify an access control policy. The specification shall be of sufficient detail to identify the cryptographic keys and CSPs that the operator has access to while performing a service, and the type(s) of access the operator has to the parameters.

The security policy shall specify:

- all roles supported by a cryptographic module,

- all services provided by a cryptographic module,

- all cryptographic keys and CSPs employed by the cryptographic module, including

  - secret, private, and public cryptographic keys (both plaintext and encrypted),

  - authentication data such as passwords or PINs, and

  - other security-relevant information (e.g., audited events and audit data),

- for each role, the services an operator is authorized to perform within that role, and

- for each service within each role, the type(s) of access to the cryptographic keys and CSPs.

C.3.3 Physical Security Policy

The cryptographic module security policy shall specify a physical security policy, including:

- the physical security mechanisms that are implemented in a cryptographic module (e.g., tamper-evident seals, locks, tamper response and zeroization switches, and alarms) and

- the actions required by the operator(s) to ensure that physical security is maintained (e.g., periodic inspection of tamper-evident seals or testing of tamper response and zeroization switches).

C.3.4 Mitigation of Other Attacks Policy

The cryptographic module security policy shall specify a security policy for mitigation of other attacks, including the security mechanisms implemented to mitigate the attacks.

C.4 Security Policy Check List Tables

The following check list tables may be used as guides to ensure the security policy is complete and contains the appropriate details:

Role	Type of Authentication	Authentication Data
...	...	... ...
...	...	... ...

Table C1. *Roles and Required Identification and Authentication*

Authentication Mechanism	Strength of Mechanism
...	...
...	...

Table C2. *Strengths of Authentication Mechanisms*

Role	Authorized Services
...	... ...
...	... ...

Table C3. *Services Authorized for Roles*

Service	Cryptographic Keys and CSPs	Type(s) of Access (e.g., RWE)
...	... ...	... ...
...	... ...	... ...

Table C4. *Access Rights within Services*

Physical Security Mechanisms	Recommended Frequency of Inspection/Test	Inspection/Test Guidance Details
...	... ...	... ...
...	... ...	... ...

Table C5. *Inspection/Testing of Physical Security Mechanisms*

Other Attacks	Mitigation Mechanism	Specific Limitations
...	... ...	... ...
...	... ...	... ...

Table C6. *Mitigation of Other Attacks*

APPENDIX D: SELECTED BIBLIOGRAPHY

American Bankers Association, *Digital Signatures using Reversible Public Key Cryptography for the Financial Services Industry (rDSA),* ANSI X9.31-1998, Washington, D.C., 1998.

American Bankers Association, *Triple Data Encryption Algorithm Modes of Operation*, ANSI X9.52-1998, Washington, D.C., 1998.

American Bankers Association, *Public Key Cryptography for the Financial Services Industry: The Elliptic Curve Digital Signature Algorithm*, American National Standard X9.62-1998, Washington, D.C., 1998.

Common Criteria Implementation Board (CCIB), *International Standard (IS) 15408, Common Criteria for Information Technology Security Evaluation*, Version 2, May 1998, ISO/IEC JTC 1 and Common Criteria Implementation Board.

Computer Security Act of 1987, 40 U.S. Code 759, (Public Law 100-235), January 8, 1988.

Department of Defense, *Department of Defense Trusted Computer System Evaluation Criteria*, DOD 5200.28-STD, December 1985.

Information Technology Management Reform Act of 1996, U.S. Code, (Public Law 104-106), 10 February 1996.

Information Technology Security Evaluation Criteria (ITSEC), Harmonized Criteria of France – Germany - the Netherlands - the United Kingdom, Version 1.1, January 1991.

Keller, Sharon and Smid, Miles, *Modes of Operation Validation System (MOVS): Requirements and Procedures*, Special Publication 800-17, Gaithersburg, MD, National Institute of Standards and Technology, February 1998.

Keller, Sharon, *Modes of Operation Validation System for the Triple Data Encryption Algorithm (TMOVS): Requirements and Procedures,* Special Publication 800-20, Gaithersburg, MD, National Institute of Standards and Technology, October 1999.

Lee, Annabelle, *Guideline for Implementing Cryptography in the Federal Government*, Special Publication 800-21, Gaithersburg, MD, National Institute of Standards and Technology, November, 1999.

National Institute of Standards and Technology, *FIPS 140-2 Annex A: Approved Security Functions*, available at URL: http://www.nist.gov/cmvp.

National Institute of Standards and Technology, *FIPS 140-2 Annex B: Approved Protection Profiles*, available at URL: http://www.nist.gov/cmvp.

National Institute of Standards and Technology, *FIPS 140-2 Annex C: Approved Random Number Generators*, available at URL: http://www.nist.gov/cmvp.

National Institute of Standards and Technology, *FIPS 140-2 Annex D: Approved Key Establishment Techniques*, available at URL: http://www.nist.gov/cmvp.

National Institute of Standards and Technology, *Computer Data Authentication*, Federal Information Processing Standards Publication 113, 30 May 1985.

National Institute of Standards and Technology, *Data Encryption Standard*, Federal Information Processing Standards Publication 46-3, October 25, 1999.

National Institute of Standards and Technology and Communications Security Establishment, *Derived Test Requirements(DTR) for FIPS PUB 140-2, Security Requirements for Cryptographic Modules*, available at URL: http://www.nist.gov/cmvp.

National Institute of Standards and Technology, *DES Modes of Operation*, Federal Information Processing Standards Publication 81, December 2, 1980.

National Institute of Standards and Technology, *Digital Signature Standard (DSS)*, Federal Information Processing Standards Publication 186-2, January 27, 2000.

National Institute of Standards and Technology, *Digital Signature Standard Validation System (DSSVS) User's Guide*, June 20, 1997.

National Institute of Standards and Technology, *Entity Authentication Using Public Key Cryptography*, Federal Information Processing Standards Publication 196, February 18, 1997.

National Institute of Standards and Technology, *Guideline for the Use of Advanced Authentication Technology Alternatives*, Federal Information Processing Standards Publication 190, September 28, 1994.

National Institute of Standards and Technology and Communications Security Establishment, *Implementation Guidance (IG) for FIPS 140-2*, available at URL: http://www.nist.gov/cmvp.

National Institute of Standards and Technology, *Key Management using ANSI X9.17*, Federal Information Processing Standards Publication 171, April 27, 1992.

National Institute of Standards and Technology, *Secure Hash Standard*, Federal Information Processing Standards Publication 180-1, April 17, 1995.

National Institute of Standards and Technology, *Security Requirements for Cryptographic Modules*, Federal Information Processing Standards Publication 140-1, January 11, 1994.

Office of Management and Budget, *Security of Federal Automated Information Resources*, Appendix III to OMB Circular No. A-130, February 8, 1996.

Telecommunications Industry Association, *Over-The-Air-Rekeying (OTAR) Protocol*, New Technology Standards Project, Digital Radio Technical Standards, TIA/EIA Telecommunications Systems Bulletin, APCO Project 25, TSB102.AACA, January 1996.

APPENDIX E: APPLICABLE INTERNET UNIFORM RESOURCE LOCATORS (URL)

Communications Security Establishment (CSE): http://www.cse-cst.gc.ca

Cryptographic Module Validation Program (CMVP): http://www.nist.gov/cmvp

NIST Information Technology Laboratory (NIST ITL): http://www.nist.gov/itl

NIST Security Publications including FIPS and Special Publications: http://csrc.nist.gov/publications

National Technical Information Service (NTIS): http://www.ntis.gov

National Voluntary Laboratory Accreditation Program (NVLAP): http://ts.nist.gov/nvlap

National Information Assurance Partnership® (NIAP): http://niap.nist.gov/

Validated Protection Profiles: http://niap.nist.gov/cc-scheme/PPRegistry.html

CHANGE NOTICES

Change Notice 1 (Superseded by Change Notice 2)

FIPS PUB 140-2, SECURITY REQUIREMENTS FOR CRYPTOGRAPHIC MODULES

U.S. DEPARTMENT OF COMMERCE
NATIONAL INSTITUTE OF STANDARDS AND TECHNOLOGY
Gaithersburg, MD 20899

DATE OF CHANGE: 2001 October 10

Federal Information Processing Standard (FIPS) 140-2, *Security Requirements for Cryptographic Modules*, specifies the security requirements that will be satisfied by a cryptographic module utilized within a security system protecting sensitive but unclassified information (hereafter referred to as sensitive information).

This change notice provides a correction to the required intervals for the length of runs test indicated in Table 3 in Section 4.9.1 Power-Up Tests.

Table 3 as originally published, incorrectly specified the required intervals. The correct intervals are indicated.

Incorrect	
Length of Run	Required Interval
1	2,343 – 2,657
2	1,135 – 1,365
3	542 – 708
4	251 – 373
5	111 – 201
6+	111 - 201

Correct	
Length of Run	Required Interval
1	2,315 – 2,685
2	1,114 – 1,386
3	527 - 723
4	240 - 384
5	103 - 209
6+	103 - 209

Questions regarding this change notice may be directed to Annabelle Lee (annabelle.lee@nist.gov, 301-975-2941).

Change Notice 2

FIPS PUB 140-2, SECURITY REQUIREMENTS FOR CRYPTOGRAPHIC MODULES

U.S. DEPARTMENT OF COMMERCE
NATIONAL INSTITUTE OF STANDARDS AND TECHNOLOGY
Gaithersburg, MD 20899

DATE OF CHANGE: 2002 December 03

TITLE: Random Number Generator Requirements

Federal Information Processing Standard (FIPS) 140-2, *Security Requirements for Cryptographic Modules*, specifies the security requirements that will be satisfied by a cryptographic module utilized within a security system protecting sensitive but unclassified information (hereafter referred to as sensitive information).

This change notice provides corrections to the requirements for random number generator used by cryptographic modules. These corrections involve paragraphs 4.7.1 and 4.9.1 of FIPS 140-2. Table 1 – *Summary of security requirements* has also been corrected and involves the random number generator requirements.

This change notice also provides a correction to the Table 1 – *Summary of security requirements*. The correction involves text found in the requirements of Physical Security at Security Level 4.

Finally, this change notice replaces the term "modes" used in paragraph 4.9.1 *Cryptographic algorithm test* with "cryptographic functions" which clarifies the standard.

In the corrected paragraphs and table below, the deleted text is struck out and the added text is underlined.

Change Notice 2 supersedes Change Notice 1.

The *Derived Test Requirements for FIPS 140-2* are also affected by these corrections.

Questions regarding this change notice may be directed to Annabelle Lee (annabelle.lee@nist.gov, 301-975-2941).

4.7.1   Random Number Generators (RNGs)

A cryptographic module may employ random number generators (RNGs). If a cryptographic module employs Approved or non-Approved RNGs in an Approved mode of operation, the data output from the RNG shall pass the continuous random number generator test as specified in Section 4.9.2. ~~Depending on the security level, the data output from an Approved RNG shall pass all statistical tests for randomness as specified in Section 4.9.1.~~ Approved ~~deterministic~~ RNGs shall be subject to the cryptographic algorithm test in Section 4.9.1. Approved RNGs are listed in Annex C to this standard.

Until such time as an Approved nondeterministic RNG standard exists, nondeterministic RNGs approved for use in classified applications may be used for key generation or to seed Approved deterministic RNGs used in key generation. Commercially available nondeterministic RNGs may be used for the purpose of generating seeds for Approved deterministic RNGs. Nondeterministic RNGs shall comply with all applicable RNG requirements of this standard.

An Approved RNG shall be used for the generation of cryptographic keys used by an Approved security function. The output from a non-Approved RNG may be used 1) as input (e.g., seed, and seed key) to an

Approved deterministic RNG or 2) to generate initialization vectors (IVs) for Approved security function(s). The seed and seed key shall not have the same value.

Documentation shall specify each RNG (Approved and non-Approved) employed by a cryptographic module.

4.9.1 Power-Up Tests

Power-up tests shall be performed by a cryptographic module when the module is powered up (after being powered off, reset, rebooted, etc.). The power-up tests shall be initiated automatically and shall not require operator intervention. When the power-up tests are completed, the results (i.e., indications of success or failure) shall be output via the "status output" interface. All data output via the data output interface shall be inhibited when the power-up tests are performed.

In addition to performing the power-up tests when powered up, a cryptographic module shall permit operators to initiate the tests on demand for periodic testing of the module. Resetting, rebooting, and power cycling are acceptable means for the on-demand initiation of power-up tests.

A cryptographic module shall perform the following power-up tests: cryptographic algorithm test, software/firmware integrity test, and critical functions test.

SECURITY LEVELS 1 AND 2

For Security Levels 1 and 2, a cryptographic module shall perform the following power-up tests: cryptographic algorithm test, software/firmware integrity test, and critical functions test. Statistical random number generator tests may be performed by the cryptographic module but are not required at Security Levels 1 and 2.

SECURITY LEVEL 3

For Security Level 3, in addition to the tests specified for Security Levels 1 and 2, a cryptographic module shall perform all of the statistical random number tests on demand by the operator and *may* perform the tests when the module is powered up.

SECURITY LEVEL 4

For Security Level 4, in addition to the tests specified for Security Levels 1,2 and 3, a cryptographic module shall also perform all of the statistical random number generator tests when the module is powered up.

Cryptographic algorithm test. A cryptographic algorithm test using a known answer shall be conducted for all ~~modes~~ cryptographic functions (e.g., encryption, decryption, authentication, and ~~deterministic~~ random number generation) of each Approved cryptographic algorithm implemented by a cryptographic module. A known-answer test involves operating the cryptographic algorithm on data for which the correct output is already known and comparing the calculated output with the previously generated output (the known answer). If the calculated output does not equal the known answer, the known-answer test shall fail.

Cryptographic algorithms whose outputs vary for a given set of inputs (e.g., the Digital Signature Algorithm) shall be tested using a known-answer test or shall be tested using a pair-wise consistency test (specified below). Message digest algorithms shall have an independent known-answer test or the known-answer test shall be included with the associated cryptographic algorithm test (e.g., the Digital Signature Standard).

If a cryptographic module includes two independent implementations of the same cryptographic algorithm, then:

- the known-answer test may be omitted,

- the outputs of two implementations shall be continuously compared, and

- if the outputs of two implementations are not equal, the cryptographic algorithm test shall fail.

Software/firmware integrity test. A software/firmware integrity test using an error detection code (EDC) or Approved authentication technique (e.g., an Approved message authentication code or digital signature algorithm) shall be applied to all validated software and firmware components within a cryptographic module when the module is powered up. The software/firmware integrity test is not required for any software and firmware components excluded from the security requirements of this standard (refer to Section 4.1). If the calculated result does not equal the previously generated result, the software/firmware test shall fail.

If an EDC is used, the EDC shall be at least 16 bits in length.

Critical functions test. Other security functions critical to the secure operation of a cryptographic module shall be tested when the module is powered up as part of the power-up tests. Other critical security functions performed under specific conditions shall be tested as conditional tests.

Documentation shall specify all security functions critical to the secure operation of a cryptographic module and shall identify the applicable power-up tests and conditional tests performed by the module.

Statistical random number generator tests. If statistical random number generator tests are required (i.e., depending on the security level), a cryptographic module employing RNGs shall perform the following statistical tests for randomness. A single bit stream of 20,000 consecutive bits of output from each RNG shall be subjected to the following four tests: monobit test, poker test, runs test, and long runs test.

The monobit test

Count the number of ones in the 20,000 bit stream. Denote this quantity by X.

The test is passed if 9,725 < X < 10,275.

The poker test

Divide the 20,000 bit stream into 5,000 consecutive 4 bit segments. Count and store the number of occurrences of the 16 possible 4 bit values. Denote $f(i)$ as the number of each 4 bit value i, where $0 \leq i \leq 15$.

Evaluate the following:

$$X = (16/5000) * \left(\sum_{i=0}^{15} [f(i)]^2 \right) - 5000$$

The test is passed if 2.16 < X < 46.17.

The runs test

57

A run is defined as a maximal sequence of consecutive bits of either all ones or all zeros that is part of the 20,000 bit sample stream. The incidences of runs (for both consecutive zeros and consecutive ones) of all lengths (≥ 1) in the sample stream should be counted and stored.

The test is passed if the runs that occur (of lengths 1 through 6) are each within the corresponding interval specified in the table below. This must hold for both the zeros and ones (i.e., all 12 counts must lie in the specified interval). For the purposes of this test, runs of greater than 6 are considered to be of length 6.

Length of Run	Required Interval
1	2,343 — 2,657
2	1,135 — 1,365
3	542 — 708
4	251 — 373
5	111 — 201
6+	111 — 201

Table 3. *Required intervals for length of runs test*

The long runs test

A long run is defined to be a run of length 26 or more (of either zeros or ones).

On the sample of 20,000 bits, the test is passed if there are no long runs.

	Security Level 1	Security Level 2	Security Level 3	Security Level 4
Cryptographic Module Specification	Specification of cryptographic module, cryptographic boundary, Approved algorithms, and Approved modes of operation. Description of cryptographic module, including all hardware, software, and firmware components. Statement of module security policy.			
Cryptographic Module Ports and Interfaces	Required and optional interfaces. Specification of all interfaces and of all input and output data paths.		Data ports for unprotected critical security parameters logically or physically separated from other data ports.	
Roles, Services, and Authentication	Logical separation of required and optional roles and services.	Role-based or identity-based operator authentication.	Identity-based operator authentication.	
Finite State Model	Specification of finite state model. Required states and optional states. State transition diagram and specification of state transitions.			
Physical Security	Production grade equipment.	Locks or tamper evidence.	Tamper detection and response for covers and doors.	Tamper detection and response envelope. EFP ~~and~~ or EFT.
Operational Environment	Single operator. Executable code. Approved integrity technique.	Referenced PPs evaluated at EAL2 with specified discretionary access control mechanisms and auditing.	Referenced PPs plus trusted path evaluated at EAL3 plus security policy modeling.	Referenced PPs plus trusted path evaluated at EAL4.
Cryptographic Key Management	Key management mechanisms: random number and key generation, key establishment, key distribution, key entry/output, key storage, and key zeroization.			
	Secret and private keys established using manual methods may be entered or output in plaintext form.		Secret and private keys established using manual methods shall be entered or output encrypted or with split knowledge procedures.	
EMI/EMC	47 CFR FCC Part 15. Subpart B, Class A (Business use). Applicable FCC requirements (for radio).		47 CFR FCC Part 15. Subpart B, Class B (Home use).	
Self-Tests	Power-up tests: cryptographic algorithm tests, software/firmware integrity tests, critical functions tests. Conditional tests.			
			~~Statistical RNG tests callable on demand.~~	~~Statistical RNG tests performed at power-up.~~
Design Assurance	Configuration management (CM). Secure installation and generation. Design and policy correspondence. Guidance documents.	CM system. Secure distribution. Functional specification.	High-level language implementation.	Formal model. Detailed explanations (informal proofs). Preconditions and postconditions.
Mitigation of Other Attacks	Specification of mitigation of attacks for which no testable requirements are currently available.			

Table 1: *Summary of security requirements*

Change Notice 3

FIPS PUB 140-2, SECURITY REQUIREMENTS FOR CRYPTOGRAPHIC MODULES

U.S. DEPARTMENT OF COMMERCE
NATIONAL INSTITUTE OF STANDARDS AND TECHNOLOGY
Gaithersburg, MD 20899

DATE OF CHANGE: 2002 December 03

TITLE: Pair-Wise Consistency Test

Federal Information Processing Standard (FIPS) 140-2, *Security Requirements for Cryptographic Modules*, specifies the security requirements that will be satisfied by a cryptographic module utilized within a security system protecting sensitive but unclassified information (hereafter referred to as sensitive information).

This change notice provides corrections to the requirements for pair-wise consistency test for public/ private keys used for key agreement. These corrections involve paragraphs 4.9.2 of FIPS 140-2.

In the corrected paragraphs below, the deleted text is struck out and the added text is underlined.

The *Derived Test Requirements for FIPS 140-2* is also affected by these corrections.

Questions regarding this change notice may be directed to Annabelle Lee (annabelle.lee@nist.gov, 301-975-2941).

4.9.2   Conditional Tests

Conditional tests shall be performed by a cryptographic module when the conditions specified for the following tests occur: pair-wise consistency test, software/firmware load test, manual key entry test, continuous random number generator test, and bypass test.

> *Pair-wise consistency test (for public and private keys).* If a cryptographic module generates public or private keys, then the following pair-wise consistency tests for public and private keys shall be performed:
>
> 1. If the keys are used to perform <u>an approved</u> key transport <u>method</u> ~~or encryption~~, then the public key shall encrypt a plaintext value. The resulting ciphertext value shall be compared to the original plaintext value. If the two values are equal, then the test shall fail. If the two values differ, then the private key shall be used to decrypt the ciphertext and the resulting value shall be compared to the original plaintext value. If the two values are not equal, the test shall fail.
>
> 2. ~~If the keys are used to perform key agreement, then the cryptographic module shall create a second, compatible key pair. The cryptographic module shall perform both sides of the key agreement algorithm and shall compare the resulting shared values. If the shared values are not equal, the test shall fail.~~
>
> 2. If the keys are used to perform the calculation and verification of digital signatures, then the consistency of the keys shall be tested by the calculation and verification of a digital signature. If the digital signature cannot be verified, the test shall fail.

Change Notice 4

FIPS PUB 140-2, SECURITY REQUIREMENTS FOR CRYPTOGRAPHIC MODULES

U.S. DEPARTMENT OF COMMERCE
NATIONAL INSTITUTE OF STANDARDS AND TECHNOLOGY
Gaithersburg, MD 20899

DATE OF CHANGE: 2002 December 03

TITLE: Limited Operational Environment

Federal Information Processing Standard (FIPS) 140-2, *Security Requirements for Cryptographic Modules*, specifies the security requirements that will be satisfied by a cryptographic module utilized within a security system protecting sensitive but unclassified information (hereafter referred to as sensitive information).

This change notice provides a correction to the definition of a *Limited Operational Environment*. This correction involves paragraph 4.6 of FIPS 140-2.

In the corrected paragraph below, the deleted text is struck out and the added text is underlined.

Questions regarding this change notice may be directed to Annabelle Lee (annabelle.lee@nist.gov, 301-975-2941).

4.6   Operational Environment

A *limited operational environment* refers to a static non-modifiable virtual operational environment (e.g., JAVA virtual machine ~~or~~ on a non-programmable PC card) with no underlying general purpose operating system upon which the operational environment uniquely resides.

FIPS PUB 180-4

FEDERAL INFORMATION PROCESSING STANDARDS PUBLICATION

Secure Hash Standard (SHS)

CATEGORY: COMPUTER SECURITY   SUBCATEGORY: CRYPTOGRAPHY

Information Technology Laboratory
National Institute of Standards and Technology
Gaithersburg, MD 20899-8900

This publication is available free of charge from:
http://dx.doi.org/10.6028/NIST.FIPS.180-4

August 2015

U.S. Department of Commerce
Penny Pritzker, Secretary

National Institute of Standards and Technology
Willie E. May, Under Secretary for Standards and Technology and Director

FOREWORD

The Federal Information Processing Standards Publication Series of the National Institute of Standards and Technology (NIST) is the official series of publications relating to standards and guidelines adopted and promulgated under the provisions of the Federal Information Security Management Act (FISMA) of 2002.

Comments concerning FIPS publications are welcomed and should be addressed to the Director, Information Technology Laboratory, National Institute of Standards and Technology, 100 Bureau Drive, Stop 8900, Gaithersburg, MD 20899-8900.

Charles H. Romine, Director
Information Technology Laboratory

Abstract

This standard specifies hash algorithms that can be used to generate digests of messages. The digests are used to detect whether messages have been changed since the digests were generated.

Key words: computer security, cryptography, message digest, hash function, hash algorithm, Federal Information Processing Standards, Secure Hash Standard.

**Federal Information
Processing Standards Publication 180-4**

August 2015

Announcing the

SECURE HASH STANDARD

Federal Information Processing Standards Publications (FIPS PUBS) are issued by the National Institute of Standards and Technology (NIST) after approval by the Secretary of Commerce pursuant to Section 5131 of the Information Technology Management Reform Act of 1996 (Public Law 104-106), and the Computer Security Act of 1987 (Public Law 100-235).

1. **Name of Standard**: Secure Hash Standard (SHS) (FIPS PUB 180-4).

2. **Category of Standard**: Computer Security Standard, Cryptography.

3. **Explanation**: This Standard specifies secure hash algorithms - SHA-1, SHA-224, SHA-256, SHA-384, SHA-512, SHA-512/224 and SHA-512/256 - for computing a condensed representation of electronic data (message). When a message of any length less than 2^{64} bits (for SHA-1, SHA-224 and SHA-256) or less than 2^{128} bits (for SHA-384, SHA-512, SHA-512/224 and SHA-512/256) is input to a hash algorithm, the result is an output called a message digest. The message digests range in length from 160 to 512 bits, depending on the algorithm. Secure hash algorithms are typically used with other cryptographic algorithms, such as digital signature algorithms and keyed-hash message authentication codes, or in the generation of random numbers (bits).

The hash algorithms specified in this Standard are called secure because, for a given algorithm, it is computationally infeasible 1) to find a message that corresponds to a given message digest, or 2) to find two different messages that produce the same message digest. Any change to a message will, with a very high probability, result in a different message digest. This will result in a verification failure when the secure hash algorithm is used with a digital signature algorithm or a keyed-hash message authentication algorithm.

This Standard supersedes FIPS 180-3 [FIPS 180-3].

4. **Approving Authority**: Secretary of Commerce.

5. **Maintenance Agency**: U.S. Department of Commerce, National Institute of Standards and Technology (NIST), Information Technology Laboratory (ITL).

6. Applicability: This Standard is applicable to all Federal departments and agencies for the protection of sensitive unclassified information that is not subject to Title 10 United States Code Section 2315 (10 USC 2315) and that is not within a national security system as defined in Title 40 United States Code Section 11103(a)(1) (40 USC 11103(a)(1)). Either this Standard or Federal Information Processing Standard (FIPS) 202 must be implemented wherever a secure hash algorithm is required for Federal applications, including as a component within other cryptographic algorithms and protocols. This Standard may be adopted and used by non-Federal Government organizations.

7. Specifications: Federal Information Processing Standard (FIPS) 180-4, Secure Hash Standard (SHS) (affixed).

8. Implementations: The secure hash algorithms specified herein may be implemented in software, firmware, hardware or any combination thereof. Only algorithm implementations that are validated by NIST will be considered as complying with this standard. Information about the validation program can be obtained at http://csrc.nist.gov/groups/STM/index.html.

9. Implementation Schedule: Guidance regarding the testing and validation to FIPS 180-4 and its relationship to FIPS 140-2 can be found in IG 1.10 of the Implementation Guidance for FIPS PUB 140-2 and the Cryptographic Module Validation Program at http://csrc.nist.gov/groups/STM/cmvp/index.html.

10. Patents: Implementations of the secure hash algorithms in this standard may be covered by U.S. or foreign patents.

11. Export Control: Certain cryptographic devices and technical data regarding them are subject to Federal export controls. Exports of cryptographic modules implementing this standard and technical data regarding them must comply with these Federal regulations and be licensed by the Bureau of Export Administration of the U.S. Department of Commerce. Information about export regulations is available at: http://www.bis.doc.gov/index.htm.

12. Qualifications: While it is the intent of this Standard to specify general security requirements for generating a message digest, conformance to this Standard does not assure that a particular implementation is secure. The responsible authority in each agency or department shall assure that an overall implementation provides an acceptable level of security. This Standard will be reviewed every five years in order to assess its adequacy.

13. Waiver Procedure: The Federal Information Security Management Act (FISMA) does not allow for waivers to a FIPS that is made mandatory by the Secretary of Commerce.

14. Where to Obtain Copies of the Standard: This publication is available electronically by accessing http://csrc.nist.gov/publications/. Other computer security publications are available at the same web site.

**Federal Information
Processing Standards Publication 180-4**

Specifications for the

SECURE HASH STANDARD

Table of Contents

1.   INTRODUCTION

This Standard specifies secure hash algorithms, SHA-1, SHA-224, SHA-256, SHA-384, SHA-512, SHA-512/224 and SHA-512/256. All of the algorithms are iterative, one-way hash functions that can process a message to produce a condensed representation called a *message digest*. These algorithms enable the determination of a message's integrity: any change to the message will, with a very high probability, result in a different message digest. This property is useful in the generation and verification of digital signatures and message authentication codes, and in the generation of random numbers or bits.

Each algorithm can be described in two stages: preprocessing and hash computation. Preprocessing involves padding a message, parsing the padded message into m-bit blocks, and setting initialization values to be used in the hash computation. The hash computation generates a *message schedule* from the padded message and uses that schedule, along with functions, constants, and word operations to iteratively generate a series of hash values. The final hash value generated by the hash computation is used to determine the message digest.

The algorithms differ most significantly in the security strengths that are provided for the data being hashed. The security strengths of these hash functions and the system as a whole when each of them is used with other cryptographic algorithms, such as digital signature algorithms and keyed-hash message authentication codes, can be found in [SP 800-57] and [SP 800-107].

Additionally, the algorithms differ in terms of the size of the blocks and words of data that are used during hashing or message digest sizes. Figure 1 presents the basic properties of these hash algorithms.

Algorithm	Message Size (bits)	Block Size (bits)	Word Size (bits)	Message Digest Size (bits)
SHA-1	$< 2^{64}$	512	32	160
SHA-224	$< 2^{64}$	512	32	224
SHA-256	$< 2^{64}$	512	32	256
SHA-384	$< 2^{128}$	1024	64	384
SHA-512	$< 2^{128}$	1024	64	512
SHA-512/224	$< 2^{128}$	1024	64	224
SHA-512/256	$< 2^{128}$	1024	64	256

Figure 1: Secure Hash Algorithm Properties

2. DEFINITIONS

2.1 Glossary of Terms and Acronyms

Bit	A binary digit having a value of 0 or 1.
Byte	A group of eight bits.
FIPS	Federal Information Processing Standard.
NIST	National Institute of Standards and Technology.
SHA	Secure Hash Algorithm.
SP	Special Publication
Word	A group of either 32 bits (4 bytes) or 64 bits (8 bytes), depending on the secure hash algorithm.

2.2 Algorithm Parameters, Symbols, and Terms

2.2.1 Parameters

The following parameters are used in the secure hash algorithm specifications in this Standard.

$a, b, c, ..., h$	Working variables that are the w-bit words used in the computation of the hash values, $H^{(i)}$.
$H^{(i)}$	The ith hash value. $H^{(0)}$ is the *initial* hash value; $H^{(N)}$ is the *final* hash value and is used to determine the message digest.
$H_j^{(i)}$	The jth word of the ith hash value, where $H_0^{(i)}$ is the left-most word of hash value i.
K_t	Constant value to be used for the iteration t of the hash computation.
k	Number of zeroes appended to a message during the padding step.
ℓ	Length of the message, M, in bits.
m	Number of bits in a message block, $M^{(i)}$.
M	Message to be hashed.

4

$M^{(i)}$	Message block i, with a size of m bits.
$M_j^{(i)}$	The jth word of the ith message block, where $M_0^{(i)}$ is the left-most word of message block i.
n	Number of bits to be rotated or shifted when a word is operated upon.
N	Number of blocks in the padded message.
T	Temporary w-bit word used in the hash computation.
w	Number of bits in a word.
W_t	The tth w-bit word of the message schedule.

2.2.2 Symbols and Operations

The following symbols are used in the secure hash algorithm specifications; each operates on w-bit words.

$\wedge$	Bitwise AND operation.
$\vee$	Bitwise OR ("inclusive-OR") operation.
$\oplus$	Bitwise XOR ("exclusive-OR") operation.
$\neg$	Bitwise complement operation.
$+$	Addition modulo 2^w.
$<<$	Left-shift operation, where $x << n$ is obtained by discarding the left-most n bits of the word x and then padding the result with n zeroes on the right.
$>>$	Right-shift operation, where $x >> n$ is obtained by discarding the right-most n bits of the word x and then padding the result with n zeroes on the left.

The following operations are used in the secure hash algorithm specifications:

$\boldsymbol{ROTL}^{\,n}(x)$	The *rotate left* (circular left shift) operation, where x is a w-bit word and n is an integer with $0 \leq n < w$, is defined by $ROTL^{\,n}(x) = (x << n) \vee (x >> w - n)$.
$\boldsymbol{ROTR}^{\,n}(x)$	The *rotate right* (circular right shift) operation, where x is a w-bit word and n is an integer with $0 \leq n < w$, is defined by $ROTR^{\,n}(x) = (x >> n) \vee (x << w - n)$.

5

SHR^n(x)   The *right shift* operation, where x is a w-bit word and n is an integer with $0 \leq n < w$, is defined by $SHR^n(x)=x >> n$.

3. NOTATION AND CONVENTIONS

3.1 Bit Strings and Integers

The following terminology related to bit strings and integers will be used.

1. A *hex digit* is an element of the set {0, 1,..., 9, a,..., f}. A hex digit is the representation of a 4-bit string. For example, the hex digit "7" represents the 4-bit string "0111", and the hex digit "a" represents the 4-bit string "1010".

2. A *word* is a *w*-bit string that may be represented as a sequence of hex digits. To convert a word to hex digits, each 4-bit string is converted to its hex digit equivalent, as described in (1) above. For example, the 32-bit string

        1010 0001 0000 0011 1111 1110 0010 0011

   can be expressed as "a103fe23", and the 64-bit string

        1010 0001 0000 0011 1111 1110 0010 0011
        0011 0010 1110 1111 0011 0000 0001 1010

   can be expressed as "a103fe2332ef301a".

   Throughout this specification, the "big-endian" convention is used when expressing both 32- and 64-bit words, so that within each word, the most significant bit is stored in the left-most bit position.

3. An *integer* may be represented as a word or pair of words. A word representation of the message length, ℓ, in bits, is required for the padding techniques of Sec. 5.1.

   An integer between 0 and 2^{32}-1 *inclusive* may be represented as a 32-bit word. The least significant four bits of the integer are represented by the right-most hex digit of the word representation. For example, the integer $291 = 2^8 + 2^5 + 2^1 + 2^0 = 256+32+2+1$ is represented by the hex word "00000123".

   The same holds true for an integer between 0 and 2^{64}-1 *inclusive*, which may be represented as a 64-bit word.

   If Z is an integer, $0 \le Z < 2^{64}$, then $Z = 2^{32}X + Y$, where $0 \le X < 2^{32}$ and $0 \le Y < 2^{32}$. Since X and Y can be represented as 32-bit words x and y, respectively, the integer Z can be represented as the pair of words (x, y). This property is used for SHA-1, SHA-224 and SHA-256.

7

If Z is an integer, $0 \leq Z < 2^{128}$, then $Z=2^{64}X + Y$, where $0 \leq X < 2^{64}$ and $0 \leq Y < 2^{64}$. Since X and Y can be represented as 64-bit words x and y, respectively, the integer Z can be represented as the pair of words (x, y). This property is used for SHA-384, SHA-512, SHA-512/224 and SHA-512/256.

4. For the secure hash algorithms, the size of the *message block* - m bits - depends on the algorithm.

   a) For **SHA-1, SHA-224** and **SHA-256**, each message block has **512 bits**, which are represented as a sequence of sixteen **32-bit words**.

   b) For **SHA-384, SHA-512, SHA-512/224** and **SHA-512/256** each message block has **1024 bits**, which are represented as a sequence of sixteen **64-bit words**.

3.2 Operations on Words

The following operations are applied to w-bit words in all five secure hash algorithms. SHA-1, SHA-224 and SHA-256 operate on 32-bit words ($w=32$), and SHA-384, SHA-512, SHA-512/224 and SHA-512/256 operate on 64-bit words ($w=64$).

1. Bitwise *logical* word operations: $\wedge$, $\vee$, $\oplus$, and $\neg$ (see Sec. 2.2.2).

2. Addition modulo 2^w.

   The operation $x + y$ is defined as follows. The words x and y represent integers X and Y, where $0 \leq X < 2^w$ and $0 \leq Y < 2^w$. For positive integers U and V, let $U \bmod V$ be the remainder upon dividing U by V. Compute

   $$Z=(X + Y) \bmod 2^w.$$

   Then $0 \leq Z < 2^w$. Convert the integer Z to a word, z, and define $z=x + y$.

3. The *right shift* operation $SHR^n(x)$, where x is a w-bit word and n is an integer with $0 \leq n < w$, is defined by

   $$SHR^n(x)=x \gg n.$$

   This operation is used in the SHA-224, SHA-256, SHA-384, SHA-512, SHA-512/224 and SHA-512/256 algorithms.

4. The *rotate right* (circular right shift) operation $ROTR^n(x)$, where x is a w-bit word and n is an integer with $0 \leq n < w$, is defined by

   $$ROTR^n(x)=(x \gg n) \vee (x \ll w - n).$$

Thus, $ROTR^n(x)$ is equivalent to a circular shift (rotation) of x by n positions to the right.

This operation is used by the SHA-224, SHA-256, SHA-384, SHA-512, SHA-512/224 and SHA-512/256 algorithms.

5. The *rotate left* (circular left shift) operation, **$ROTL^n(x)$**, where x is a w-bit word and n is an integer with $0 \leq n < w$, is defined by

$$ROTL^n(x) = (x << n) \lor (x >> w - n).$$

Thus, $ROTL^n(x)$ is equivalent to a circular shift (rotation) of x by n positions to the left.

This operation is used only in the SHA-1 algorithm.

6. Note the following equivalence relationships, where w is fixed in each relationship:

$$ROTL^n(x) \approx ROTR^{w-n}(x)$$

$$ROTR^n(x) \approx ROTL^{w-n}(x)$$

4. FUNCTIONS AND CONSTANTS

4.1 Functions

This section defines the functions that are used by each of the algorithms. Although the SHA-224, SHA-256, SHA-384,SHA-512, SHA-512/224 and SHA-512/256 algorithms all use similar functions, their descriptions are separated into sections for SHA-224 and SHA-256 (Sec. 4.1.2) and for SHA-384, SHA-512, SHA-512/224 and SHA-512/256 (Sec. 4.1.3), since the input and output for these functions are words of different sizes. Each of the algorithms include $Ch(x, y, z)$ and $Maj(x, y, z)$ functions; the exclusive-OR operation ($\oplus$) in these functions may be replaced by a bitwise OR operation ($\vee$) and produce identical results.

4.1.1 SHA-1 Functions

SHA-1 uses a sequence of logical functions, $f_0, f_1, \ldots, f_{79}$. Each function f_t, where $0 \leq t \leq 79$, operates on three 32-bit words, x, y, and z, and produces a 32-bit word as output. The function f_t (x, y, z) is defined as follows:

$$
f_t(x, y, z) = \begin{cases}
Ch(x, y, z) = (x \wedge y) \oplus (\neg x \wedge z) & 0 \leq t \leq 19 \\[2ex]
Parity(x, y, z) = x \oplus y \oplus z & 20 \leq t \leq 39 \\[2ex]
Maj(x, y, z) = (x \wedge y) \oplus (x \wedge z) \oplus (y \wedge z) & 40 \leq t \leq 59 \\[2ex]
Parity(x, y, z) = x \oplus y \oplus z & 60 \leq t \leq 79.
\end{cases} \tag{4.1}
$$

4.1.2 SHA-224 and SHA-256 Functions

SHA-224 and SHA-256 both use six logical functions, where *each function operates on 32-bit words*, which are represented as x, y, and z. The result of each function is a new 32-bit word.

$$Ch(x, y, z) = (x \wedge y) \oplus (\neg x \wedge z) \tag{4.2}$$

$$Maj(x, y, z) = (x \wedge y) \oplus (x \wedge z) \oplus (y \wedge z) \tag{4.3}$$

$$\sum_{0}^{\{256\}}(x) = ROTR^2(x) \oplus ROTR^{13}(x) \oplus ROTR^{22}(x) \tag{4.4}$$

$$\sum_{1}^{\{256\}}(x) = ROTR^6(x) \oplus ROTR^{11}(x) \oplus ROTR^{25}(x) \tag{4.5}$$

$$\sigma_0^{\{256\}}(x) = ROTR^7(x) \oplus ROTR^{18}(x) \oplus SHR^3(x) \tag{4.6}$$

$$\sigma_1^{\{256\}}(x) = ROTR^{17}(x) \oplus ROTR^{19}(x) \oplus SHR^{10}(x) \tag{4.7}$$

10

4.1.3 SHA-384, SHA-512, SHA-512/224 and SHA-512/256 Functions

SHA-384, SHA-512, SHA-512/224 and SHA-512/256 use six logical functions, where *each function operates on 64-bit words*, which are represented as *x*, *y*, and *z*. The result of each function is a new 64-bit word.

$$Ch(x,y,z) = (x \wedge y) \oplus (\neg x \wedge z) \tag{4.8}$$

$$Maj(x,y,z) = (x \wedge y) \oplus (x \wedge z) \oplus (y \wedge z) \tag{4.9}$$

$$\sum\nolimits_{0}^{\{512\}}(x) = ROTR^{28}(x) \oplus ROTR^{34}(x) \oplus ROTR^{39}(x) \tag{4.10}$$

$$\sum\nolimits_{1}^{\{512\}}(x) = ROTR^{14}(x) \oplus ROTR^{18}(x) \oplus ROTR^{41}(x) \tag{4.11}$$

$$\sigma_{0}^{\{512\}}(x) = ROTR^{1}(x) \oplus ROTR^{8}(x) \oplus SHR^{7}(x) \tag{4.12}$$

$$\sigma_{1}^{\{512\}}(x) = ROTR^{19}(x) \oplus ROTR^{61}(x) \oplus SHR^{6}(x) \tag{4.13}$$

4.2 Constants

4.2.1 SHA-1 Constants

SHA-1 uses a sequence of eighty constant 32-bit words, $K_0, K_1, \ldots, K_{79}$, which are given by

$$K_t = \begin{cases} \text{5a827999} & 0 \leq t \leq 19 \\ \text{6ed9eba1} & 20 \leq t \leq 39 \\ \text{8f1bbcdc} & 40 \leq t \leq 59 \\ \text{ca62c1d6} & 60 \leq t \leq 79 \end{cases} \tag{4.14}$$

4.2.2 SHA-224 and SHA-256 Constants

SHA-224 and SHA-256 use the same sequence of sixty-four constant 32-bit words, $K_0^{\{256\}}, K_1^{\{256\}}, \ldots, K_{63}^{\{256\}}$. These words represent the first thirty-two bits of the fractional parts of the cube roots of the first sixty-four prime numbers. In hex, these constant words are (from left to right)

```
428a2f98 71374491 b5c0fbcf e9b5dba5 3956c25b 59f111f1 923f82a4 ab1c5ed5
d807aa98 12835b01 243185be 550c7dc3 72be5d74 80deb1fe 9bdc06a7 c19bf174
e49b69c1 efbe4786 0fc19dc6 240ca1cc 2de92c6f 4a7484aa 5cb0a9dc 76f988da
983e5152 a831c66d b00327c8 bf597fc7 c6e00bf3 d5a79147 06ca6351 14292967
27b70a85 2e1b2138 4d2c6dfc 53380d13 650a7354 766a0abb 81c2c92e 92722c85
a2bfe8a1 a81a664b c24b8b70 c76c51a3 d192e819 d6990624 f40e3585 106aa070
19a4c116 1e376c08 2748774c 34b0bcb5 391c0cb3 4ed8aa4a 5b9cca4f 682e6ff3
748f82ee 78a5636f 84c87814 8cc70208 90befffa a4506ceb bef9a3f7 c67178f2
```

4.2.3   SHA-384, SHA-512, SHA-512/224 and SHA-512/256 Constants

SHA-384, SHA-512, SHA-512/224 and SHA-512/256 use the same sequence of eighty constant 64-bit words, $K_0^{\{512\}}, K_1^{\{512\}}, \ldots, K_{79}^{\{512\}}$. These words represent the first sixty-four bits of the fractional parts of the cube roots of the first eighty prime numbers. In hex, these constant words are (from left to right)

```
428a2f98d728ae22  7137449123ef65cd  b5c0fbcfec4d3b2f  e9b5dba58189dbbc
3956c25bf348b538  59f111f1b605d019  923f82a4af194f9b  ab1c5ed5da6d8118
d807aa98a3030242  12835b0145706fbe  243185be4ee4b28c  550c7dc3d5ffb4e2
72be5d74f27b896f  80deb1fe3b1696b1  9bdc06a725c71235  c19bf174cf692694
e49b69c19ef14ad2  efbe4786384f25e3  0fc19dc68b8cd5b5  240ca1cc77ac9c65
2de92c6f592b0275  4a7484aa6ea6e483  5cb0a9dcbd41fbd4  76f988da831153b5
983e5152ee66dfab  a831c66d2db43210  b00327c898fb213f  bf597fc7beef0ee4
c6e00bf33da88fc2  d5a79147930aa725  06ca6351e003826f  142929670a0e6e70
27b70a8546d22ffc  2e1b21385c26c926  4d2c6dfc5ac42aed  53380d139d95b3df
650a73548baf63de  766a0abb3c77b2a8  81c2c92e47edaee6  92722c851482353b
a2bfe8a14cf10364  a81a664bbc423001  c24b8b70d0f89791  c76c51a30654be30
d192e819d6ef5218  d69906245565a910  f40e35855771202a  106aa07032bbd1b8
19a4c116b8d2d0c8  1e376c085141ab53  2748774cdf8eeb99  34b0bcb5e19b48a8
391c0cb3c5c95a63  4ed8aa4ae3418acb  5b9cca4f7763e373  682e6ff3d6b2b8a3
748f82ee5defb2fc  78a5636f43172f60  84c87814a1f0ab72  8cc702081a6439ec
90befffa23631e28  a4506cebde82bde9  bef9a3f7b2c67915  c67178f2e372532b
ca273eceea26619c  d186b8c721c0c207  eada7dd6cde0eb1e  f57d4f7fee6ed178
06f067aa72176fba  0a637dc5a2c898a6  113f9804bef90dae  1b710b35131c471b
28db77f523047d84  32caab7b40c72493  3c9ebe0a15c9bebc  431d67c49c100d4c
4cc5d4becb3e42b6  597f299cfc657e2a  5fcb6fab3ad6faec  6c44198c4a475817
```

5. PREPROCESSING

Preprocessing consists of three steps: padding the message, M (Sec. 5.1), parsing the message into message blocks (Sec. 5.2), and setting the initial hash value, $H^{(0)}$ (Sec. 5.3).

5.1 Padding the Message

The purpose of this padding is to ensure that the padded message is a multiple of 512 or 1024 bits, depending on the algorithm. Padding can be inserted before hash computation begins on a message, or at any other time during the hash computation prior to processing the block(s) that will contain the padding.

5.1.1 SHA-1, SHA-224 and SHA-256

Suppose that the length of the message, M, is ℓ bits. Append the bit "1" to the end of the message, followed by k zero bits, where k is the smallest, non-negative solution to the equation $\ell + 1 + k \equiv 448 \bmod 512$. Then append the 64-bit block that is equal to the number ℓ expressed using a binary representation. For example, the (8-bit ASCII) message "**abc**" has length $8 \times 3 = 24$, so the message is padded with a one bit, then $448 - (24 + 1) = 423$ zero bits, and then the message length, to become the 512-bit padded message

$$
\underbrace{01100001}_{\text{"a"}} \quad \underbrace{01100010}_{\text{"b"}} \quad \underbrace{01100011}_{\text{"c"}} \quad 1 \quad \overbrace{00...00}^{423} \quad \underbrace{\overbrace{00...011000}^{64}}_{\ell = 24}
$$

The length of the padded message should now be a multiple of 512 bits.

5.1.2 SHA-384, SHA-512, SHA-512/224 and SHA-512/256

Suppose the length of the message M, in bits, is ℓ bits. Append the bit "1" to the end of the message, followed by k zero bits, where k is the smallest non-negative solution to the equation $\ell + 1 + k \equiv 896 \bmod 1024$. Then append the 128-bit block that is equal to the number ℓ expressed using a binary representation. For example, the (8-bit ASCII) message "**abc**" has length $8 \times 3 = 24$, so the message is padded with a one bit, then $896 - (24 + 1) = 871$ zero bits, and then the message length, to become the 1024-bit padded message

$$
\underbrace{01100001}_{\text{"a"}} \quad \underbrace{01100010}_{\text{"b"}} \quad \underbrace{01100011}_{\text{"c"}} \quad 1 \quad \overbrace{00...00}^{871} \quad \underbrace{\overbrace{00...011000}^{128}}_{\ell = 24}
$$

The length of the padded message should now be a multiple of 1024 bits.

5.2   Parsing the Message

The message and its padding must be parsed into N m-bit blocks.

5.2.1   SHA-1, SHA-224 and SHA-256

For SHA-1, SHA-224 and SHA-256, the message and its padding are parsed into N 512-bit blocks, $M^{(1)}$, $M^{(2)}$,..., $M^{(N)}$. Since the 512 bits of the input block may be expressed as sixteen 32-bit words, the first 32 bits of message block i are denoted $M_0^{(i)}$, the next 32 bits are $M_1^{(i)}$, and so on up to $M_{15}^{(i)}$.

5.2.2   SHA-384, SHA-512, SHA-512/224 and SHA-512/256

For SHA-384, SHA-512, SHA-512/224 and SHA-512/256, the message and its padding are parsed into N 1024-bit blocks, $M^{(1)}$, $M^{(2)}$,..., $M^{(N)}$. Since the 1024 bits of the input block may be expressed as sixteen 64-bit words, the first 64 bits of message block i are denoted $M_0^{(i)}$, the next 64 bits are $M_1^{(i)}$, and so on up to $M_{15}^{(i)}$.

5.3   Setting the Initial Hash Value ($H^{(0)}$)

Before hash computation begins for each of the secure hash algorithms, the initial hash value, $H^{(0)}$, must be set. The size and number of words in $H^{(0)}$ depends on the message digest size.

5.3.1   SHA-1

For SHA-1, the initial hash value, $H^{(0)}$, shall consist of the following five 32-bit words, in hex:

$$H_0^{(0)} = \texttt{67452301}$$
$$H_1^{(0)} = \texttt{efcdab89}$$
$$H_2^{(0)} = \texttt{98badcfe}$$
$$H_3^{(0)} = \texttt{10325476}$$
$$H_4^{(0)} = \texttt{c3d2e1f0}$$

5.3.2   SHA-224

For SHA-224, the initial hash value, $H^{(0)}$, shall consist of the following eight 32-bit words, in hex:

$$H_0^{(0)} = \texttt{c1059ed8}$$
$$H_1^{(0)} = \texttt{367cd507}$$
$$H_2^{(0)} = \texttt{3070dd17}$$
$$H_3^{(0)} = \texttt{f70e5939}$$
$$H_4^{(0)} = \texttt{ffc00b31}$$
$$H_5^{(0)} = \texttt{68581511}$$
$$H_6^{(0)} = \texttt{64f98fa7}$$

$$H_7^{(0)} = \texttt{befa4fa4}$$

5.3.3 SHA-256

For SHA-256, the initial hash value, $H^{(0)}$, shall consist of the following eight 32-bit words, in hex:

$$H_0^{(0)} = \texttt{6a09e667}$$
$$H_1^{(0)} = \texttt{bb67ae85}$$
$$H_2^{(0)} = \texttt{3c6ef372}$$
$$H_3^{(0)} = \texttt{a54ff53a}$$
$$H_4^{(0)} = \texttt{510e527f}$$
$$H_5^{(0)} = \texttt{9b05688c}$$
$$H_6^{(0)} = \texttt{1f83d9ab}$$
$$H_7^{(0)} = \texttt{5be0cd19}$$

These words were obtained by taking the first thirty-two bits of the fractional parts of the square roots of the first eight prime numbers.

5.3.4 SHA-384

For SHA-384, the initial hash value, $H^{(0)}$, shall consist of the following eight 64-bit words, in hex:

$$H_0^{(0)} = \texttt{cbbb9d5dc1059ed8}$$
$$H_1^{(0)} = \texttt{629a292a367cd507}$$
$$H_2^{(0)} = \texttt{9159015a3070dd17}$$
$$H_3^{(0)} = \texttt{152fecd8f70e5939}$$
$$H_4^{(0)} = \texttt{67332667ffc00b31}$$
$$H_5^{(0)} = \texttt{8eb44a8768581511}$$
$$H_6^{(0)} = \texttt{db0c2e0d64f98fa7}$$
$$H_7^{(0)} = \texttt{47b5481dbefa4fa4}$$

These words were obtained by taking the first sixty-four bits of the fractional parts of the square roots of the ninth through sixteenth prime numbers.

5.3.5 SHA-512

For SHA-512, the initial hash value, $H^{(0)}$, shall consist of the following eight 64-bit words, in hex:

$$H_0^{(0)} = \texttt{6a09e667f3bcc908}$$
$$H_1^{(0)} = \texttt{bb67ae8584caa73b}$$

15

$$H_2^{(0)} = \text{3c6ef372fe94f82b}$$
$$H_3^{(0)} = \text{a54ff53a5f1d36f1}$$
$$H_4^{(0)} = \text{510e527fade682d1}$$
$$H_5^{(0)} = \text{9b05688c2b3e6c1f}$$
$$H_6^{(0)} = \text{1f83d9abfb41bd6b}$$
$$H_7^{(0)} = \text{5be0cd19137e2179}$$

These words were obtained by taking the first sixty-four bits of the fractional parts of the square roots of the first eight prime numbers.

5.3.6 SHA-512/*t*

"SHA-512/*t*" is the general name for a *t*-bit hash function based on SHA-512 whose output is truncated to *t* bits. Each hash function requires a distinct initial hash value. This section provides a procedure for determining the initial value for SHA-512/ *t* for a given value of *t*.

For SHA-512/*t*, *t* is any positive integer without a leading zero such that $t < 512$, and *t* is not 384. For example: *t* is 256, but not 0256, and "SHA-512/*t*" is "SHA-512/256" (an 11 character long ASCII string), which is equivalent to 53 48 41 2D 35 31 32 2F 32 35 36 in hexadecimal.

The initial hash value for SHA-512/*t*, for a given value of *t*, shall be generated by the *SHA-512/t IV Generation Function* below.

SHA-512/t IV Generation Function

(begin:)

Denote $H^{(0)'}$ to be the initial hash value of SHA-512 as specified in Section 5.3.5 above.

Denote $H^{(0)''}$ to be the initial hash value computed below.

$H^{(0)}$ is the IV for SHA-512/*t*.

For $i = 0$ to 7
  {
    $H_i^{(0)''} = H_i^{(0)'} \oplus \text{a5a5a5a5a5a5a5a5}$(in hex).
  }

$H^{(0)} = \text{SHA-512}$ ("SHA-512/*t*") using $H^{(0)''}$ as the IV, where *t* is the specific truncation value.

(end.)

SHA-512/224 (t = 224) and SHA-512/256 (t = 256) are **approved** hash algorithms. Other SHA-512/t hash algorithms with different t values may be specified in [SP 800-107] in the future as the need arises. Below are the IVs for SHA-512/224 and SHA-512/256.

5.3.6.1 SHA-512/224

For SHA-512/224, the initial hash value, $H^{(0)}$, shall consist of the following eight 64-bit words, in hex:

$$H_0^{(0)} = \text{8C3D37C819544DA2}$$
$$H_1^{(0)} = \text{73E1996689DCD4D6}$$
$$H_2^{(0)} = \text{1DFAB7AE32FF9C82}$$
$$H_3^{(0)} = \text{679DD514582F9FCF}$$
$$H_4^{(0)} = \text{0F6D2B697BD44DA8}$$
$$H_5^{(0)} = \text{77E36F7304C48942}$$
$$H_6^{(0)} = \text{3F9D85A86A1D36C8}$$
$$H_7^{(0)} = \text{1112E6AD91D692A1}$$

These words were obtained by executing the *SHA-512/t IV Generation Function* with t = 224.

5.3.6.2 SHA-512/256

For SHA-512/256, the initial hash value, $H^{(0)}$, shall consist of the following eight 64-bit words, in hex:

$$H_0^{(0)} = \text{22312194FC2BF72C}$$
$$H_1^{(0)} = \text{9F555FA3C84C64C2}$$
$$H_2^{(0)} = \text{2393B86B6F53B151}$$
$$H_3^{(0)} = \text{963877195940EABD}$$
$$H_4^{(0)} = \text{96283EE2A88EFFE3}$$
$$H_5^{(0)} = \text{BE5E1E2553863992}$$
$$H_6^{(0)} = \text{2B0199FC2C85B8AA}$$
$$H_7^{(0)} = \text{0EB72DDC81C52CA2}$$

These words were obtained by executing the *SHA-512/t IV Generation Function* with t = 256.

6. SECURE HASH ALGORITHMS

In the following sections, the hash algorithms are not described in ascending order of size. SHA-256 is described before SHA-224 because the specification for SHA-224 is identical to SHA-256, except that different initial hash values are used, and the final hash value is truncated to 224 bits for SHA-224. The same is true for SHA-512, SHA-384, SHA-512/224 and SHA-512/256, except that the final hash value is truncated to 224 bits for SHA-512/224, 256 bits for SHA-512/256 or 384 bits for SHA-384.

For each of the secure hash algorithms, there may exist alternate computation methods that yield identical results; one example is the alternative SHA-1 computation described in Sec. 6.1.3. Such alternate methods may be implemented in conformance to this standard.

6.1 SHA-1

SHA-1 may be used to hash a message, M, having a length of ℓ bits, where $0 \le \ell < 2^{64}$. The algorithm uses 1) a message schedule of eighty 32-bit words, 2) five working variables of 32 bits each, and 3) a hash value of five 32-bit words. The final result of SHA-1 is a 160-bit message digest.

The words of the message schedule are labeled $W_0, W_1, \ldots, W_{79}$. The five working variables are labeled a, b, c, d, and e. The words of the hash value are labeled $H_0^{(i)}, H_1^{(i)}, \ldots, H_4^{(i)}$, which will hold the initial hash value, $H^{(0)}$, replaced by each successive intermediate hash value (after each message block is processed), $H^{(i)}$, and ending with the final hash value, $H^{(N)}$. SHA-1 also uses a single temporary word, T.

6.1.1 SHA-1 Preprocessing

1. Set the initial hash value, $H^{(0)}$, as specified in Sec. 5.3.1.

2. The message is padded and parsed as specified in Section 5.

6.1.2 SHA-1 Hash Computation

The SHA-1 hash computation uses functions and constants previously defined in Sec. 4.1.1 and Sec. 4.2.1, respectively. Addition (+) is performed modulo 2^{32}.

Each message block, $M^{(1)}$, $M^{(2)}$, ..., $M^{(N)}$, is processed in order, using the following steps:

For i=1 to N:
{
1. Prepare the message schedule, $\{W_t\}$:

$$
W_t = \begin{cases} M_t^{(i)} & 0 \leq t \leq 15 \\[2em] ROTL^1(W_{t-3} \oplus W_{t-8} \oplus W_{t-14} \oplus W_{t-16}) & 16 \leq t \leq 79 \end{cases}
$$

2. Initialize the five working variables, a, b, c, d, and e, with the $(i-1)^{\text{st}}$ hash value:

$$a = H_0^{(i-1)}$$
$$b = H_1^{(i-1)}$$
$$c = H_2^{(i-1)}$$
$$d = H_3^{(i-1)}$$
$$e = H_4^{(i-1)}$$

3. For t=0 to 79:
    {
$$T = ROTL^5(a) + f_t(b,c,d) + e + K_t + W_t$$
$$e = d$$
$$d = c$$
$$c = ROTL^{30}(b)$$
$$b = a$$
$$a = T$$
    }

4. Compute the ith intermediate hash value $H^{(i)}$:

$$H_0^{(i)} = a + H_0^{(i-1)}$$
$$H_1^{(i)} = b + H_1^{(i-1)}$$
$$H_2^{(i)} = c + H_2^{(i-1)}$$
$$H_3^{(i)} = d + H_3^{(i-1)}$$
$$H_4^{(i)} = e + H_4^{(i-1)}$$
}

After repeating steps one through four a total of N times (i.e., after processing $M^{(N)}$), the resulting 160-bit message digest of the message, M, is

$$H_0^{(N)} \| H_1^{(N)} \| H_2^{(N)} \| H_3^{(N)} \| H_4^{(N)}$$

6.1.3 Alternate Method for Computing a SHA-1 Message Digest

The SHA-1 hash computation method described in Sec. 6.1.2 assumes that the message schedule $W_0, W_1, \ldots, W_{79}$ is implemented as an array of eighty 32-bit words. This is efficient from the standpoint of the minimization of execution time, since the addresses of $W_{t-3}, \ldots, W_{t-16}$ in step (2) of Sec. 6.1.2 are easily computed.

However, if memory is limited, an alternative is to regard $\{W_t\}$ as a circular queue that may be implemented using an array of sixteen 32-bit words, $W_0, W_1, \ldots, W_{15}$. The alternate method that is described in this section yields the same message digest as the SHA-1 computation method described in Sec. 6.1.2. Although this alternate method saves sixty-four 32-bit words of storage, it is likely to lengthen the execution time due to the increased complexity of the address computations for the $\{W_t\}$ in step (3).

For this alternate SHA-1 method, let $MASK$=0000000f (in hex). As in Sec. 6.1.1, addition is performed modulo 2^{32}. Assuming that the preprocessing as described in Sec. 6.1.1 has been performed, the processing of $M^{(i)}$ is as follows:

For i=1 to N:
{
    1. For t=0 to 15:
        {
$$W_t = M_t^{(i)}$$
        }

    2. Initialize the five working variables, a, b, c, d, and e, with the $(i\text{-}1)^{\text{st}}$ hash value:

$$a = H_0^{(i-1)}$$
$$b = H_1^{(i-1)}$$
$$c = H_2^{(i-1)}$$
$$d = H_3^{(i-1)}$$
$$e = H_4^{(i-1)}$$

    3. For t=0 to 79:
        {
$$s = t \wedge MASK$$

20

If $t \geq 16$ then
{

$$W_s = ROTL^1 (W_{(s+13) \wedge MASK} \oplus W_{(s+8) \wedge MASK} \oplus W_{(s+2) \wedge MASK} \oplus W_s)$$

}

$T = ROTL^5 (a) + f_t(b,c,d) + e + K_t + W_s$

$e = d$

$d = c$

$c = ROTL^{30} (b)$

$b = a$

$a = T$

}

4. Compute the ith intermediate hash value $H^{(i)}$:

$H_0^{(i)} = a + H_0^{(i-1)}$

$H_1^{(i)} = b + H_1^{(i-1)}$

$H_2^{(i)} = c + H_2^{(i-1)}$

$H_3^{(i)} = d + H_3^{(i-1)}$

$H_4^{(i)} = e + H_4^{(i-1)}$

}

After repeating steps one through four a total of N times (i.e., after processing $M^{(N)}$), the resulting 160-bit message digest of the message, M, is

$$H_0^{(N)} \| H_1^{(N)} \| H_2^{(N)} \| H_3^{(N)} \| H_4^{(N)}$$

6.2   SHA-256

SHA-256 may be used to hash a message, M, having a length of ℓ bits, where $0 \leq \ell < 2^{64}$. The algorithm uses 1) a message schedule of sixty-four 32-bit words, 2) eight working variables of 32 bits each, and 3) a hash value of eight 32-bit words. The final result of SHA-256 is a 256-bit message digest.

The words of the message schedule are labeled W_0, W_1,…, W_{63}. The eight working variables are labeled a, b, c, d, e, f, g, and h. The words of the hash value are labeled $H_0^{(i)}, H_1^{(i)}, \dots, H_7^{(i)}$, which will hold the initial hash value, $H^{(0)}$, replaced by each successive intermediate hash value (after each message block is processed), $H^{(i)}$, and ending with the final hash value, $H^{(N)}$. SHA-256 also uses two temporary words, T_1 and T_2.

6.2.1   SHA-256 Preprocessing

1. Set the initial hash value, $H^{(0)}$, as specified in Sec. 5.3.3.

2. The message is padded and parsed as specified in Section 5.

6.2.2   SHA-256 Hash Computation

The SHA-256 hash computation uses functions and constants previously defined in Sec. 4.1.2 and Sec. 4.2.2, respectively. Addition (+) is performed modulo 2^{32}.

Each message block, $M^{(1)}$, $M^{(2)}$, ..., $M^{(N)}$, is processed in order, using the following steps:

For i=1 to N:
{
1. Prepare the message schedule, $\{W_t\}$:

$$W_t = \begin{cases} M_t^{(i)} & 0 \le t \le 15 \\ \\ \sigma_1^{\{256\}}(W_{t-2}) + W_{t-7} + \sigma_0^{\{256\}}(W_{t-15}) + W_{t-16} & 16 \le t \le 63 \end{cases}$$

2. Initialize the eight working variables, a, b, c, d, e, f, g, and h, with the $(i\text{-}1)^{\text{st}}$ hash value:

$$a = H_0^{(i-1)}$$
$$b = H_1^{(i-1)}$$
$$c = H_2^{(i-1)}$$
$$d = H_3^{(i-1)}$$
$$e = H_4^{(i-1)}$$
$$f = H_5^{(i-1)}$$
$$g = H_6^{(i-1)}$$
$$h = H_7^{(i-1)}$$

3. For t=0 to 63:

{

$$T_1 = h + \sum_1^{\{256\}}(e) + Ch(e,f,g) + K_t^{\{256\}} + W_t$$

$$T_2 = \sum_0^{\{256\}}(a) + Maj(a,b,c)$$

$$h = g$$

$$g = f$$

$$f = e$$

$$e = d + T_1$$

$$d = c$$

$$c = b$$

$$b = a$$

$$a = T_1 + T_2$$

}

4. Compute the ith intermediate hash value $H^{(i)}$:

$$H_0^{(i)} = a + H_0^{(i-1)}$$

$$H_1^{(i)} = b + H_1^{(i-1)}$$

$$H_2^{(i)} = c + H_2^{(i-1)}$$

$$H_3^{(i)} = d + H_3^{(i-1)}$$

$$H_4^{(i)} = e + H_4^{(i-1)}$$

$$H_5^{(i)} = f + H_5^{(i-1)}$$

$$H_6^{(i)} = g + H_6^{(i-1)}$$

$$H_7^{(i)} = h + H_7^{(i-1)}$$

}

After repeating steps one through four a total of N times (i.e., after processing $M^{(N)}$), the resulting 256-bit message digest of the message, M, is

$$H_0^{(N)} \| H_1^{(N)} \| H_2^{(N)} \| H_3^{(N)} \| H_4^{(N)} \| H_5^{(N)} \| H_6^{(N)} \| H_7^{(N)}$$

6.3   SHA-224

SHA-224 may be used to hash a message, M, having a length of ℓ bits, where $0 \le \ell < 2^{64}$. The function is defined in the exact same manner as SHA-256 (Section 6.2), with the following two exceptions:

1. The initial hash value, $H^{(0)}$, shall be set as specified in Sec. 5.3.2; and

2. The 224-bit message digest is obtained by truncating the final hash value, $H(N)$, to its left-most 224 bits:

$$H_0^{(N)} \| H_1^{(N)} \| H_2^{(N)} \| H_3^{(N)} \| H_4^{(N)} \| H_5^{(N)} \| H_6^{(N)}$$

6.4 SHA-512

SHA-512 may be used to hash a message, M, having a length of ℓ bits, where $0 \le \ell < 2^{128}$. The algorithm uses 1) a message schedule of eighty 64-bit words, 2) eight working variables of 64 bits each, and 3) a hash value of eight 64-bit words. The final result of SHA-512 is a 512-bit message digest.

The words of the message schedule are labeled W_0, W_1,..., W_{79}. The eight working variables are labeled a, b, c, d, e, f, g, and h. The words of the hash value are labeled $H_0^{(i)}, H_1^{(i)}, ..., H_7^{(i)}$, which will hold the initial hash value, $H^{(0)}$, replaced by each successive intermediate hash value (after each message block is processed), $H^{(i)}$, and ending with the final hash value, $H^{(N)}$. SHA-512 also uses two temporary words, T_1 and T_2.

6.4.1 SHA-512 Preprocessing

1. Set the initial hash value, $H^{(0)}$, as specified in Sec. 5.3.5.

2. The message is padded and parsed as specified in Section 5.

6.4.2 SHA-512 Hash Computation

The SHA-512 hash computation uses functions and constants previously defined in Sec. 4.1.3 and Sec. 4.2.3, respectively. Addition (+) is performed modulo 2^{64}.

Each message block, $M^{(1)}$, $M^{(2)}$, ..., $M^{(N)}$, is processed in order, using the following steps:

For i=1 to N:
{
1. Prepare the message schedule, $\{W_t\}$:

$$W_t = \begin{cases} M_t^{(i)} & 0 \le t \le 15 \\ \\ \sigma_1^{\{512\}}(W_{t-2}) + W_{t-7} + \sigma_0^{\{512\}}(W_{t-15}) + W_{t-16} & 16 \le t \le 79 \end{cases}$$

2. Initialize the eight working variables, a, b, c, d, e, f, g, and h, with the $(i$-$1)^{st}$ hash value:

$$a = H_0^{(i-1)}$$
$$b = H_1^{(i-1)}$$
$$c = H_2^{(i-1)}$$
$$d = H_3^{(i-1)}$$
$$e = H_4^{(i-1)}$$
$$f = H_5^{(i-1)}$$
$$g = H_6^{(i-1)}$$
$$h = H_7^{(i-1)}$$

3. For t=0 to 79:
   {

   $$T_1 = h + \sum_1^{\{512\}}(e) + Ch(e,f,g) + K_t^{\{512\}} + W_t$$
   $$T_2 = \sum_0^{\{512\}}(a) + Maj(a,b,c)$$
   $$h = g$$
   $$g = f$$
   $$f = e$$
   $$e = d + T_1$$
   $$d = c$$
   $$c = b$$
   $$b = a$$
   $$a = T_1 + T_2$$

   }

4. Compute the ith intermediate hash value $H^{(i)}$:

   $$H_0^{(i)} = a + H_0^{(i-1)}$$
   $$H_1^{(i)} = b + H_1^{(i-1)}$$
   $$H_2^{(i)} = c + H_2^{(i-1)}$$
   $$H_3^{(i)} = d + H_3^{(i-1)}$$
   $$H_4^{(i)} = e + H_4^{(i-1)}$$
   $$H_5^{(i)} = f + H_5^{(i-1)}$$
   $$H_6^{(i)} = g + H_6^{(i-1)}$$
   $$H_7^{(i)} = h + H_7^{(i-1)}$$

}

After repeating steps one through four a total of N times (i.e., after processing $M^{(N)}$), the resulting 512-bit message digest of the message, M, is

$$H_0^{(N)} \| H_1^{(N)} \| H_2^{(N)} \| H_3^{(N)} \| H_4^{(N)} \| H_5^{(N)} \| H_6^{(N)} \| H_7^{(N)}$$

6.5   SHA-384

SHA-384 may be used to hash a message, M, having a length of ℓ bits, where $0 \le \ell < 2^{128}$. The algorithm is defined in the exact same manner as SHA-512 (Sec. 6.4), with the following two exceptions:

1. The initial hash value, $H^{(0)}$, shall be set as specified in Sec. 5.3.4; and

2. The 384-bit message digest is obtained by truncating the final hash value, $H^{(N)}$, to its left-most 384 bits:

$$H_0^{(N)} \| H_1^{(N)} \| H_2^{(N)} \| H_3^{(N)} \| H_4^{(N)} \| H_5^{(N)}$$

6.6   SHA-512/224

SHA-512/224 may be used to hash a message, M, having a length of ℓ bits, where $0 \le \ell < 2^{128}$. The algorithm is defined in the exact same manner as SHA-512 (Sec. 6.4), with the following two exceptions:

1. The initial hash value, $H^{(0)}$, shall be set as specified in Sec. 5.3.6.1; and

2. The 224-bit message digest is obtained by truncating the final hash value, $H^{(N)}$, to its left-most 224 bits.

6.7   SHA-512/256

SHA-512/256 may be used to hash a message, M, having a length of ℓ bits, where $0 \le \ell < 2^{128}$. The algorithm is defined in the exact same manner as SHA-512 (Sec. 6.4), with the following two exceptions:

1. The initial hash value, $H^{(0)}$, shall be set as specified in Sec. 5.3.6.2; and

2. The 256-bit message digest is obtained by truncating the final hash value, $H^{(N)}$, to its left-most 256 bits.

7.   TRUNCATION OF A MESSAGE DIGEST

Some application may require a hash function with a message digest length different than those provided by the hash functions in this Standard. In such cases, a truncated message digest may be used, whereby a hash function with a larger message digest length is applied to the data to be hashed, and the resulting message digest is truncated by selecting an appropriate number of the leftmost bits. For guidelines on choosing the length of the truncated message digest and information about its security implications for the cryptographic application that uses it, see SP 800-107 [SP 800-107].

APPENDIX A: Additional Information

A.1 Security of the Secure Hash Algorithms

The security of the five hash algorithms, SHA-1, SHA-224, SHA-256, SHA-384, SHA-512, SHA-512/224 and SHA-512/256 is discussed in [SP 800-107].

A.2 Implementation Notes

Examples of SHA-1, SHA-224, SHA-256, SHA-384, SHA-512, SHA-512/224 and SHA-512/256 are available at http://csrc.nist.gov/groups/ST/toolkit/examples.html.

A.3 Object Identifiers

Object identifiers (OIDs) for the SHA-1, SHA-224, SHA-256, SHA-384, SHA-512, SHA-512/224 and SHA-512/256 algorithms are posted at http://csrc.nist.gov/groups/ST/crypto_apps_infra/csor/algorithms.html.

APPENDIX B: REFERENCES

[FIPS 180-3]   NIST, Federal Information Processing Standards Publication 180-3, *Secure Hash Standards (SHS)*, October 2008.

[SP 800-57]   NIST Special Publication (SP) 800-57, Part 1, *Recommendation for Key Management: General*, (Draft) May 2011.

[SP 800-107]   NIST Special Publication (SP) 800-107, *Recommendation for Applications Using Approved Hash Algorithms*, (Revised), (Draft) September 2011.

APPENDIX C: Technical Changes from FIPS 180-3

1. In FIPS 180-3, padding was inserted before hash computation begins. FIPS 140-4 removed this restriction. Padding can be inserted before hash computation begins or at any other time during the hash computation prior to processing the message block(s) containing the padding.

2. FIPS 180-4 adds two additional algorithms: SHA-512/224 and SHA-512/256 to the Standard and the method for determining the initial value for SHA-512/t for a given value of t.

ERRATUM

The following change has been incorporated into FIPS 180-4, as of the date indicated in the table.

DATE	TYPE	CHANGE	PAGE NUMBER
5/9/2014	Editorial	Change "$t < 79$" to "$t \leq 79$"	Page 10, Section 4.1.1, Line 1

FIPS PUB 186-4

FEDERAL INFORMATION PROCESSING STANDARDS PUBLICATION

Digital Signature Standard (DSS)

CATEGORY: COMPUTER SECURITY   SUBCATEGORY: CRYPTOGRAPHY

Information Technology Laboratory

National Institute of Standards and Technology

Gaithersburg, MD 20899-8900

Issued July 2013

U.S. Department of Commerce

Cameron F. Kerry, Acting Secretary

National Institute of Standards and Technology

Patrick D. Gallagher, Under Secretary of Commerce for Standards and Technology and Director

FOREWORD

The Federal Information Processing Standards Publication Series of the National Institute of Standards and Technology (NIST) is the official series of publications relating to standards and guidelines adopted and promulgated under the provisions of the Federal Information Security Management Act (FISMA) of 2002.

Comments concerning FIPS publications are welcomed and should be addressed to the Director, Information Technology Laboratory, National Institute of Standards and Technology, 100 Bureau Drive, Stop 8900, Gaithersburg, MD 20899-8900.

Charles Romine, Director
Information Technology Laboratory

Abstract

This Standard specifies a suite of algorithms that can be used to generate a digital signature. Digital signatures are used to detect unauthorized modifications to data and to authenticate the identity of the signatory. In addition, the recipient of signed data can use a digital signature as evidence in demonstrating to a third party that the signature was, in fact, generated by the claimed signatory. This is known as non-repudiation, since the signatory cannot easily repudiate the signature at a later time.

Key words: computer security, cryptography, digital signatures, Federal Information Processing Standards, public key cryptography.

Federal Information Processing Standards Publication 186-4

July 2013

Announcing the
DIGITAL SIGNATURE STANDARD (DSS)

Federal Information Processing Standards Publications (FIPS PUBS) are issued by the National Institute of Standards and Technology (NIST) after approval by the Secretary of Commerce pursuant to Section 5131 of the Information Technology Management Reform Act of 1996 (Public Law 104-106), and the Computer Security Act of 1987 (Public Law 100-235).

1. **Name of Standard**: Digital Signature Standard (DSS) (FIPS 186-4).

2. **Category of Standard**: Computer Security. **Subcategory.** Cryptography.

3. **Explanation**: This Standard specifies algorithms for applications requiring a digital signature, rather than a written signature. A digital signature is represented in a computer as a string of bits. A digital signature is computed using a set of rules and a set of parameters that allow the identity of the signatory and the integrity of the data to be verified. Digital signatures may be generated on both stored and transmitted data.

Signature generation uses a private key to generate a digital signature; signature verification uses a public key that corresponds to, but is not the same as, the private key. Each signatory possesses a private and public key pair. Public keys may be known by the public; private keys are kept secret. Anyone can verify the signature by employing the signatory's public key. Only the user that possesses the private key can perform signature generation.

A hash function is used in the signature generation process to obtain a condensed version of the data to be signed; the condensed version of the data is often called a message digest. The message digest is input to the digital signature algorithm to generate the digital signature. The hash functions to be used are specified in the Secure Hash Standard (SHS), FIPS 180. FIPS **approved** digital signature algorithms **shall** be used with an appropriate hash function that is specified in the SHS.

The digital signature is provided to the intended verifier along with the signed data. The verifying entity verifies the signature by using the claimed signatory's public key and the same hash function that was used to generate the signature. Similar procedures may be used to generate and verify signatures for both stored and transmitted data.

4. **Approving Authority:** Secretary of Commerce.

i

5. Maintenance Agency: Department of Commerce, National Institute of Standards and Technology, Information Technology Laboratory, Computer Security Division.

6. Applicability: This Standard is applicable to all Federal departments and agencies for the protection of sensitive unclassified information that is not subject to section 2315 of Title 10, United States Code, or section 3502 (2) of Title 44, United States Code. This Standard **shall** be used in designing and implementing public key-based signature systems that Federal departments and agencies operate or that are operated for them under contract. The adoption and use of this Standard is available to private and commercial organizations.

7. Applications: A digital signature algorithm allows an entity to authenticate the integrity of signed data and the identity of the signatory. The recipient of a signed message can use a digital signature as evidence in demonstrating to a third party that the signature was, in fact, generated by the claimed signatory. This is known as non-repudiation, since the signatory cannot easily repudiate the signature at a later time. A digital signature algorithm is intended for use in electronic mail, electronic funds transfer, electronic data interchange, software distribution, data storage, and other applications that require data integrity assurance and data origin authentication.

8. Implementations: A digital signature algorithm may be implemented in software, firmware, hardware or any combination thereof. NIST has developed a validation program to test implementations for conformance to the algorithms in this Standard. Information about the validation program is available at http://csrc.nist.gov/cryptval. Examples for each digital signature algorithm are available at http://csrc.nist.gov/groups/ST/toolkit/examples.html.

Agencies are advised that digital signature key pairs **shall not** be used for other purposes.

9. Other Approved Security Functions: Digital signature implementations that comply with this Standard **shall** employ cryptographic algorithms, cryptographic key generation algorithms, and key establishment techniques that have been approved for protecting Federal government sensitive information. Approved cryptographic algorithms and techniques include those that are either:

  a. specified in a Federal Information Processing Standard (FIPS),

  b. adopted in a FIPS or a NIST Recommendation, or

  c. specified in the list of approved security functions for FIPS 140.

10. Export Control: Certain cryptographic devices and technical data regarding them are subject to Federal export controls. Exports of cryptographic modules implementing this Standard and technical data regarding them must comply with these Federal regulations and be licensed by the Bureau of Industry and Security of the U.S. Department of Commerce. Information about export regulations is available at: http://www.bis.doc.gov.

11. Patents: The algorithms in this Standard may be covered by U.S. or foreign patents.

12. Implementation Schedule: This Standard becomes effective immediately upon approval by the Secretary of Commerce. A transition strategy for validating algorithms and cryptographic modules will be posted on NIST's Web page at http://csrc.nist.gov/groups/STM/cmvp/index.html under Notices. The transition plan addresses the transition by Federal agencies from modules tested and validated for compliance to previous versions of this Standard to modules tested and validated for compliance to FIPS 186-4 under the Cryptographic Module Validation Program. The transition plan allows Federal agencies and vendors to make a smooth transition to FIPS 186-4.

13. Specifications: Federal Information Processing Standard (FIPS) 186-4 Digital Signature Standard (affixed).

14. Cross Index: The following documents are referenced in this Standard. Unless a specific version or date is indicated with the document number, the latest version of the given document is intended as the reference.

- a. FIPS PUB 140, Security Requirements for Cryptographic Modules.

- b. FIPS PUB 180 Secure Hash Standard.

- c. ANS X9.31-1998, Digital Signatures Using Reversible Public Key Cryptography for the Financial Services Industry (rDSA).

- d. ANS X9.62-2005, Public Key Cryptography for the Financial Services Industry: The Elliptic Curve Digital Signature Algorithm (ECDSA).

- e. ANS X9.80, Prime Number Generation, Primality Testing and Primality Certificates.

- f. Public Key Cryptography Standard (PKCS) #1, RSA Encryption Standard.

- g. Special Publication (SP) 800-57, Recommendation for Key Management.

- h. Special Publication (SP) 800-89, Recommendation for Obtaining Assurances for Digital Signature Applications.

- i. Special Publication (SP) 800-90A, Recommendation for Random Number Generation Using Deterministic Random Bit Generators.

- j. Special Publication (SP) 800-102, Recommendation for Digital Signature Timeliness.

- k. Special Publication (SP) 800-131A, Transitions: Recommendation for Transitioning the Use of Cryptographic Algorithms and Key Lengths.

- l. IEEE Std. 1363-2000, Standard Specifications for Public Key Cryptography.

15. Qualifications: The security of a digital signature system is dependent on maintaining the secrecy of the signatory's private keys. Signatories **shall**, therefore, guard against the disclosure of their private keys. While it is the intent of this Standard to specify general security requirements for generating digital signatures, conformance to this Standard does not assure that a particular implementation is secure. It is the responsibility of an implementer to ensure that any module that implements a digital signature capability is designed and built in a secure manner.

Similarly, the use of a product containing an implementation that conforms to this Standard does not guarantee the security of the overall system in which the product is used. The responsible authority in each agency or department **shall** assure that an overall implementation provides an acceptable level of security.

Since a standard of this nature must be flexible enough to adapt to advancements and innovations in science and technology, this Standard will be reviewed every five years in order to assess its adequacy.

16. Waiver Procedure: The Federal Information Security Management Act (FISMA) does not allow for waivers to Federal Information Processing Standards (FIPS) that are made mandatory by the Secretary of Commerce.

17. Where to Obtain Copies of the Standard: This publication is available by accessing http://csrc.nist.gov/publications/. Other computer security publications are available at the same web site.

Table of Contents

Federal Information Processing Standards Publication 186-4

July 2013

Specifications for the
DIGITAL SIGNATURE STANDARD (DSS)

1.   Introduction

This Standard defines methods for digital signature generation that can be used for the protection of binary data (commonly called a message), and for the verification and validation of those digital signatures. Three techniques are approved.

(1) The Digital Signature Algorithm (DSA) is specified in this Standard. The specification includes criteria for the generation of domain parameters, for the generation of public and private key pairs, and for the generation and verification of digital signatures.

(2) The RSA digital signature algorithm is specified in American National Standard (ANS) X9.31 and Public Key Cryptography Standard (PKCS) #1. FIPS 186-4 approves the use of implementations of either or both of these standards and specifies additional requirements.

(3) The Elliptic Curve Digital Signature Algorithm (ECDSA) is specified in ANS X9.62. FIPS 186-4 approves the use of ECDSA and specifies additional requirements. Recommended elliptic curves for Federal Government use are provided herein.

This Standard includes requirements for obtaining the assurances necessary for valid digital signatures. Methods for obtaining these assurances are provided in NIST Special Publication (SP) 800-89, *Recommendation for Obtaining Assurances for Digital Signature Applications*.

2. Glossary of Terms, Acronyms and Mathematical Symbols

2.1 Terms and Definitions

Approved	FIPS-approved and/or NIST-recommended. An algorithm or technique that is either 1) specified in a FIPS or NIST Recommendation, or 2) adopted in a FIPS or NIST Recommendation or 3) specified in a list of NIST approved security functions.
Assurance of domain parameter validity	Confidence that the domain parameters are arithmetically correct.
Assurance of possession	Confidence that an entity possesses a private key and any associated keying material.
Assurance of public key validity	Confidence that the public key is arithmetically correct.
Bit string	An ordered sequence of 0's and 1's. The leftmost bit is the most significant bit of the string. The rightmost bit is the least significant bit of the string.
Certificate	A set of data that uniquely identifies a key pair and an owner that is authorized to use the key pair. The certificate contains the owner's public key and possibly other information, and is digitally signed by a Certification Authority (i.e., a trusted party), thereby binding the public key to the owner.
Certification Authority (CA)	The entity in a Public Key Infrastructure (PKI) that is responsible for issuing certificates and exacting compliance with a PKI policy.
Claimed signatory	From the verifier's perspective, the claimed signatory is the entity that purportedly generated a digital signature.
Digital signature	The result of a cryptographic transformation of data that, when properly implemented, provides a mechanism for verifying origin authentication, data integrity and signatory non-repudiation.
Domain parameter seed	A string of bits that is used as input for a domain parameter generation or validation process.
Domain parameters	Parameters used with cryptographic algorithms that are usually common to a domain of users. A DSA or ECDSA cryptographic key pair is associated with a specifc set of domain parameters.

Entity	An individual (person), organization, device or process. Used interchangeably with "party".
Equivalent process	Two processes are equivalent if, when the same values are input to each process (either as input parameters or as values made available during the process or both), the same output is produced.
Hash function	A function that maps a bit string of arbitrary length to a fixed length bit string. Approved hash functions are specified in FIPS 180 and are designed to satisfy the following properties: 1. (One-way) It is computationally infeasible to find any input that maps to any new pre-specified output, and 2. (Collision resistant) It is computationally infeasible to find any two distinct inputs that map to the same output.
Hash value	See "message digest".
Intended signatory	An entity that intends to generate digital signatures in the future.
Key	A parameter used in conjunction with a cryptographic algorithm that determines its operation. Examples applicable to this Standard include: 1. The computation of a digital signature from data, and 2. The verification of a digital signature.
Key pair	A public key and its corresponding private key.
Message	The data that is signed. Also known as "signed data" during the signature verification and validation process.
Message digest	The result of applying a hash function to a message. Also known as "hash value".
Non-repudiation	A service that is used to provide assurance of the integrity and origin of data in such a way that the integrity and origin can be verified and validated by a third party as having originated from a specific entity in possession of the private key (i.e., the signatory).
Owner	A key pair owner is the entity that is authorized to use the private key of a key pair.
Party	An individual (person), organization, device or process. Used interchangeably with "entity".
Per-message secret number	A secret random number that is generated prior to the generation of each digital signature.

Public Key Infrastructure (PKI)	A framework that is established to issue, maintain and revoke public key certificates.
Prime number generation seed	A string of random bits that is used to determine a prime number with the required characteristics.
Private key	A cryptographic key that is used with an asymmetric (public key) cryptographic algorithm. For digital signatures, the private key is uniquely associated with the owner and is not made public. The private key is used to compute a digital signature that may be verified using the corresponding public key.
Probable prime	An integer that is believed to be prime, based on a probabilistic primality test. There should be no more than a negligible probability that the so-called probable prime is actually composite.
Provable prime	An integer that is either constructed to be prime or is calculated to be prime using a primality-proving algorithm.
Pseudorandom	A process or data produced by a process is said to be pseudorandom when the outcome is deterministic, yet also effectively random as long as the internal action of the process is hidden from observation. For cryptographic purposes, "effectively" means "within the limits of the intended security strength."
Public key	A cryptographic key that is used with an asymmetric (public key) cryptographic algorithm and is associated with a private key. The public key is associated with an owner and may be made public. In the case of digital signatures, the public key is used to verify a digital signature that was signed using the corresponding private key.
Security strength	A number associated with the amount of work (that is, the number of operations) that is required to break a cryptographic algorithm or system. Sometimes referred to as a security level.
Shall	Used to indicate a requirement of this Standard.
Should	Used to indicate a strong recommendation, but not a requirement of this Standard.
Signatory	The entity that generates a digital signature on data using a private key.
Signature generation	The process of using a digital signature algorithm and a private key to generate a digital signature on data.

Signature validation	The (mathematical) verification of the digital signature and obtaining the appropriate assurances (e.g., public key validity, private key possession, etc.).
Signature verification	The process of using a digital signature algorithm and a public key to verify a digital signature on data.
Signed data	The data or message upon which a digital signature has been computed. Also, see "message".
Subscriber	An entity that has applied for and received a certificate from a Certificate Authority.
Trusted third party (TTP)	An entity other than the owner and verifier that is trusted by the owner or the verifier or both. Sometimes shortened to "trusted party".
Verifier	The entity that verifies the authenticity of a digital signature using the public key.

2.2   Acronyms

ANS	American National Standard.
CA	Certification Authority.
DSA	Digital Signature Algorithm; specified in this Standard.
ECDSA	Elliptic Curve Digital Signature Algorithm; specified in ANS X9.62.
FIPS	Federal Information Processing Standard.
NIST	National Institute of Standards and Technology.
PKCS	Public Key Cryptography Standard.
PKI	Public Key Infrastructure.
RBG	Random Bit Generator.
RSA	Algorithm developed by Rivest, Shamir and Adleman; specified in ANS X9.31 and PKCS #1.
SHA	Secure Hash Algorithm; specified in FIPS 180.
SP	NIST Special Publication
TTP	Trusted Third Party.

2.3   Mathematical Symbols

$a \bmod n$	The unique remainder r, $0 \le r \le (n-1)$, when integer a is divided by the positive integer n. For example, 23 mod 7 = 2.
$b \equiv a \bmod n$	There exists an integer k such that $b - a = kn$; equivalently, $a \bmod n = b \bmod n$.
counter	The counter value that results from the domain parameter generation process when the domain parameter seed is used to generate DSA domain parameters.
d	1. For RSA, the private signature exponent of a private key. 2. For ECDSA, the private key.
domain_parameter_seed	A seed used for the generation of domain parameters.
e	The public verification exponent of an RSA public key.
g	One of the DSA domain parameters; g is a generator of the q-order cyclic group of $GF(p)^*$; that is, an element of order q in the multiplicative group of $GF(p)$.
GCD (a, b)	Greatest common divisor of the integers a and b.
Hash (M)	The result of a hash computation (message digest or hash value) on message M using an approved hash function.
index	A value used in the generation of g to indicate its intended use (e.g., for digital signatures).
k	For DSA and ECDSA, a per-message secret number.
L	For DSA, the length of the parameter p in bits.
(L, N)	The associated pair of length parameters for a DSA key pair, where L is the length of p, and N is the length of q.
LCM (a, b)	The least common multiple of the integers a and b.
len (a)	The length of a in bits; the integer L, where $2^{L-1} \le a < 2^L$.
M	The message that is signed using the digital signature algorithm.
m	For ECDSA, the degree of the finite field GF_{2^m}.
N	For DSA, the length of the parameter q in bits.

n	1. For RSA, the modulus; the bit length of n is considered to be the key size.
	2. For ECDSA, the order of the base point of the elliptic curve; the bit length of n is considered to be the key size.
(n, d)	An RSA private key, where n is the modulus, and d is the private signature exponent.
(n, e)	An RSA public key, where n is the modulus, and e is the public verification exponent.
$nlen$	The length of the RSA modulus n in bits.
p	1. For DSA, one of the DSA domain parameters; a prime number that defines the Galois Field GF(p) and is used as a modulus in the operations of GF(p).
	2. For RSA, a prime factor of the modulus n.
q	1. For DSA, one of the DSA domain parameters; a prime factor of $p - 1$.
	2. For RSA, a prime factor of the modulus n.
Q	An ECDSA public key.
r	One component of a DSA or ECDSA digital signature. See the definition of (r, s).
(r, s)	A DSA or ECDSA digital signature, where r and s are the digital signature components.
s	One component of a DSA or ECDSA digital signature. See the definition of (r, s).
$seedlen$	The length of the *domain_parameter_seed* in bits.
SHA$x(M)$	The result when M is the input to the SHA-x hash function, where SHA-x is specified in FIPS 180.
x	The DSA private key.
y	The DSA public key.
$\oplus$	Bitwise logical "exclusive-or" on bit strings of the same length; for corresponding bits of each bit string, the result is determined as follows: $0 \oplus 0 = 0$, $0 \oplus 1 = 1$, $1 \oplus 0 = 1$, or $1 \oplus 1 = 0$.
	Example: $01101 \oplus 11010 = 10111$
$+$	Addition.

*	Multiplication.
/	Division.
$a \parallel b$	The concatenation of two strings a and b. Either a and b are both bit strings, or both are byte strings.
$\lceil a \rceil$	The ceiling of a: the smallest integer that is greater than or equal to a. For example, $\lceil 5 \rceil = 5$, $\lceil 5.3 \rceil = 6$, and $\lceil -2.1 \rceil = -2$.
$\lfloor a \rfloor$	The floor of a; the largest integer that is less than or equal to a. For example, $\lfloor 5 \rfloor = 5$, $\lfloor 5.3 \rfloor = 5$, and $\lfloor -2.1 \rfloor = -3$.
$\lvert a \rvert$	The absolute value of a; $\lvert a \rvert$ is $-a$ if $a < 0$; otherwise, it is simply a. For example, $\lvert 2 \rvert = 2$, and $\lvert -2 \rvert = 2$.
$[a, b]$	The interval of integers between and including a and b. For example, $[1, 4]$ consists of the integers 1, 2, 3 and 4.
$\{, a, b, \ldots\}$	Used to indicate optional information.
0x	The prefix to a bit string that is represented in hexadecimal characters.

3.   General Discussion

A digital signature is an electronic analogue of a written signature; the digital signature can be used to provide assurance that the claimed signatory signed the information. In addition, a digital signature may be used to detect whether or not the information was modified after it was signed (i.e., to detect the integrity of the signed data). These assurances may be obtained whether the data was received in a transmission or retrieved from storage. A properly implemented digital signature algorithm that meets the requirements of this Standard can provide these services.

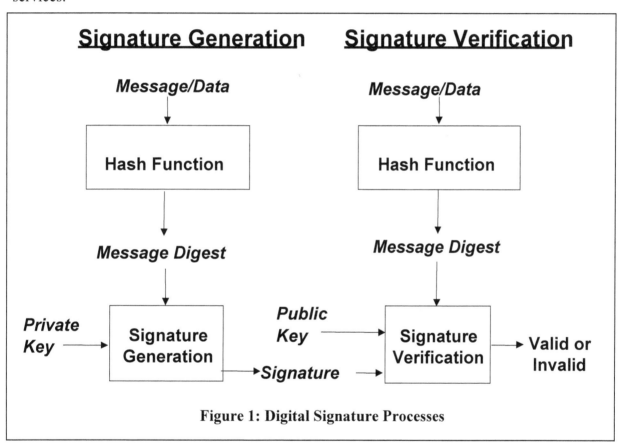

Figure 1: Digital Signature Processes

A digital signature algorithm includes a signature generation process and a signature verification process. A signatory uses the generation process to generate a digital signature on data; a verifier uses the verification process to verify the authenticity of the signature. Each signatory has a public and private key and is the owner of that key pair. As shown in Figure 1, the private key is used in the signature generation process. The key pair owner is the only entity that is authorized to use the private key to generate digital signatures. In order to prevent other entities from claiming to be the key pair owner and using the private key to generate fraudulent signatures, the private key must remain secret. The approved digital signature algorithms are designed to prevent an adversary who does not know the signatory's private key from generating the same signature as the signatory on a different message. In other words, signatures are designed so that they cannot be forged. A number of alternative terms are used in this Standard to refer to the signatory or key pair owner. An entity that intends to generate digital signatures in the future may be referred to as the *intended signatory*. Prior to the verification of a signed message, the signatory is referred to as the *claimed signatory* until such time as adequate assurance can be obtained of the actual identity of the signatory.

The public key is used in the signature verification process (see Figure 1). The public key need not be kept secret, but its integrity must be maintained. Anyone can verify a correctly signed message using the public key.

For both the signature generation and verification processes, the message (i.e., the signed data) is converted to a fixed-length representation of the message by means of an approved hash function. Both the original message and the digital signature are made available to a verifier.

A verifier requires assurance that the public key to be used to verify a signature belongs to the entity that claims to have generated a digital signature (i.e., the claimed signatory). That is, a verifier requires assurance that the signatory is the actual owner of the public/private key pair used to generate and verify a digital signature. A binding of an owner's identity and the owner's public key **shall** be effected in order to provide this assurance.

A verifier also requires assurance that the key pair owner actually possesses the private key associated with the public key, and that the public key is a mathematically correct key.

By obtaining these assurances, the verifier has assurance that if the digital signature can be correctly verified using the public key, the digital signature is valid (i.e., the key pair owner really signed the message). Digital signature validation includes both the (mathematical) verification of the digital signature and obtaining the appropriate assurances. The following are reasons why such assurances are required.

1. If a verifier does not obtain assurance that a signatory is the actual owner of the key pair whose public component is used to verify a signature, the problem of forging a signature is reduced to the problem of falsely claiming an identity. For example, anyone in possession of a mathematically consistent key pair can sign a message and claim that the signatory was the President of the United States. If a verifier does not require assurance that the President is actually the owner of the public key that is used to mathematically verify the message's signature, then successful signature verification provides assurance that the message has not been altered since it was signed, but does not provide assurance that the message came from the President (i.e., the verifier has assurance of the data's integrity, but source authentication is lacking).

2. If the public key used to verify a signature is not mathematically valid, the arguments used to establish the cryptographic strength of the signature algorithm may not apply.

The owner may not be the only party who can generate signatures that can be verified with that public key.

3. If a public key infrastructure cannot provide assurance to a verifier that the owner of a key pair has demonstrated knowledge of a private key that corresponds to the owner's public key, then it may be possible for an unscrupulous entity to have their identity (or an assumed identity) bound to a public key that is (or has been) used by another party. The unscrupulous entity may then claim to be the source of certain messages signed by that other party. Or, it may be possible that an unscrupulous entity has managed to obtain ownership of a public key that was chosen with the sole purpose of allowing for the verification of a signature on a specific message.

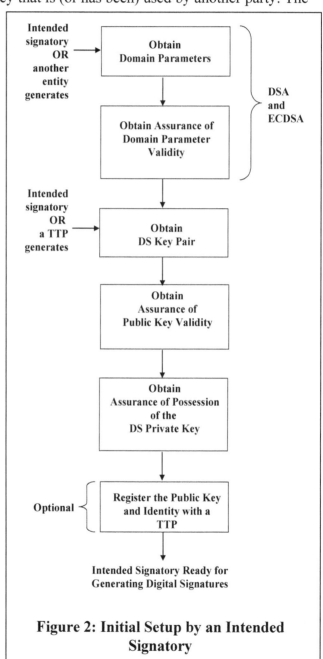

Figure 2: Initial Setup by an Intended Signatory

Technically, a key pair used by a digital signature algorithm could also be used for purposes other than digital signatures (e.g., for key establishment). However, a key pair used for digital signature generation and verification as specified in this Standard **shall not** be used for any other purpose. See SP 800-57 on Key Usage for further information.

A number of steps are required to enable a digital signature generation or verification capability in accordance with this Standard. All parties that generate digital signatures **shall** perform the initial setup process as discussed in Section 3.1. Digital signature generation **shall** be performed as discussed in Section 3.2. Digital signature verification and validation **shall** be performed as discussed in Section 3.3.

3.1   Initial Setup

Figure 2 depicts the steps that are performed prior to generating a digital

11

signature by an entity intending to act as a signatory.

For the DSA and ECDSA algorithms, the intended signatory **shall** first obtain appropriate domain parameters, either by generating the domain parameters itself, or by obtaining domain parameters that another entity has generated. Having obtained the set of domain parameters, the intended signatory **shall** obtain assurance of the validity of those domain parameters; approved methods for obtaining this assurance are provided in SP 800-89. Note that the RSA algorithm does not use domain parameters.

Each intended signatory **shall** obtain a digital signature key pair that is generated as specified for the appropriate digital signature algorithm, either by generating the key pair itself or by obtaining the key pair from a trusted party. The intended signatory is authorized to use the key pair and is the owner of that key pair. Note that if a trusted party generates the key pair, that party needs to be trusted not to masquerade as the owner, even though the trusted party knows the private key.

After obtaining the key pair, the intended signatory (now the key pair owner) **shall** obtain (1) assurance of the validity of the public key and (2) assurance that he/she actually possesses the associated private key. Approved methods for obtaining these assurances are provided in SP 800-89.

A digital signature verifier requires assurance of the identity of the signatory. Depending on the environment in which digital signatures are generated and verified, the key pair owner (i.e., the intended signatory) may register the public key and establish proof of identity with a mutually trusted party. For example, a certification authority (CA) could sign credentials containing an owner's public key and identity to form a certificate after being provided with proof of the owner's identity. Systems for certifying credentials and distributing certificates are beyond the scope of this Standard. Other means of establishing proof of identity (e.g., by providing identity credentials along with the public key directly to a prospective verifier) are allowed.

3.2 Digital Signature Generation

Figure 3 depicts the steps that are performed by an intended signatory (i.e., the entity that generates a digital signature).

Prior to the generation of a digital signature, a message digest **shall** be generated on the information to be signed using an appropriate approved hash function.

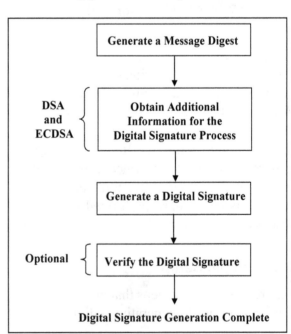

Figure 3: Digital Signature Generation

12

Depending on the digital signature algorithm to be used, additional information **shall** be obtained. For example, a random per-message secret number **shall** be obtained for DSA and ECDSA.

Using the selected digital signature algorithm, the signature private key, the message digest, and any other information required by the digital signature process, a digital signature **shall** be generated in accordance with this Standard.

The signatory may optionally verify the digital signature using the signature verification process and the associated public key. This optional verification serves as a final check to detect otherwise undetected signature generation computation errors; this verification may be prudent when signing a high-value message, when multiple users are expected to verify the signature, or if the verifier will be verifying the signature at a much later time.

3.3   Digital Signature Verification and Validation

Figure 4 depicts the digital signature verification and validation process that are performed by a verifier (e.g., the intended recipient of the signed data and associated digital signature). Note that the figure depicts a successful verification and validation process (i.e., no errors are detected).

In order to verify a digital signature, the verifier **shall** obtain the public key of the claimed signatory, (usually) based on the claimed identity. If DSA or ECDSA has been used to generate the digital signature, the verifier **shall** also obtain the domain parameters. The public key and domain parameters may be obtained, for example, from a certificate created by a trusted party (e.g., a CA) or directly from the claimed signatory. A message digest **shall** be generated on the data whose signature is to be verified (i.e., not on the received digital signature) using the same hash function that was used during the digital signature generation process. Using the appropriate digital signature algorithm, the domain parameters (if appropriate), the public key and the newly computed message digest, the received digital signature is verified in accordance with this Standard. If the verification process fails, no inference can be made as to whether the data is correct, only that in using the specified public key and the specified signature format, the digital signature cannot be verified for that data.

Before accepting the verified digital signature as valid, the verifier **shall** have (1) assurance of the signatory's claimed identity, (2) assurance of the validity of the domain parameters (for DSA and ECDSA), (3) assurance of the validity of the public key, and (4) assurance that the claimed signatory actually possessed the private key that was used to generate the digital signature at the time that the signature was generated. Methods for the verifier to obtain these assurances are provided in SP 800-89. Note that assurance of domain parameter validity may have been obtained during initial setup (see Section 3.1).

If the verification and assurance processes are successful, the digital signature and signed data **shall** be considered valid. However, if a verification or assurance process fails, the digital signature **should** be considered invalid. An organization's policy **shall** govern the action to be taken for an invalid digital signature. Such policy is outside the scope of this Standard.

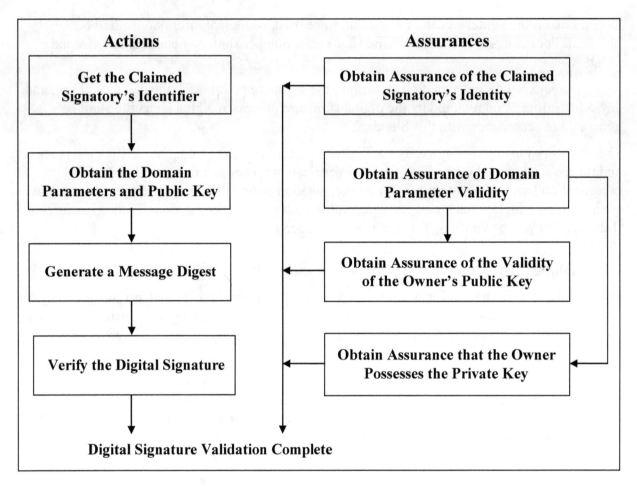

Figure 4: Digital Signature Verification and Validation

4 The Digital Signature Algorithm (DSA)

4.1 DSA Parameters

A DSA digital signature is computed using a set of domain parameters, a private key x, a per-message secret number k, data to be signed, and a hash function. A digital signature is verified using the same domain parameters, a public key y that is mathematically associated with the private key x used to generate the digital signature, data to be verified, and the same hash function that was used during signature generation. These parameters are defined as follows:

p a prime modulus, where $2^{L-1} < p < 2^L$, and L is the bit length of p. Values for L are provided in Section 4.2.

q a prime divisor of $(p - 1)$, where $2^{N-1} < q < 2^N$, and N is the bit length of q. Values for N are provided in Section 4.2.

g a generator of a subgroup of order q in the multiplicative group of GF(p), such that $1 < g < p$.

x the private key that must remain secret; x is a randomly or pseudorandomly generated integer, such that $0 < x < q$, i.e., x is in the range $[1, q-1]$.

y the public key, where $y = g^x \bmod p$.

k a secret number that is unique to each message; k is a randomly or pseudorandomly generated integer, such that $0 < k < q$, i.e., k is in the range $[1, q-1]$.

4.2 Selection of Parameter Sizes and Hash Functions for DSA

This Standard specifies the following choices for the pair L and N (the bit lengths of p and q, respectively):

$L = 1024, N = 160$

$L = 2048, N = 224$

$L = 2048, N = 256$

$L = 3072, N = 256$

Federal Government entities **shall** generate digital signatures using use one or more of these choices.

An approved hash function, as specified in FIPS 180, **shall** be used during the generation of digital signatures. The security strength associated with the DSA digital signature process is no greater than the minimum of the security strength of the (L, N) pair and the security strength of the hash function that is employed. Both the security strength of the hash function used and the security strength of the (L, N) pair **shall** meet or exceed the security strength required for the digital signature process. The security strength for each (L, N) pair and hash function is provided in SP 800-57.

SP 800-57 provides information about the selection of the appropriate (L, N) pair in accordance with a desired security strength for a given time period for the generation of digital signatures. An (L, N) pair **shall** be chosen that protects the signed information during the entire expected lifetime of that information. For example, if a digital signature is generated in 2009 for information that needs to be protected for five years, and a particular (L, N) pair is invalid after 2010, then a larger (L, N) pair **shall** be used that remains valid for the entire period of time that the information needs to be protected.

It is recommended that the security strength of the (L, N) pair and the security strength of the hash function used for the generation of digital signatures be the same unless an agreement has been made between participating entities to use a stronger hash function. When the length of the output of the hash function is greater than N (i.e., the bit length of q), then the leftmost N bits of the hash function output block **shall** be used in any calculation using the hash function output during the generation or verification of a digital signature. A hash function that provides a lower security strength than the (L, N) pair ordinarily **should not** be used, since this would reduce the security strength of the digital signature process to a level no greater than that provided by the hash function.

A Federal Government entity other than a Certification Authority (CA) **should** use only the first three (L, N) pairs (i.e., the (1024, 160), (2048, 224) and (2048, 256) pairs). A CA **shall** use an (L, N) pair that is equal to or greater than the (L, N) pairs used by its subscribers. For example, if subscribers are using the (2048, 224) pair, then the CA **shall** use either the (2048, 224), (2048, 256) or (3072, 256) pair. Possible exceptions to this rule include cross certification between CAs, certifying keys for purposes other than digital signatures and transitioning from one key size or algorithm to another. See SP 800-57 for further guidance.

4.3   DSA Domain Parameters

DSA requires that the private/public key pairs used for digital signature generation and verification be generated with respect to a particular set of domain parameters. These domain parameters may be common to a group of users and may be public. A user of a set of domain parameters (i.e., both the signatory and the verifier) **shall** have assurance of their validity prior to using them (see Section 3). Although domain parameters may be public information, they **shall** be managed so that the correct correspondence between a given key pair and its set of domain parameters is maintained for all parties that use the key pair. A set of domain parameters may remain fixed for an extended time period.

The domain parameters for DSA are the integers p, q, and g, and optionally, the *domain_parameter_seed* and *counter* that were used to generate p and q (i.e., the full set of domain parameters is $(p, q, g\ \{, domain\_parameter\_seed, counter\}))$.

16

4.3.1 Domain Parameter Generation

Domain parameters may be generated by a trusted third party (a TTP, such as a CA) or by an entity other than a TTP. Assurance of domain parameter validity **shall** be obtained prior to key pair generation, digital signature generation or digital signature verification (see Section 3).

The integers p and q **shall** be generated as specified in Appendix A.1. The input to the generation process is the selected values of L and N (see Section 4.2); the output of the generation process is the values for p and q, and optionally, the values of the *domain_parameter_seed* and *counter*.

The generator g **shall** be generated as specified in Appendix A.2.

The security strength of a hash function used during the generation of the domain parameters **shall** meet or exceed the security strength associated with the (L, N) pair. Note that this is more restrictive than the hash function that can be used for the digital signature process (see Section 4.2).

4.3.2 Domain Parameter Management

Each digital signature key pair **shall** be correctly associated with one specific set of domain parameters (e.g., by a public key certificate that identifies the domain parameters associated with the public key). The domain parameters **shall** be protected from unauthorized modification until the set is deactivated (if and when the set is no longer needed). The same domain parameters may be used for more than one purpose (e.g., the same domain parameters may be used for both digital signatures and key establishment). However, using different values for the generator g reduces the risk that key pairs generated for one purpose could be accidentally used (successfully) for another purpose.

4.4 Key Pairs

Each signatory has a key pair: a private key x and a public key y that are mathematically related to each other. The private key **shall** be used for only a fixed period of time (i.e., the private key cryptoperiod) in which digital signatures may be generated; the public key may continue to be used as long as digital signatures that were generated using the associated private key need to be verified (i.e., the public key may continue to be used beyond the cryptoperiod of the associated private key). See SP 800-57 for further guidance.

4.4.1 DSA Key Pair Generation

A digital signature key pair x and y is generated for a set of domain parameters (p, q, g {, *domain_parameter_seed, counter*}). Methods for the generation of x and y are provided in Appendix B.1.

4.4.2 Key Pair Management

Guidance on the protection of key pairs is provided in SP 800-57. The secure use of digital signatures depends on the management of an entity's digital signature key pair as follows:

1. The validity of the domain parameters **shall** be assured prior to the generation of the key pair, or the verification and validation of a digital signature (see Section 3).

2. Each key pair **shall** be associated with the domain parameters under which the key pair was generated.

3. A key pair **shall** only be used to generate and verify signatures using the domain parameters associated with that key pair.

4. The private key **shall** be used only for signature generation as specified in this Standard and **shall** be kept secret; the public key **shall** be used only for signature verification and may be made public.

5. An intended signatory **shall** have assurance of possession of the private key prior to or concurrently with using it to generate a digital signature (see Section 3.1).

6. A private key **shall** be protected from unauthorized access, disclosure and modification.

7. A public key **shall** be protected from unauthorized modification (including substitution). For example, public key certificates that are signed by a CA may provide such protection.

8. A verifier **shall** be assured of a binding between the public key, its associated domain parameters and the key pair owner (see Section 3).

9. A verifier **shall** obtain public keys in a trusted manner (e.g., from a certificate signed by a CA that the entity trusts, or directly from the intended or claimed signatory, provided that the entity is trusted by the verifier and can be authenticated as the source of the signed information that is to be verified).

10. Verifiers **shall** be assured that the claimed signatory is the key pair owner, and that the owner possessed the private key that was used to generate the digital signature at the time that the signature was generated (i.e., the private key that is associated with the public key that will be used to verify the digital signature) (see Section 3.3).

11. A signatory and a verifier **shall** have assurance of the validity of the public key (see Sections 3.1 and 3.3).

4.5 DSA Per-Message Secret Number

A new secret random number k **shall** be generated prior to the generation of each digital signature for use during the signature generation process. This secret number **shall** be protected from unauthorized disclosure and modification.

k^{-1} is the multiplicative inverse of k with respect to multiplication modulo q; i.e., $0 < k^{-1} < q$

and $1 = (k^{-1}\ k)$ mod q. This inverse is required for the signature generation process (see Section 4.6). A technique is provided in Appendix C.1 for deriving k^{-1} from k.

k and k^{-1} may be pre-computed, since knowledge of the message to be signed is not required for the computations. When k and k^{-1} are pre-computed, their confidentiality and integrity **shall** be protected.

Methods for the generation of the per-message secret number are provided in Appendix B.2.

4.6   DSA Signature Generation

The intended signatory **shall** have assurances as specified in Section 3.1.

Let N be the bit length of q. Let **min**(N, *outlen*) denote the minimum of the positive integers N and *outlen*, where *outlen* is the bit length of the hash function output block.

The signature of a message M consists of the pair of numbers r and s that is computed according to the following equations:

$r = (g^k \bmod p) \bmod q$.

$z =$ the leftmost **min**(N, *outlen*) bits of **Hash**(M).

$s = (k^{-1}(z + xr)) \bmod q$.

When computing s, the string z obtained from **Hash**(M) **shall** be converted to an integer. The conversion rule is provided in Appendix C.2.

Note that r may be computed whenever k, p, q and g are available, e.g., whenever the domain parameters p, q and g are known, and k has been pre-computed (see Section 4.5), r may also be pre-computed, since knowledge of the message to be signed is not required for the computation of r. Pre-computed k, k^{-1} and r values **shall** be protected in the same manner as the the private key x until s has been computed (see SP 800-57).

The values of r and s **shall** be checked to determine if $r = 0$ or $s = 0$. If either $r = 0$ or $s = 0$, a new value of k **shall** be generated, and the signature **shall** be recalculated. It is extremely unlikely that $r = 0$ or $s = 0$ if signatures are generated properly.

The signature (r, s) may be transmitted along with the message to the verifier.

4.7   DSA Signature Verification and Validation

Signature verification may be performed by any party (i.e., the signatory, the intended recipient or any other party) using the signatory's public key. A signatory may wish to verify that the computed signature is correct, perhaps before sending the signed message to the intended recipient. The intended recipient (or any other party) verifies the signature to determine its authenticity.

Prior to verifying the signature of a signed message, the domain parameters, and the claimed signatory's public key and identity **shall** be made available to the verifier in an authenticated manner. The public key may, for example, be obtained in the form of a certificate signed by a trusted entity (e.g., a CA) or in a face-to-face meeting with the public key owner.

Let M', r', and s' be the received versions of M, r, and s, respectively; let y be the public key of the claimed signatory; and let N be the bit length of q. Also, let $\mathbf{min}(N, outlen)$ denote the minimum of the positive integers N and $outlen$, where $outlen$ is the bit length of the hash function output block.

The signature verification process is as follows:

1. The verifier **shall** check that $0 < r' < q$ and $0 < s' < q$; if either condition is violated, the signature **shall** be rejected as invalid.

2. If the two conditions in step 1 are satisfied, the verifier computes the following:

   $w = (s')^{-1} \bmod q.$

   $z = $ the leftmost $\mathbf{min}(N, outlen)$ bits of $\mathbf{Hash}(M')$.

   $u1 = (zw) \bmod q.$

   $u2 = ((r')w) \bmod q.$

   $v = (((g)^{u1} (y)^{u2}) \bmod p) \bmod q.$

   A technique is provided in Appendix C.1 for deriving $(s')^{-1}$ (i.e., the multiplicative inverse of $s' \bmod q$).

   The string z obtained from $\mathbf{Hash}(M')$ **shall** be converted to an integer. The conversion rule is provided in Appendix C.2.

3. If $v = r'$, then the signature is verified. For a proof that $v = r'$ when $M' = M$, $r' = r$, and $s' = s$, see Appendix E.

4. If v does not equal r', then the message or the signature may have been modified, there may have been an error in the signatory's generation process, or an imposter (who did not know the private key associated with the public key of the claimed signatory) may have attempted to forge the signature. The signature **shall** be considered invalid. No inference can be made as to whether the data is valid, only that when using the public key to verify the signature, the signature is incorrect for that data.

5. Prior to accepting the signature as valid, the verifier **shall** have assurances as specified in Section 3.3.

An organization's policy may govern the action to be taken for invalid digital signatures. Such policy is outside the scope of this Standard. Guidance about determining the timeliness of digitally signed messages is addressed in SP 800-102, Recommendation for Digital Signature Timeliness.

5. The RSA Digital Signature Algorithm

The use of the RSA algorithm for digital signature generation and verification is specified in American National Standard (ANS) X9.31 and Public Key Cryptography Standard (PKCS) #1. While each of these standards uses the RSA algorithm, the format of the ANS X9.31 and PKCS #1 data on which the digital signature is generated differs in details that make the algorithms non-interchangeable.

5.1 RSA Key Pair Generation

An RSA digital signature key pair consists of an RSA private key, which is used to compute a digital signature, and an RSA public key, which is used to verify a digital signature. An RSA key pair used for digital signatures **shall** only be used for one digital signature scheme (e.g., ANS X9.31, RSASSA-PKCS1 v1.5 or RSASSA-PSS; see Sections 5.4 and 5.5). In addition, an RSA digital signature key pair **shall not** be used for other purposes (e.g., key establishment).

An RSA public key consists of a modulus n, which is the product of two positive prime integers p and q (i.e., $n = pq$), and a public key exponent e. Thus, the RSA public key is the pair of values (n, e) and is used to verify digital signatures. The size of an RSA key pair is commonly considered to be the length of the modulus n in bits ($nlen$).

The corresponding RSA private key consists of the same modulus n and a private key exponent d that depends on n and the public key exponent e. Thus, the RSA private key is the pair of values (n, d) and is used to generate digital signatures. Note that an alternative method for representing (n, d) using the Chinese Remainder Theorem (CRT) is allowed.

In order to provide security for the digital signature process, the two integers p and q, and the private key exponent d **shall** be kept secret. The modulus n and the public key exponent e may be made known to anyone. Guidance on the protection of these values is provided in SP 800-57.

This Standard specifies three choices for the length of the modulus (i.e., $nlen$): 1024, 2048 and 3072 bits. Federal Government entities **shall** generate digital signatures using one or more of these choices.

An approved hash function, as specified in FIPS 180, **shall** be used during the generation of key pairs and digital signatures. When used during the generation of an RSA key pair (as specified in this Standard), the length in bits of the hash function output block **shall** meet or exceed the security strength associated with the bit length of the modulus n (see SP 800-57).

The security strength associated with the RSA digital signature process is no greater than the minimum of the security strength associated with the bit length of the modulus and the security strength of the hash function that is employed. The security strength for each modulus length and hash function used during the digital signature process is provided in SP 800-57. Both the security strength of the hash function used and the security strength associated with the bit length of the modulus n **shall** meet or exceed the security strength required for the digital signature process.

It is recommended that the security strength of the modulus and the security strength of the hash function be the same unless an agreement has been made between participating entities to use a stronger hash function. A hash function that provides a lower security strength than the security strength associated with the bit length of the modulus ordinarily **should not** be used, since this would reduce the security strength of the digital signature process to a level no greater than that provided by the hash function.

Federal Government entities other than CAs **should** use only the first two choices (i.e., $nlen =$ 1024 or 2048) during the timeframes indicated in SP 800-57. A CA **should** use a modulus whose length $nlen$ is equal to or greater than the moduli used by its subscribers. For example, if the subscribers are using $nlen = 2048$, then the CA **should** use $nlen \geq 2048$. SP 800-57 provides further information about the selection of the bit length of n. Possible exceptions to this rule include cross certification between CAs, certifying keys for purposes other than digital signatures and transitioning from one key size or algorithm to another.

Criteria for the generation of RSA key pairs are provided in Appendix B.3.1.

When RSA parameters are randomly generated (i.e., the primes p and q, and optionally, the public key exponent e), they **shall** be generated using an approved random bit generator. The (pseudo) random bits produced by the random bit generator **shall** be used as seeds for generating RSA parameters (e.g., the (pseudo) random number is used as a prime number generation seed). Prime number generation seeds **shall** be kept secret or destroyed when the modulus n is computed. If any prime number generation seed is retained (e.g., to regenerate the RSA modulus n, or as evidence that the generated prime factors p and q were generated in compliance with this Standard, then the seed **shall** be kept secret and **shall** be protected. The strength of this protection **shall** be (at least) equivalent to the protection required for the associated private key.

5.2   Key Pair Management

The secure use of digital signatures depends on the management of an entity's digital signature key pair. Key pair management requirements for RSA are provided in Section 4.4.2, requirements 4 – 11. Note that the first three requirements in Section 4.4.2, which address the relationship between domain parameters and key pairs, are not applicable to RSA.

5.3   Assurances

The intended signatory **shall** have assurances as specified in Section 3.1. Prior to accepting a digital signature as valid, the verifier **shall** have assurances as specified in Section 3.3.

23

5.4 ANS X9.31

ANS X9.31, *Digital Signatures Using Reversible Public Key Cryptography for the Financial Services Industry (rDSA)*, was developed for the American National Standards Institute by the Accredited Standards Committee on Financial Services, X9. See http://www.x9.org for information about obtaining copies of ANS X9.31 and any associated errata. The following discussions are based on the version of ANS X9.31 that was approved in 1998.

Methods for the generation of the private prime factors p and q are provided in Appendix B.3.

In ANS X9.31, the length of the modulus n is allowed in increments of 256 bits beyond a minimum of 1024 bits. Implementations claiming conformance to FIPS 186-4 **shall** include one or more of the modulus sizes specified in Section 5.1.

Two methods for the generation of digital signatures are included in ANS X9.31. When the public signature verification exponent e is odd, the digital signature algorithm is commonly known as RSA; when the public signature verification exponent e is even, the digital signature algorithm is commonly known as Rabin-Williams. This Standard (i.e., FIPS 186-4) adopts the use of RSA, but does not adopt the use of Rabin-Williams.

During signature verification, the extraction of the hash value $H(M)'$ from the data structure IR' **shall** be accomplished by either:

- Selecting the *hashlen* bytes of the data structure IR' that immediately precedes the two bytes of trailer information, where *hashlen* is the length in bytes of the hash function used, regardless of the length of the padding, or

- If the hash value $H(M)'$ is selected by its location with respect to the last byte of padding (i.e., 0xBA), including a check that the hash value is followed by only two bytes containing the expected trailer value.

ANS X9.31 contains an annex on random number generation. However, implementations of ANS X9.31 **shall** use approved random number generation methods.

Annexes in ANS X9.31 provide informative discussions of security and implementation considerations.

5.5 PKCS #1

Public-Key Cryptography Standard (PKCS) #1, *RSA Cryptography Standard*, defines mechanisms for encrypting and signing data using the RSA algorithm. PKCS #1 v2.1 specifies two digital signature processes and corresponding formats: RSASSA-PKCS1-v1.5 and RSASSA-PSS. Both signature schemes are approved for use, but additional constraints are imposed beyond those specified in PKCS #1 v2.1.

(a) Implementations that generate RSA key pairs **shall** use the criteria and methods in Appendix B.3 to generate those key pairs,

24

(b) Only approved hash functions **shall** be used.

(c) Only two prime factors p and q **shall** be used to form the modulus n.

(d) Random numbers **shall** be generated using an **approved** random bit generator.

(e) For RSASSA-PSS:

- If $nlen$ = 1024 bits (i.e., 128 bytes), and the output length of the **approved** hash function output block is 512 bits (i.e., 64 bytes), then the length (in bytes) of the salt ($sLen$) **shall** satisfy $0 \leq sLen \leq hLen - 2$,

- Otherwise, the length (in bytes) of the salt ($sLen$) **shall** satisfy $0 \leq sLen \leq hLen$,

where $hLen$ is the length of the hash function output block (in bytes).

(f) For RSASSA-PKCS-v1.5, when the hash value is recovered from the encoded message EM during the verification of the digital signature[1], the extraction of the hash value **shall** be accomplished by either:

- Selecting the rightmost (least significant) bits of EM, based on the size of the hash function used, regardless of the length of the padding, or

- If the hash value is selected by its location with respect to the last byte of padding, including a check that the hash value is located in the rightmost (least significant) bytes of EM (i.e., no other information follows the hash value in the encoded message).

Note: PKCS #1 was initially developed by RSA Laboratories in 1991 and has been revised as multiple versions. At the time of the approval of FIPS 186-4, three versions of PKSC #1 were available: version 1.5, version 2.0 and version 2.1. This Standard references only version 2.1.

---

[1] PKCS #1, v2.1 provides two methods for comparing the hash values: by comparing the encoded messages EM and EM', and by extracting the hash value from the decoding of the encoded message (see the Note in PKCS #1, v2.1). Step (f) above applies to the latter case.

6. The Elliptic Curve Digital Signature Algorithm (ECDSA)

ANS X9.62, *Public Key Cryptography for the Financial Services Industry: The Elliptic Curve Digital Signature Standard (ECDSA)*, was developed for the American National Standards Institute by the Accredited Standards Committee on Financial Services, X9. Information about obtaining copies of ANS X9.62 is available at http://www.x9.org. The following discussions are based on the version of ANS X9.62 that was approved in 2005. This version of ANS X9.62 **shall** be used, subject to the transition period referenced in the implementation schedule of this Standard.

ANS X9.62 defines methods for digital signature generation and verification using the Elliptic Curve Digital Signature Algorithm (ECDSA). Specifications for the generation of the domain parameters used during the generation and verification of digital signatures are also included in ANS X9.62. ECDSA is the elliptic curve analog of DSA. ECDSA keys **shall not** be used for any other purpose (e.g., key establishment).

6.1   ECDSA Domain Parameters

ECDSA requires that the private/public key pairs used for digital signature generation and verification be generated with respect to a particular set of domain parameters. These domain parameters may be common to a group of users and may be public. Domain parameters may remain fixed for an extended time period.

Domain parameters for ECDSA are of the form (q, *FR*, a, b {, *domain_parameter_seed*}, G, n, h), where q is the field size; *FR* is an indication of the basis used; a and b are two field elements that define the equation of the curve; *domain_parameter_seed* is the domain parameter seed and is an optional bit string that is present if the elliptic curve was randomly generated in a verifiable fashion, G is a base point of prime order on the curve (i.e., $G = (x_G, y_G)$), n is the order of the point G, and h is the cofactor (which is equal to the order of the curve divided by n).

6.1.1   Domain Parameter Generation

This Standard specifies five ranges for n (see Table 1). For each range, a maximum cofactor size is also specified. Note that the specification of a cofactor h in a set of domain parameters is optional in ANS X9.62, whereas implementations conforming to this Standard (i.e., FIPS 186-4) **shall** specify the cofactor h in the set of domain parameters. Table 1 provides the maximum sizes for the cofactor h.

Table 1: ECDSA Security Parameters

Bit length of n	Maximum Cofactor (h)
160 - 223	2^{10}
224 - 255	2^{14}
256 - 383	2^{16}
384 - 511	2^{24}
≥ 512	2^{32}

ECDSA is defined for two arithmetic fields: the finite field GF_p and the finite field GF_{2^m}. For the field GF_p, p is required to be an odd prime.

NIST Recommended curves are provided in Appendix D of this Standard (i.e., FIPS 186-4). Three types of curves are provided:

1. Curves over prime fields, which are identified as P-xxx,

2. Curves over Binary fields, which are identified as B-xxx, and

3. Koblitz curves, which are identified as K-xxx,

where xxx indicates the bit length of the field size.

Alternatively, ECDSA domain parameters may be generated as specified in ANS X9.62; when ECDSA domain parameters are generated (i.e., the NIST Recommended curves are not used), the value of G **should** be generated canonically (verifiably random). An approved hash function, as specified in FIPS 180, **shall** be used during the generation of ECDSA domain parameters. When generating these domain parameters, the security strength of a hash function used **shall** meet or exceed the security strength associated with the bit length of n (see footnote 2 below).

An approved hash function, as specified in FIPS 180, is required during the generation of domain parameters. The security strength of the hash function used **shall** meet or exceed the security strength associated with the bit length of n. The security strengths for the ranges of n and the hash functions are provided in SP 800-57. It is recommended that the security strength associated with the bit length of n and the security strength of the hash function be the same

---

[2] The NIST Recommended curves were generated prior to the formulation of this guidance and using SHA-1, which was the only approved hash function available at that time. Since SHA-1 was considered secure at the time of generation, the curves were made public, and SHA-1 will only be used to validate those curves, the NIST Recommended curves are still considered secure and appropriate for Federal government use.

unless an agreement has been made between participating entities to use a stronger hash function; a hash function that provides a lower security strength than is associated with the bit length of n **shall not** be used. If the length of the output of the hash function is greater than the bit length of n, then the leftmost n bits of the hash function output block **shall** be used in any calculation using the hash function output during the generation or verification of a digital signature.

Normally, a CA **should** use a bit length of n whose assessed security strength is equal to or greater than the assessed security strength associated with the bit length of n used by its subscribers. For example, if subscribers are using a bit length of n with an assessed security strength of 112 bits, then CAs **should** use a bit length of n whose assessed security strength is equal to or greater than 112 bits. SP 800-57 provides further information about the selection of a bit length of n. Possible exceptions to this rule include cross certification between CAs, certifying keys for purposes other than digital signatures and transitioning from one key size or algorithm to another. However, these exceptions require further analysis.

6.1.2 Domain Parameter Management

Each ECDSA key pair **shall** be correctly associated with one specific set of domain parameters (e.g., by a public key certificate that identifies the domain parameters associated with the public key). The domain parameters **shall** be protected from unauthorized modification until the set is deactivated (if and when the set is no longer needed). The same domain parameters may be used for more than one purpose (e.g., the same domain parameters may be used for both digital signatures and key establishment). However, using different domain parameters reduces the risk that key pairs generated for one purpose could be accidentally used (successfully) for another purpose.

6.2 Private/Public Keys

An ECDSA key pair consists of a private key d and a public key Q that is associated with a specific set of ECDSA domain parameters; d, Q and the domain parameters are mathematically related to each other. The private key is normally used for a period of time (i.e., the cryptoperiod); the public key may continue to be used as long as digital signatures that have been generated using the associated private key need to be verified (i.e., the public key may continue to be used beyond the cryptoperiod of the associated private key). See SP 800-57 for further guidance.

ECDSA keys **shall** only be used for the generation and verification of ECDSA digital signatures.

6.2.1 Key Pair Generation

A digital signature key pair d and Q is generated for a set of domain parameters (q, *FR*, *a*, *b* {, *domain_parameter_seed*}, *G*, *n*, *h*). Methods for the generation of d and Q are provided in Appendix B.4.

6.2.2 Key Pair Management

The secure use of digital signatures depends on the management of an entity's digital signature key pair as specified in Section 4.4.2.

6.3 Secret Number Generation

A new secret random number k **shall** be generated prior to the generation of each digital signature for use during the signature generation process. This secret number **shall** be protected from unauthorized disclosure and modification. Methods for the generation of the per-message secret number are provided in Appendix B.5.

k^{-1} is the multiplicative inverse of k with respect to multiplication modulo n; i.e., $0 < k^{-1} < n$ and $1 = (k^{-1} k) \bmod n$. This inverse is required for the signature generation process. A technique is provided in Appendix C.1 for deriving k^{-1} from k.

k and k^{-1} may be pre-computed, since knowledge of the message to be signed is not required for the computations. When k and k^{-1} are pre-computed, their confidentiality and integrity **shall** be protected.

6.4 ECDSA Digital Signature Generation and Verification

An ECDSA digital signature (r, s) **shall** be generated as specified in ANS X9.62, using:

1. Domain parameters that are generated in accordance with Section 6.1.1,

2. A private key that is generated as specified in Section 6.2.1,

3. A per-message secret number that is generated as specified in Section 6.3,

4. An approved hash function as discussed below, and

5. An approved random bit generator.

An ECDSA digital signature **shall** be verified as specified in ANS X9.62, using the same domain parameters and hash function that were used during signature generation.

An approved hash function, as specified in FIPS 180, **shall** be used during the generation of digital signatures. The security strength associated with the ECDSA digital signature process is no greater than the minimum of the security strength associated with the bit length of n and the security strength of the hash function that is employed. Both the security strength of the hash function used and the security strength associated with the bit length of n **shall** meet or exceed the security strength required for the digital signature process. The security strengths for the ranges of the bit lengths of n and for each hash function is provided in SP 800-57.

It is recommended that the security strength associated with the bit length of n and the security strength of the hash function be the same unless an agreement has been made between participating entities to use a stronger hash function. When the length of the output of the hash function is greater than the bit length of n, then the leftmost n bits of the hash function output block **shall** be used in any calculation using the hash function output during the generation or verification of a digital signature. A hash function that provides a lower security strength than the security strength associated with the bit length of n ordinarily **should not** be used, since this would reduce the security strength of the digital signature process to a level no greater than that provided by the hash function.

6.5 Assurances

The intended signatory **shall** have assurances as specified in Section 3.1. Prior to accepting a signature as valid, the verifier **shall** have assurances as specified in Section 3.3.

APPENDIX A: Generation and Validation of FFC Domain Parameters

Finite field cryptography (FFC) is a method of implementing discrete logarithm cryptography using finite field mathematics. DSA, as specified in this Standard, is an example of FFC. The Diffie-Hellman and MQV key establishment algorithms specified in SP 800-56A can also be implemented as FFC.

The domain parameters for FFC consist of the set of values (p, q, g {, *domain_parameter_seed*, *counter*}). This appendix specifies techniques for the generation of the FFC domain parameters p, q and g and performing an explicit domain parameter validation. During the generation process, the values for *domain_parameter_seed* and *counter* are obtained.

A.1   Generation of the FFC Primes *p* and *q*

This section provides methods for generating the primes p and q that fulfill the criteria specified in Sections 4.1 and 4.2. One of these methods **shall** be used when generating these primes. A method is provided in Appendix A.1.1 to generate random candidate integers and then test them for primality using a probabilistic algorithm. A second method is provided in Appendix A.1.2 that constructs integers from smaller integers so that the constructed integer is guaranteed to be prime.

During the generation, validation and testing processes, conversions between bit strings and integers are required. Appendix C.2 provides methods for these conversions.

A.1.1   Generation and Validation of Probable Primes

Previous versions of this Standard contained a method for the generation of the domain parameters p and q using SHA-1 and probabilistic methods. This method is no longer approved for domain parameter generation; however, the validation process for this method is provided in Appendix A.1.1.1 to validate previously generated domain parameters.

A method for the generation and validation of the primes p and q using probabilistic methods is provided in Appendix A.1.1.2 and is based on the use of an approved hash function; this method **shall** be used for generating probable primes. The validation process for this method is provided in Appendix A.1.1.3.

The probabilistic methods use a hash function and an arbitrary seed (*domain_parameter_seed*). Arbitrary seeds could be anything, e.g., a user's favorite number or a random or pseudorandom number output by an approved random number generator. The *domain_parameter_seed* determines a sequence of candidates for p and q in the required intervals that are then tested for primality using a probabilistic primality test (see Appendix C.3). The test determines that the candidate is either not a prime (i.e., it is a composite integer) or is "probably a prime" (i.e., there is a very small probability that a composite integer will be declared to be a prime). p and q **shall** be the first candidate set that passes the primality tests. Note that the *domain_parameter_seed*

shall be unique for every unique set of domain parameters that are generated using the same method.

A.1.1.1 Validation of the Probable Primes *p* and *q* that were Generated Using SHA-1 as Specified in Prior Versions of this Standard

This prime validation algorithm is used to validate that the primes *p* and *q* that were generated by the prime generation algorithm specified in previous versions of this Standard. The algorithm requires the values of *p*, *q*, *domain_parameter_seed* and *counter*, which were output from the prime generation algorithm.

Let **SHA1( )** be the SHA-1 hash function specified in FIPS 180. The following process or its equivalent **shall** be used to validate *p* and *q* for this method.

Input:

1. *p, q*   The generated primes *p* and *q*.

2. *domain_parameter_seed*   A seed that was used to generate *p* and *q*.

3. *counter*   A count value that was determined during generation.

Output:

1. *status*   The status returned from the validation procedure, where status is either **VALID** or **INVALID**.

Process:

1. If ($\mathbf{len}\,(p) \neq 1024$) or ($\mathbf{len}\,(q) \neq 160$), then return **INVALID**.

2. If (*counter* > 4095), then return **INVALID**.

3. *seedlen* = **len** (*domain_parameter_seed*).

4. If (*seedlen* < 160), then return **INVALID**.

5. *computed_q* = **SHA1**(*domain_parameter_seed*) $\oplus$ **SHA1**((*domain_parameter_seed* + 1) mod $2^{seedlen}$).

6. Set the first and last bits of *computed_q* equal to 1 (i.e., the 159th and 0th bits).

7. Test whether or not *computed_q* is prime as specified in Appendix C.3. If (*computed_q* $\neq$ *q*) or (*computed_q* is not prime), then return **INVALID**.

8. *offset* = 2.

9. For *i* = 0 to *counter* do

   9.1   For *j* = 0 to 6 do

          V_j = **SHA1**((*domain_parameter_seed* + *offset* + *j*) mod $2^{seedlen}$).

   9.2 $W = V_0 + (V_1 * 2^{160}) + (V_2 * 2^{320}) + (V_3 * 2^{480}) + (V_4 * 2^{640}) + (V_5 * 2^{800}) +$

32

$$((V_6 \bmod 2^{63}) * 2^{960}).$$

9.3 $X = W + 2^{1023}$.   Comment: $0 \leq W < 2^{L-1}$.

9.4 $c = X \bmod 2q$.

9.5 $computed\_p = X - (c - 1)$. Comment: $computed\_p \equiv 1 \ (\bmod \ 2q)$.

9.6   If ($computed\_p < 2^{1023}$), then go to step 9.8.

9.7   Test whether or not $computed\_p$ is prime as specified in Appendix C.3. If $computed\_p$ is determined to be prime, then go to step 10.

9.8 $offset = offset + 7$.

10. If (($i \neq counter$) or ($computed\_p \neq p$) or ($computed\_p$ is not prime)), then return **INVALID.**

11. Return **VALID**.

A.1.1.2   Generation of the Probable Primes *p* and *q* Using an Approved Hash Function

This method uses an approved hash function and may be used for the generation of the primes *p* and *q* for any application (e.g., digital signatures or key establishment). The security strength of the hash function **shall** be equal to or greater than the security strength associated with the (L, N) pair.

An arbitrary *domain_parameter_seed* of *seedlen* bits is also used, where *seedlen* **shall** be equal to or greater than N.

The generation process returns a set of integers *p* and *q* that have a very high probability of being prime. For another entity to validate that the primes were generated correctly using the validation process in Appendix A.1.1.3, the value of the *domain_parameter_seed* and the *counter* used to generate the primes must also be returned and made available to the validating entity; the *domain_parameter_seed* and *counter* need not be kept secret. Let **Hash( )** be the selected hash function, and let *outlen* be the bit length of the output block, where *outlen* **shall** be equal to or greater than N.

The following process or its equivalent **shall** be used to generate *p* and *q* for this method.

Input:

1. L The desired length of the prime *p* (in bits).
2. N The desired length of the prime *q* (in bits).
3. *seedlen*   The desired length of the domain parameter seed; *seedlen* **shall** be equal to or greater than N.

Output:

1. *status*   The status returned from the generation procedure, where status is

either **VALID** or **INVALID**. If **INVALID** is returned as the *status*, either no values for the other output parameters **shall** be returned, or invalid values **shall** be returned (e.g., zeros or Null strings).

2. *p, q*   The generated primes p and q.

3. *domain_parameter_seed*

   (Optional) A seed that was used to generate p and q.

4. *counter*   (Optional) A count value that was determined during generation.

Process:

1. Check that the (L, N) pair is in the list of acceptable $(L, N$ pairs) (see Section 4.2). If the pair is not in the list, then return **INVALID**.

2. If $(seedlen < N)$, then return **INVALID**.

3. $n = \lceil L / outlen \rceil - 1$.

4. $b = L - 1 - (n * outlen)$.

5. Get an arbitrary sequence of *seedlen* bits as the *domain_parameter_seed*.

6. $U = \textbf{Hash}\,(domain\_parameter\_seed) \bmod 2^{N-1}$.

7. $q = 2^{N-1} + U + 1 - (\,U \bmod 2)$.

8. Test whether or not q is prime as specified in Appendix C.3.

9. If q is not a prime, then go to step 5.

10. $offset = 1$.

11. For *counter* = 0 to $(4L - 1)$ do

    11.1   For $j = 0$ to n do

           $V_j = \textbf{Hash}\,((domain\_parameter\_seed + offset + j) \bmod 2^{seedlen})$.

    11.2 $W = V_0 + (V_1 * 2^{outlen}) + \ldots + (V_{n-1} * 2^{(n-1)*outlen}) + ((V_n \bmod 2^b) * 2^{n*outlen})$.

    11.3 $X = W + 2^{L-1}$.   Comment: $0 \leq W < 2^{L-1}$; hence, $2^{L-1} \leq X < 2^L$.

    11.4 $c = X \bmod 2q$.

    11.5 $p = X - (c - 1)$.   Comment: $p \equiv 1 \pmod{2q}$.

    11.6   If $(p < 2^{L-1})$, then go to step 11.9.

    11.7   Test whether or not p is prime as specified in Appendix C.3.

    11.8   If p is determined to be prime, then return **VALID** and the values of p, q and (optionally) the values of *domain_parameter_seed and counter*.

34

11.9   *offset* = *offset* + *n* + 1.   Comment: Increment *offset*; then, as part of
                                                  the loop in step 11, increment *counter*; if
                                                  counter < 4*L*, repeat steps 11.1 through 11.8.

12. Go to step 5.

A.1.1.3   Validation of the Probable Primes *p* and *q* that were Generated Using an Approved Hash Function

This prime validation algorithm is used to validate that the integers *p* and *q* were generated by the prime generation algorithm given in Appendix A.1.1.2. The validation algorithm requires the values of *p*, *q*, *domain_parameter_seed* and *counter*, which were output from the prime generation algorithm. Let **Hash( )** be the hash function used to generate *p* and *q*, and let *outlen* be its output block length.

The following process or its equivalent **shall** be used to validate *p* and *q* for this method.

Input:

1. *p, q*   The generated primes *p* and *q*.

3. *domain_parameter_seed*   The domain parameter seed that was used to generate *p* and *q*.

4. *counter*   A count value that was determined during generation.

Output:

1. *status*   The status returned from the validation procedure, where status is either **VALID** or **INVALID**.

Process:

1. *L* = **len** (*p*).

2. *N* = **len** (*q*).

3. Check that the (*L, N*) pair is in the list of acceptable (*L, N*) pairs (see Section 4.2). If the pair is not in the list, return **INVALID**.

4. If (*counter* > (4*L* − 1)), then return **INVALID**.

5. *seedlen* = **len** (*domain_parameter_seed*).

6. If (*seedlen* < *N*), then return **INVALID**.

7. *U* = **Hash**(*domain_parameter_seed*) mod 2^{N-1}.

8. *computed_q* = 2^{N-1} + *U* + 1 − (*U* mod 2).

9. Test whether or not *computed_q* is prime as specified in Appendix C.3. If (*computed_q* ≠ *q*) or (*computed_q* is not prime), then return **INVALID.**

10. $n = \lceil L / outlen \rceil - 1$.

11. $b = L - 1 - (n * outlen)$.

12. $offset = 1$.

13. For $i = 0$ to $counter$ do

13.1 For $j = 0$ to n do

$V_j = \textbf{Hash}((domain\_parameter\_seed + offset + j) \bmod 2^{seedlen})$.

13.2 $W = V_0 + (V_1 * 2^{outlen}) + \ldots + (V_{n-1} * 2^{(n-1) * outlen}) + ((V_n \bmod 2^b) * 2^{n * outlen})$.

13.3 $X = W + 2^{L-1}$.

13.4 $c = X \bmod 2q$.

13.5 $computed\_p = X - (c - 1)$.

13.6 If $(computed\_p < 2^{L-1})$, then go to step 13.9

13.7 Test whether or not $computed\_p$ is prime as specified in Appendix C.3.

13.8 If $computed\_p$ is determined to be a prime, then go to step 14.

13.9 $offset = offset + n + 1$.

14. If $((i \neq counter)$ or $(computed\_p \neq p)$ or $(computed\_p$ is not a prime$))$, then return **INVALID**.

15. Return **VALID**.

A.1.2 Construction and Validation of the Provable Primes p and q

Primes can be generated so that they are guaranteed to be prime. The following algorithm for generating p and q uses an approved hash function and an arbitrary seed (*firstseed*) to construct p and q in the required intervals. The security strength of the hash function **shall** be equal to or greater than the security strength associated with the (L, N) pair.

Arbitrary seeds can be anything, e.g., a user's favorite number or a random or pseudorandom number that is output from a random number generator. Note that the *firstseed* must be unique to produce a unique set of domain parameters. Candidate primes are tested for primality using a deterministic primality test that proves whether or not the candidate is prime. The resulting p and q are guaranteed to be primes.

A.1.2.1 Construction of the Primes p and q Using the Shawe-Taylor Algorithm

For each set of domain parameters generated, an arbitrary initial seed (*firstseed*) of at least *seedlen* bits **shall** be determined, where *seedlen* **shall** be $\geq N$.

The generation process returns a set of integers p and q that are guaranteed to be prime. For another entity to validate that the primes were generated correctly (using the validation process in Appendix A.1.2.2), the value of the *firstseed*, the two computed seeds (*pseed* and *qseed*) and the counters used to generate the primes (*pgen_counter* and *qgen_counter*) must be made available to the validating entity; the seeds and the counters need not be kept secret. The domain parameters for DSA are identified in Section 4.3 as (p, q, g {, *domain_parameter_seed*, *counter*}). When using the Shawe-Taylor algorithm for generating p and q, the *domain_parameter_seed* consists of three seed values (*firstseed, pseed,* and *qseed*), and the *counter* consists of the pair of counter values (*pgen_counter* and *qgen_counter*).

Let **Hash( )** be the selected hash function (see Appendix A.1.2), and let *outlen* be the bit length of the output block of that hash function.

A.1.2.1.1 Get the First Seed

The following process or its equivalent **shall** be used to generate *firstseed* for this constructive method.

Input:

1. N — The length of q in bits.

2. *seedlen* — The length of firstseed, where *seedlen* $\geq N$.

Output:

1. *status* — The status returned from the generation procedure, where *status* is either **SUCCESS** or **FAILURE.** If **FAILURE** is returned, then either no *firstseed* value **shall** be provided or an invalid value **shall** be returned.

2. *firstseed* — The first seed generated.

Process:

1. *firstseed* = 0.

2. Check that N is in the list of acceptable (L, N) pairs (see Section 4.2). If not, then return **FAILURE**.

3. If (*seedlen* < N), then return **FAILURE**.

4. While *firstseed* < 2^{N-1}.

   Get an arbitrary sequence of *seedlen* bits as *firstseed*.

5. Return **SUCCESS** and the value of *firstseed*.

Note: This routine could be incorporated into the beginning of the constructive prime generation procedure in Appendix A.1.2.1.2. However, this was not done in this specification so that the validation process in Appendix A.1.2.2 could also call the constructive prime generation procedure and provide the value of *firstseed* as input.

A.1.2.1.2 Constructive Prime Generation

The following process or its equivalent **shall** be used to generate p and q for this constructive method.

Input:

1. L — The requested length for p (in bits).

2. N — The requested length for q (in bits).

3. *firstseed* — The first seed to be used. This was obtained as specified in Appendix A.1.2.1.1.

Output:

1. *status* — The status returned from the generation procedure, where *status* is either **SUCCESS** or **FAILURE**. If **FAILURE** is returned, then either no other values **shall** be returned, or invalid values **shall** be returned.

2. p, q — The requested primes.

3. *pseed, qseed* — (Optional) Computed seed values that were used to generate p and q. The entire *seed* for the generation of p and q consists of *firstseed, pseed* and *qseed*.

4. *pgen_counter, qgen_counter* — (Optional) The count values that were determined during generation.

Process:

1. Check that the (L, N) pair is in the list of acceptable (L, N) pairs (see Section 4.2). If the pair is not in the list, return **FAILURE**.

   > Comment: Use the Shawe-Taylor random prime routine in Appendix C.6 to generate random primes.

2. Using N as the length and *firstseed* as the *input_seed*, use the random prime generation routine in Appendix C.6 to obtain q, *qseed* and *qgen_counter*. If **FAILURE** is returned, then return **FAILURE**.

3. Using $\lceil L / 2 + 1 \rceil$ as the *length* and *qseed* as the *input_seed*, use the random prime routine in Appendix C.6 to obtain p_0, *pseed,* and *pgen_counter*. If **FAILURE** is returned, then return **FAILURE**.

4. $iterations = \lceil L / outlen \rceil - 1$.

5. $old\_counter = pgen\_counter$.

Comment: Generate a (pseudo) random x in the interval $[2^{L-1}, 2^L]$.

6. $x = 0$.

7. For $i = 0$ to $iterations$ do

   $x = x + (\mathbf{Hash}(pseed + i) * 2^{i * outlen})$.

8. $pseed = pseed + iterations + 1$.

9. $x = 2^{L-1} + (x \bmod 2^{L-1})$.

Comment: Generate p, a candidate for the prime, in the interval $[2^{L-1}, 2^L]$.

10. $t = \lceil x / (2q\, p_0) \rceil$.

11. If $(2tq\, p_0 + 1) > 2^L$, then $t = \lceil 2^{L-1} / (2q\, p_0) \rceil$.

12. $p = 2tq\, p_0 + 1$.

13. $pgen\_counter = pgen\_counter + 1$.

Comment: Test p for primality; choose an integer a in the interval $[2, p-2]$.

14. $a = 0$

15. For $i = 0$ to $iterations$ do

   $a = a + (\mathbf{Hash}(pseed + i) * 2^{i * outlen})$.

16. $pseed = pseed + iterations + 1$.

17. $a = 2 + (a \bmod (p-3))$.

18. $z = a^{2tq} \bmod p$.

19. If $((1 = \mathbf{GCD}(z-1, p))$ and $(1 = z^{p_0} \bmod p))$, then return **SUCCESS** and the values of p, q and (optionally) $pseed, qseed, pgen\_counter,$ and $qgen\_counter$.

20. If $(pgen\_counter > (4L + old\_counter))$, then **return FAILURE.**

21. $t = t + 1$.

22. Go to step 11.

A.1.2.2 Validation of the DSA Primes p and q that were Constructed Using the Shawe-Taylor Algorithm

The validation of the primes p and q that were generated by the method described in Appendix A.1.2.1.2 may be performed if the values of *firstseed, pseed, qseed, pgen_counter* and *qgen_counter* were saved and are provided for use in the following algorithm.

The following process or its equivalent **shall** be used to validate p and q for this constructive method.

Input:

1. p, q The primes to be validated.

2. *firstseed, pseed, qseed*   Seed values that were used to generate p and q.

3. *pgen_counter, qgen_counter*

                                    The count values that were determined during generation.

Output:

1. *status*   The status returned from the validation procedure, where *status* is either **SUCCESS** or **FAILURE.**

Process:

1. $L = \mathbf{len}\,(p)$.

2. $N = \mathbf{len}\,(q)$.

3. Check that the (L, N) pair is in the list of acceptable (L, N) pairs (see Section 4.2). If the pair is not in the list, then return **FAILURE.**

4. If $(firstseed < 2^{N-1})$, then return **FAILURE.**

5. If $(2^N \leq q)$, then return **FAILURE**).

6. If $(2^L \leq p)$, then return **FAILURE.**

7. If $((p-1) \bmod q \neq 0)$, then return **FAILURE.**

8. Using L, N and *firstseed*, perform the constructive prime generation procedure in Appendix A.1.2.1.2 to obtain *p_val, q_val, pseed_val, qseed_val, pgen_counter_val,* and *qgen_counter_val*. If **FAILURE** is returned, or if ($q\_val \neq q$) or ($qseed\_val \neq$

qseed) or (*qgen_counter_val* ≠ *qgen_counter*) or (*p_val* ≠ *p*) or (*pseed_val* ≠ *pseed*) or (*pgen_counter_val* ≠ *pgen_counter*), then return **FAILURE.**

9. Return **SUCCESS.**

A.2 Generation of the Generator *g*

The generator *g* depends on the values of *p* and *q*. Two methods for determining the generator *g* are provided; one of these methods **shall** be used. The first method, discussed in Appendix A.2.1, may be used when complete validation of the generator *g* is not required; it is recommended that this method be used only when the party generating *g* is trusted to not deliberately generate a *g* that has a potentially exploitable relationship to another generator *g'*. For example, it must be hard to determine an exponential relationship between the generators such that $g = (g')^x \bmod p$ for a known value of *x*. (Note: Read $(g')^x$ as *g* prime to the *x*.)

Appendix A.2.2 provides a method for partial validation when the method of generation in Appendix A.2.1 is used. The second method for generating *g*, discussed in Appendix A.2.3, **shall** be used when validation of the generator *g* is required; the method for the validation of a generator determined using the method in Appendix A.2.3 is provided in Appendix A.2.4.

A.2.1 Unverifiable Generation of the Generator *g*

This method is used to determine a value for *g*, based on the values of *p* and *q*. It may be used when validation of the generator *g* is not required. The correct generation of *g* cannot be completely validated (see Appendix A.2.2). Note that this generation method for *g* was also specified in previous versions of this Standard.

The following process or its equivalent **shall** be used to generate the generator *g* for this method.

Input:

1. *p, q*   The generated primes.

Output:

1. *g*   The requested value of *g*.

Process:

1. $e = (p - 1)/q$.

2. Set *h* = any integer satisfying $1 < h < (p - 1)$, such that *h* differs from any value previously tried. Note that *h* could be obtained from a random number generator or from a counter that changes after each use.

3. $g = h^e \bmod p$.

4. If $(g = 1)$, then go to step 2.

5. Return g.

A.2.2 Assurance of the Validity of the Generator g

The order of the generator g that was generated using Appendix A.2.1 can be partially validated by checking the range and order, thereby performing a partial validation of g.

The following process or its equivalent **shall** be used when partial validation of the generator g is required:

Input:

   1. p, q, g The domain parameters.

Output:

   1. *status*   The status returned from the generation routine, where *status* is either **PARTIALLY VALID** or **INVALID**.

Process:

1. Verify that $2 \le g \le (p-1)$. If not true, return **INVALID**.

2. If $(g^q = 1 \bmod p)$, then return **PARTIALLY VALID**.

3. Return **INVALID**.

The non-existence of a potentially exploitable relationship of g to another generator g' (that is known to the entity that generated g, but may not be known by other entities) cannot be checked. In this sense, the correct generation of g cannot be completely validated.

A.2.3 Verifiable Canonical Generation of the Generator g

The generation of g is based on the values of p, q and *domain_parameter_seed* (which are outputs of the generation processes in Appendix A.1). When p and q were generated using the method in Appendix A.1.1.2, the *domain_parameter_seed* value must have been returned from the generation routine. When p and q were generated using the method in Appendix A.1.2.1, the *firstseed*, *pseed*, and *qseed* values must have been returned from the generation routine; in this case, *domain_parameter_seed = firstseed* || *pseed* || *qseed* **shall** be used in the following process.

This method of generating a generator g can be validated (see Appendix A.2.4).

This generation method supports the generation of multiple values of g for specific values of p and q. The use of different values of g for the same p and q may be used to support key separation; for example, using the g that is generated with *index* = 1 for digital signatures and with *index* = 2 for key establishment.

Let **Hash( )** be the hash function used to generate p and q (see Appendix A.1). The following process or its equivalent **shall** be used to generate the generator g.

Input:

1. p, q The primes.

2. *domain_parameter_seed*   The seed used during the generation of p and q.

3. *index*   The index to be used for generating g. *index* is a bit string of length 8 that represents an unsigned integer.

Output:

1. *status*   The status returned from the generation routine, where *status* is either **VALID** or **INVALID.**

2. g The value of g that was generated.

Process: Note: *count* is an unsigned 16-bit integer.

Comment: Check that a valid value of the *index* has been provided (see above).

1. If (*index* is incorrect), then return **INVALID.**

2. $N = $ **len**(q).

3. $e = (p - 1)/q$.

4. *count* $= 0$.

5. *count* $=$ *count* $+ 1$.

Comment: Check that *count* does not wrap around to 0.

6. If (*count* $= 0$), then return **INVALID**.

Comment: the length of the *domain_parameter_seed* has already been checked. "ggen" is the bit string 0x6767656E.

7. $U = $ *domain_parameter_seed* $\|$ "ggen" $\|$ *index* $\|$ *count*.

8. $W = $ **Hash**(U).

9. $g = W^e \bmod p$.

10. If ($g < 2$), then go to step 5.   Comment: If a generator has not been found.

11. Return **VALID** and the value of g.

A.2.4 Validation Routine when the Canonical Generation of the Generator g Routine Was Used

This algorithm **shall** be used to validate the value of g that was generated using the process in Appendix A.2.3, based on the values of p, q, *domain_parameter_seed,* and the appropriate value of *index*. It is assumed that the values of p and q have been previously validated according to Appendix A.1. Note that the method specified in Appendix A.2.3 for the generation of g was not included in previous versions of this Standard; therefore, this validation method is not appropriate for that case.

The *domain_parameter_seed* is an output from the generation of p and q. When p and q were generated using the method in Appendix A.1.1.2, the *domain_parameter_seed* must have been returned from the generation routine and made available to the validating party. When p and q were generated using the method in Appendix A.1.2.1, the *firstseed, pseed,* and *qseed* values must have been returned from the generation routine and made available; *firstseed, pseed,* and *qseed* **shall** be concatenated to form the *domain_parameter_seed* used in the following process. Let **Hash( )** be the hash function used to generate g (i.e., the hash function also used to generate p and q).

The input *index* is the index number for the generator g. See Appendix A.2.3 for more details.

The following process or its equivalent **shall** be used to validate the generator g for this method.

Input:

1.	p, q	The primes.
2.	*domain_parameter_seed*	The seed used to generate p and q.
3.	*index*	The index used in Appendix A.2.3 to generate x. *index* is a bit string of length 8 that represents an unsigned integer.
4.	g	The value of g to be validated.

Output:

1.	*status*	The status returned from the generation routine, where *status* is either **VALID** or **INVALID.**

Process: Note: *count* is an unsigned 16-bit integer.

Comment: Check that a valid value of the *index* has been provided (see above).

1. If (*index* is incorrect), then return **INVALID.**

2. Verify that $2 \le g \le (p-1)$. If not true, return **INVALID.**

3. If ($g^q \ne 1 \bmod p$), then return **INVALID.**

44

4. $N = \textbf{len}(q)$.

5. $e = (p - 1)/q$.

6. $count = 0$.

7. $count = count + 1$.

> Comment: Check that $count$ does not wrap around to 0.

8. If $(count = 0)$, then return **INVALID**.

> Comment: "ggen" is the bit string 0x6767656E.

9. $U = domain\_parameter\_seed \,||\, \text{"ggen"} \,||\, index \,||\, count$.

10. $W = \textbf{Hash}(U)$.

11. $computed\_g = W^e \bmod p$.

12. If $(computed\_g < 2)$, then go to step 7. Comment: If a generator has not been found.

13. If $(computed\_g = g)$, then return **VALID**, else return **INVALID**.

APPENDIX B: Key Pair Generation

Discrete logarithm cryptography (DLC) is divided into finite field cryptography (FFC) and elliptic curve cryptography (ECC); the difference between the two is the type of math that is used. DSA is an example of FFC; ECDSA is an example of ECC. Other examples of DLC are the Diffie-Hellman and MQV key agreement algorithms, which have both FFC and ECC forms.

The most common example of integer factorization cryptography (IFC) is RSA.

This appendix specifies methods for the generation of FFC and ECC key pairs and secret numbers, and the generation of IFC key pairs. All generation methods require the use of an approved, properly instantiated random bit generator (RBG); the RBG **shall** have a security strength equal to or greater than the security strength associated with the key pairs and secret numbers to be generated. See SP 800-57 for guidance on security strengths and key sizes.

This appendix does not indicate the required conversions between bit strings and integers. When required by a process in this appendix, the conversion **shall** be accomplished as specified in Appendix C.2.

B.1   FFC Key Pair Generation

An FFC key pair (x, y) is generated for a set of domain parameters $(p, q, g$ {, *domain_parameter_seed, counter*}). Two methods are provided for the generation of the FFC private key x and public key y; one of these two methods **shall** be used. Prior to generating DSA key pairs, assurance of the validity of the domain parameters (p, q and g) **shall** have been obtained as specified in Section 3.1.

For DSA, the valid values of L and N are provided in Section 4.2.

B.1.1 Key Pair Generation Using Extra Random Bits

In this method, 64 more bits are requested from the RBG than are needed for x so that bias produced by the mod function in step 6 is negligible.

The following process or its equivalent may be used to generate an FFC key pair.

Input:

(p, q, g) The subset of the domain parameters that are used for this process. p, q and g **shall** either be provided as integers during input, or **shall** be converted to integers prior to use.

Output:

1. *status*   The status returned from the key pair generation process. The status will indicate **SUCCESS** or an **ERROR**.

2. *(x, y)*   The generated private and public keys. If an error is encountered during the generation process, invalid values for *x* and *y* **should** be returned, as represented by *Invalid_x* and *Invalid_y* in the following specification. *x* and *y* are returned as integers. The generated private key *x* is in the range [1, *q*–1], and the public key is in the range [1, *p*–1].

Process:

1. $N = \textbf{len}(q); L = \textbf{len}(p)$.

    Comment: Check that the (*L, N*) pair is specified in Section 4.2.

2. If the (*L, N*) pair is invalid, then return an **ERROR** indicator, *Invalid_x*, and *Invalid_y*.

3. *requested_security_strength* = the security strength associated with the (*L, N*) pair; see SP 800-57.

4. Obtain a string of *N*+64 *returned_bits* from an **RBG** with a security strength of *requested_security_strength* or more. If an **ERROR** indication is returned, then return an **ERROR** indication, *Invalid_x*, and *Invalid_y*.

5. Convert *returned_bits* to the (non-negative) integer *c* (see Appendix C.2.1).

6. $x = (c \bmod (q–1)) + 1$.   Comment: $0 \leq c \bmod (q–1) \leq q–2$ and implies that $1 \leq x \leq q–1$.

7. $y = g^x \bmod p$.

8. Return **SUCCESS**, *x*, and *y*.

B.1.2 Key Pair Generation by Testing Candidates

In this method, a random number is obtained and tested to determine that it will produce a value of *x* in the correct range. If *x* is out-of-range, another random number is obtained (i.e., the process is iterated until an acceptable value of *x* is obtained.

The following process or its equivalent may be used to generate an FFC key pair.

Input:

(p, q, g)   The subset of the domain parameters that are used for this process. *p, q* and *g* **shall** either be provided as integers during input, or **shall** be converted to integers prior to use.

47

Output:

1. *status*   The status returned from the key pair generation process. The status will indicate **SUCCESS** or an **ERROR**.

2. *(x, y)*   The generated private and public keys. If an error is encountered during the generation process, invalid values for *x* and *y* **should** be returned, as represented by *Invalid_x* and *Invalid_y* in the following specification. *x* and *y* are returned as integers. The generated private key *x* is in the range [1, *q*–1], and the public key is in the range [1, *p*–1].

Process:

1. $N = \mathbf{len}(q); L = \mathbf{len}(p)$.

> Comment: Check that the (*L*, *N*) pair is specified in Section 4.2.

2. If the (*L*, *N*) pair is invalid, then return an **ERROR** indication, *Invalid_x*, and *Invalid_y*.

3. *requested_security_strength* = the security strength associated with the (*L*, *N*) pair; see SP 800-57.

4. Obtain a string of *N returned_bits* from an **RBG** with a security strength of *requested_security_strength* or more. If an **ERROR** indication is returned, then return an **ERROR** indication, *Invalid_x*, and *Invalid_y*.

5. Convert *returned_bits* to the (non-negative) integer *c* (see Appendix C.2.1).

6. If ($c > q$–2), then go to step 4.

7. $x = c + 1$.

8. $y = g^x \bmod p$.

9. Return **SUCCESS**, *x*, and *y*.

B.2   FFC Per-Message Secret Number Generation

DSA requires the generation of a new random number *k* for each message to be signed. Two methods are provided for the generation of *k*; one of these two methods or another approved method **shall** be used.

The valid values of *N* are provided in Section 4.2. Let **inverse**(*k*, *q*) be a function that computes the inverse of a (non-negative) integer *k* with respect to multiplication modulo the prime number *q*. A technique for computing the inverse is provided in Appendix C.1.

B.2.1 Per-Message Secret Number Generation Using Extra Random Bits

In this method, 64 more bits are requested from the RBG than are needed for k so that bias produced by the mod function in step 6 is not readily apparent.

The following process or its equivalent may be used to generate a per-message secret number.

Input:

(p, q, g) DSA domain parameters that are generated as specified in Section 4.3.1.

Output:

1. *status*   The status returned from the secret number generation process. The status will indicate **SUCCESS** or an **ERROR**.

2. (k, k^{-1}) The per-message secret number k and its mod q inverse, k^{-1}. If an error is encountered during the generation process, invalid values for k and k^{-1} **should** be returned, as represented by *Invalid_k* and *Invalid_k_inverse* in the following specification. k and k^{-1} are in the range $[1, q-1]$.

Process:

1. $N = \mathbf{len}(q); L = \mathbf{len}(p)$.

> Comment: Check that the (L, N) pair is specified in Section 4.2.

2. If the (L, N) pair is invalid, then return an **ERROR** indication, *Invalid_k*, and *Invalid_k_inverse*.

3. *requested_security_strength* = the security strength associated with the (L, N) pair; see SP 800-57.

4. Obtain a string of $N+64$ *returned_bits* from an **RBG** with a security strength of *requested_security_strength* or more. If an **ERROR** indication is returned, then return an **ERROR** indication, *Invalid_k*, and *Invalid_k_inverse*.

5. Convert *returned_bits* to the (non-negative) integer c (see Appendix C.2.1).

6. $k = (c \bmod (q-1)) + 1$.

7. $(status, k^{-1}) = \mathbf{inverse}\ (k, q)$.

8. Return *status*, k, and k^{-1}.

B.2.2 Per-Message Secret Number Generation by Testing Candidates

In this method, a random number is obtained and tested to determine that it will produce a value of k in the correct range. If k is out-of-range, another random number is obtained (i.e., the process is iterated until an acceptable value of k is obtained.

The following process or its equivalent may be used to generate a per-message secret number.

Input:

(p, q, g) DSA domain parameters that are generated as specified in Section 4.3.1.

Output:

1. *status*   The status returned from the secret number generation process. The status will indicate **SUCCESS** or an **ERROR**.

2. (k, k^{-1}) The per-message secret number k and its inverse, k^{-1}. If an error is encountered during the generation process, invalid values for k and k^{-1} **should** be returned, as represented by *Invalid_k* and *Invalid_k_inverse* in the following specification. k and k^{-1} are in the range $[1, q-1]$.

Process:

1. $N = \mathbf{len}(q); L = \mathbf{len}(p)$.

> Comment: Check that the (L, N) pair is specified in Section 4.2).

2. If the (L, N) pair is invalid, then return an **ERROR** indication, *Invalid_k*, and *Invalid_k_inverse*.

3. *requested_security_strength* = the security strength associated with the (L, N) pair; see SP 800-57.

4. Obtain a string of N *returned_bits* from an **RBG** with a security strength of *requested_security_strength* or more. If an **ERROR** indication is returned, then return an **ERROR** indication, *Invalid_k*, and *Invalid_k_inverse*.

5. Convert *returned_bits* to the (non-negative) integer c (see Appendix C.2.1).

6. If $(c > q-2)$, then go to step 4.

7. $k = c + 1$.

8. $(status, k^{-1}) = \mathbf{inverse}(k, q)$.

9. Return *status*, k, and k^{-1}.

B.3   IFC Key Pair Generation

B.3.1   Criteria for IFC Key Pairs

Key pairs for IFC consist of a public key (n, e), and a private key (n, d), where n is the modulus and is the product of two prime numbers p and q. The security of IFC depends on the quality and secrecy of these primes and the private exponent d. The primes p and q **shall** be generated using one of the following methods:

    A. Both p and q are randomly generated prime numbers (Random Primes), where p and q **shall** both be either :

        1. Provable primes (see Appendix B.3.2), or

        2. Probable primes (see Appendix B.3.3).

Using methods 1 and 2, p and q with lengths of 1024 or 1536 bits may be generated; p and q with lengths of 512 bits **shall not** be generated using these methods. Instead, p and q with lengths of 512 bits **shall** be generated using the conditions based on auxiliary primes (see Appendices B.3.4, B.3.5, or B.3.6).

    B. Both p and q are randomly generated prime numbers that satisfy the following additional conditions (Primes with Conditions):

- $(p{-}1)$ has a prime factor p_1
- $(p{+}1)$ has a prime factor p_2
- $(q{-}1)$ has a prime factor q_1
- $(q{+}1)$ has a prime factor q_2

where p_1, p_2, q_1 and q_2 are called auxiliary primes of p and q.

Using this method, one of the following cases **shall** apply:

        1. The primes p_1, p_2, q_1, q_2, p and q **shall** all be provable primes (see Appendix B.3.4),

        2. The primes p_1, p_2, q_1 and q_2 **shall** be provable primes, and the primes p and q **shall** be probable primes (see Appendix B.3.5), or

        3 The primes p_1, p_2, q_1, q_2, p and q **shall** all be probable primes (see Appendix B.3.6).

The minimum lengths for each of the auxiliary primes p_1, p_2, q_1 and q_2 are dependent on *nlen*, where *nlen* is the length of the modulus n in bits. Note that *nlen* is also called the key size. The lengths of the auxiliary primes may be fixed or randomly chosen, subject to the restrictions in Table B.1. The maximum length is determined by *nlen* (the sum of the length of each auxiliary prime pair) and whether the primes p and q are probable primes or provable primes (e.g., for the auxiliary prime pair p_1 and p_2, $\mathbf{len}(p_1) + \mathbf{len}(p_2)$ **shall** be less than a value determined by *nlen*, whether p_1 and p_2 are generated to be probable or provable primes)[3].

---

[3] For the probable primes p and q: $\mathbf{len}(p_1) + \mathbf{len}(p_2) < \mathbf{len}(p) - \log_2(\mathbf{len}(p)) - 6$; similarly for $\mathbf{len}(q_1) + \mathbf{len}(q_2)$ and $\mathbf{len}(q)$. For the provable primes p and q: $\mathbf{len}(p_1) + \mathbf{len}(p_2) < \mathbf{len}(p)/2 - \log_2(\mathbf{len}(p)) - 7$; similarly for $\mathbf{len}(q_1) + \mathbf{len}(q_2)$

Table B.1. Minimum and maximum lengths of p_1, p_2, q_1 and q_2

nlen	Min. length of auxiliary primes p_1, p_2, q_1 and q_2	Max. length of len(p_1) + len(p_2) and len(q_1) + len(q_2)	
		p, q Probable primes	p, q Provable primes
1024	> 100 bits	< 496 bits	< 239 bits
2048	> 140 bits	< 1007 bits	< 494 bits
3072	> 170 bits	< 1518 bits	< 750 bits

For different values of *nlen* (i.e., different key sizes), the methods allowed for the generation of *p* and *q* are specified in Table B.2.

Table B.2. Allowable Prime Generation Methods

nlen	Random Primes	Primes with Conditions
1024	No	Yes
2048	Yes	Yes
3072	Yes	Yes

In addition, all IFC keys **shall** meet the following criteria in order to conform to FIPS 186-4:

1. The public exponent *e* **shall** be selected with the following constraints:

   (a) The public verification exponent *e* **shall** be selected prior to generating the primes *p* and *q*, and the private signature exponent *d*.

   (b) The exponent *e* **shall** be an odd positive integer such that:

   $$2^{16} < e < 2^{256}.$$

   Note that the value of *e* may be any value that meets constraint 1(b), i.e., *e* may be either a fixed value or a random value.

2. The primes *p* and *q* **shall** be selected with the following constraints:

   (a) (p–1) and (q–1) **shall** be relatively prime to the public exponent *e*.

   (b) The private prime factor *p* **shall** be selected randomly and **shall** satisfy

---

and **len**(q). In each case, **len**(p) = **len**(q) = *nlen*/2.

$(\sqrt{2})(2^{(nlen/2)-1}) \le p \le (2^{nlen/2}-1)$, where *nlen* is the appropriate length for the desired *security_strength*.

(c) The private prime factor *q* **shall** be selected randomly and **shall** satisfy
$(\sqrt{2})(2^{(nlen/2)-1}) \le q \le (2^{nlen/2}-1)$, where *nlen* is the appropriate length for the desired *security_strength*.

(d) $|p-q| > 2^{(nlen/2)-100}$.

3. The private signature exponent *d* **shall** be selected with the following constraints after the generation of *p* and *q*:

(a) The exponent *d* **shall** be a positive integer value such that
$2^{nlen/2} < d < \text{LCM}(p-1, q-1)$, and

(b) $d = e^{-1} \bmod (\text{LCM}(p-1, q-1))$.

That is, the inequality in (a) holds, and $1 \equiv (ed) \ (\bmod \ \text{LCM}(p-1, q-1))$.

In the extremely rare event that $d \le 2^{nlen/2}$, then new values for *p*, *q* and *d* **shall** be determined. A different value of *e* may be used, although this is not required.

Any hash function used during the generation of the key pair **shall** be approved (i.e., specified in FIPS 180).

B.3.2 Generation of Random Primes that are Provably Prime

An approved method that satisfies the constraints of Appendix B.3.1 **shall** be used for the generation of IFC random primes *p* and *q* that are provably prime (see case A.1). One such method is provided in Appendix B.3.2.1 and B.3.2.2. For this method, a random seed is initially required (see Appendix B.3.2.1); the length of the seed is equal to twice the security strength associated with the modulus *n*. After the seed is obtained, the primes can be generated (see Appendix B.3.2.2).

B.3.2.1 Get the Seed

The following process or its equivalent **shall** be used to generate the seed for this method.

Input:

nlen The intended bit length of the modulus *n*.

Output:

status The status to be returned, where *status* is either **SUCCESS** or **FAILURE**.

seed The seed. If *status* = **FAILURE**, a value of zero is returned as the *seed*.

Process:

1. If *nlen* is not valid (see Section 5.1), then Return (**FAILURE**, 0).

2. Let *security_strength* be the security strength associated with *nlen*, as specified in SP 800-57, Part 1.

3. Obtain a string *seed* of (2 * *security_strength*) bits from an **RBG** that supports the *security_strength*.

4. Return (**SUCCESS**, *seed*).

B.3.2.2 Construction of the Provable Primes *p* and *q*

The following process or its equivalent **shall** be used to construct the random primes *p* and *q* (to be used as factors of the RSA modulus *n*) that are provably prime:

Input:

nlen	The intended bit length of the modulus *n*.
e	The public verification exponent.
seed	The seed obtained using the method in Appendix B.3.2.1.

Output:

status	The status of the generation process, where *status* is either **SUCCESS** or **FAILURE**. When **FAILURE** is returned, zero values **shall** be returned as the other parameters.
p and *q*	The private prime factors of *n*.

Process:

1. If *nlen* is neither 2048 nor 3072, then return (**FAILURE**, 0, 0).

2. If (($e \leq 2^{16}$) OR ($e \geq 2^{256}$) OR (*e* is not odd)), then return (**FAILURE**, 0, 0).

3. Set the value of *security_strength* in accordance with the value of *nlen*, as specified in SP 800-57, Part 1.

4. If (**len**(*seed*) $\neq$ 2 * *security_strength*), then return (**FAILURE**, 0, 0).

5. *working_seed* = *seed*.

6. Generate *p*:

   6.1 Using $L = nlen/2$, $N_1 = 1$, $N_2 = 1$, *first_seed* = *working_seed* and *e*, use the provable prime construction method in Appendix C.10 to obtain *p* and *pseed*. If **FAILURE** is returned, then return (**FAILURE**, 0, 0).

   6.2 *working_seed* = *pseed*.

7. Generate q:

   7.1 Using $L = nlen/2$, $N_1 = 1$, $N_2 = 1$, *first_seed* = *working_seed* and e, use the provable prime construction method in Appendix C.10 to obtain q and *qseed*. If **FAILURE** is returned, then return (**FAILURE**, 0, 0).

   7.2 *working_seed* = *qseed*.

8. If ($|p - q| \leq 2^{nlen/2 - 100}$), then go to step 7.

9. Zeroize the internally generated seeds:

   9.1 *pseed* = 0;

   9.2 *qseed* = 0;

   9.3 *working_seed* = 0.

10. Return (**SUCCESS**, p, q).

B.3.3 Generation of Random Primes that are Probably Prime

An approved method that satisfies the constraints of Appendix B.3.1 **shall** be used for the generation of IFC random primes p and q that are probably prime (see case A.2).

The following process or its equivalent **shall** be used to construct the random probable primes p and q (to be used as factors of the RSA modulus n):

Input:

   nlen   The intended bit length of the modulus n.

   e The public verification exponent.

Output:

   status   The status of the generation process, where *status* is either **SUCCESS** or **FAILURE**.

   p and q The private prime factors of n. When **FAILURE** is returned, zero values **shall** be returned as p and q.

Process:

1. If *nlen* is neither 2048 nor 3072, return (**FAILURE**, 0, 0).

2. If (($e \leq 2^{16}$) OR ($e \geq 2^{256}$) OR (e is not odd)), then return (**FAILURE**, 0, 0).

3. Set the value of *security_strength* in accordance with the value of *nlen*, as specified in SP 800-57, Part 1.

4. Generate p:

   4.1 $i = 0$.

55

4.2 Obtain a string p of ($nlen$/2) bits from an **RBG** that supports the *security_strength*.

4.3 If (p is not odd), then $p = p + 1$.

4.4 If (($p < (\sqrt{2})(2^{(nlen/2)-1})$)), then go to step 4.2.

4.5 If (**GCD**(p–1, e) = 1), then

      4.5.1 Test p for primality as specified in Appendix C.3, using an appropriate value from Table C-2 or C-3 in Appendix C.3 as the number of iterations.

      4.5.2 If p is **PROBABLY PRIME**, then go to step 5.

4.6 $i = i + 1$.

4.7 If ($i \geq 5(nlen/2)$), then return (**FAILURE**, 0, 0)

    Else go to step 4.2.

5. Generate q:

    5.1 $i = 0$.

    5.2 Obtain a string q of ($nlen$/2) bits from an **RBG** that supports the *security_strength*

    5.3 If (q is not odd), then $q = q + 1$.

    5.4 If ($|p - q| \leq 2^{nlen/2 - 100}$), then go to step 5.2.

    5.5 If (($q < (\sqrt{2})(2^{(nlen/2)-1})$)), then go to step 5.2.

    5.6 If (**GCD**(q–1, e) = 1) then

        5.6.1 Test q for primality as specified in Appendix C.3, using an appropriate value from Table C-2 or C-3 in Appendix C.3 as the number of iterations.

        5.6.2 If q is **PROBABLY PRIME**, then return (**SUCCESS**, p, q).

    5.7 $i = i + 1$.

    5.8 If ($i \geq 5(nlen/2)$), then return (**FAILURE**, 0, 0)

    Else go to step 5.2.

B.3.4 Generation of Provable Primes with Conditions Based on Auxiliary Provable Primes

This section specifies an approved method for the generation of the IFC primes p and q with the additional conditions specified in Appendix B.3.1, case B.1, where p, p_1, p_2, q, q_1 and q_2 are all provable primes. For this method, a random seed is initially required (see Appendix B.3.2.1); the length of the seed is equal to twice the security strength associated with the modulus n. After the first seed is obtained, the primes can be generated.

Let $bitlen_1$, $bitlen_2$, $bitlen_3$, and $bitlen_4$ be the bit lengths for p_1, p_2, q_1 and q_2, respectively, in accordance with Table B.1. The following process or its equivalent **shall** be used to generate the provable primes:

Input:

nlen	The intended bit length of the modulus *n*.
e	The public verification exponent.
seed	The seed obtained using the method in Appendix B.3.2.1.

Output:

status	The status of the generation process, where *status* is either **SUCCESS** or **FAILURE**. If **FAILURE** is returned then zeros **shall** be returned as the values for *p* and *q*.
p and *q*	The private prime factors of *n*.

Process:

1. If *nlen* is neither 1024, 2048, nor 3072, then return (**FAILURE**, 0, 0).

2. If $((e \leq 2^{16})$ OR $(e \geq 2^{256})$ OR (e is not odd)), then return (**FAILURE**, 0, 0).

3. Set the value of *security_strength* in accordance with the value of *nlen*, as specified in SP 800-57, Part 1.

4. If (**len**(*seed*) $\neq 2$ * *security_strength*), then return (**FAILURE**, 0, 0).

5. *working_seed* = *seed*.

6. Generate *p*:

    6.1 Using $L = nlen/2$, $N_1 = bitlen_1$, $N_2 = bitlen_2$, *firstseed* = *working_seed* and *e*, use the provable prime construction method in Appendix C.10 to obtain p, p_1, p_2 and *pseed*. If **FAILURE** is returned, return (**FAILURE**, 0, 0).

    6.2 *working_seed* = *pseed*.

7. Generate *q*:

    7.1 Using $L = nlen/2$, $N_1 = bitlen_3$, $N_2 = bitlen_4$ and *firstseed* = *working_seed* and *e*, use the provable prime construction method in Appendix C.10 to obtain q, q_1, q_2 and *qseed*. If **FAILURE** is returned, return (**FAILURE**, 0, 0).

    7.2 *working_seed* = *qseed*.

8. If ($|p - q| \leq 2^{nlen/2 - 100}$), then go to step 7.

9. Zeroize the internally generated seeds:

    9.1 *pseed* = 0.

9.2 *qseed* = 0.

9.3 *working_seed* = 0.

10. Return (**SUCCESS**, *p*, *q*).

B.3.5 Generation of Probable Primes with Conditions Based on Auxiliary Provable Primes

This section specifies an approved method for the generation of the IFC primes *p* and *q* with the additional conditions specified in Appendix B.3.1, case B.2, where p_1, p_2, q_1 and q_2 are provably prime, and *p* and *q* are probably prime. For this method, a random seed is initially required (see Appendix B.3.2.1); the length of the seed is equal to twice the security strength associated with the modulus *n*. After the first seed is obtained, the primes can be generated.

Let $bitlen_1$, $bitlen_2$, $bitlen_3$, and $bitlen_4$ be the bit lengths for p_1, p_2, q_1 and q_2, respectively in accordance with Table B.1. The following process or its equivalent **shall** be used to construct *p* and *q*.

Input:

nlen	The intended bit length of the modulus *n*.
e	The public verification exponent.
seed	The seed obtained using the method in Appendix B.3.2.1.

Output:

status	The status of the generation process, where *status* is either **SUCCESS** or **FAILURE**. If **FAILURE** is returned then zeros **shall** be returned as the values for *p* and *q*.
p and *q*	The private prime factors of *n*.

Process:

1. If *nlen* is neither 1024, 2048, nor 3072, then return (**FAILURE**, 0, 0).

2. If $((e \le 2^{16})$ OR $(e \ge 2^{256})$ OR (*e* is not odd)), then return (**FAILURE**, 0, 0).

3. Set the value of *security_strength* in accordance with the value of *nlen*, as specified in SP 800-57, Part 1.

4. If (**len**(*seed*) ≠ 2 * *security_strength*), then return (**FAILURE**, 0, 0).

> Comment: Generate four primes p_1, p_2, q_1 and q_2 that are provably prime.

58

5. Generate p:

    5.1   Using $bitlen_1$ as the length, and *seed* as the *input_seed*, use the random prime generation routine in Appendix C.6 to obtain p_1 and *prime_seed*. If **FAILURE** is returned, the return (**FAILURE**, 0, 0).

    5.2   Using $bitlen_2$ as the length, and *prime_seed* as the *input_seed*, use the random prime generation routine in Appendix C.6 to obtain p_2 and a new value for *prime_seed*. If **FAILURE** is returned, the return (**FAILURE**, 0, 0).

    5.3   Generate a prime p using the routine in Appendix C.9 with inputs of $p_1, p_2,$ *nlen, e* and *security_strength*, also obtaining X_p. If **FAILURE** is returned, return (**FAILURE**, 0, 0).

6. Generate q:

    6.1. Using $bitlen_3$ as the length, and *prime_seed* as the *input_seed*, use the random prime generation routine in Appendix C.6 to obtain q_1 and a new value for *prime_seed*. If **FAILURE** is returned, the return (**FAILURE**, 0, 0).

    6.2   Using $bitlen_4$ as the length, and *prime_seed* as the *input_seed*, use the random prime generation routine in Appendix C.6 to obtain q_2 and a new value for *prime_seed*. If **FAILURE** is returned, the return (**FAILURE**, 0, 0).

    6.3   Generate a prime q using the routine in Appendix C.9 with inputs of $q_1, q_2,$ *nlen, e* and *security_strength*, also obtaining X_q. If **FAILURE** is returned, return (**FAILURE**, 0, 0).

7. If $((|p - q| \le 2^{nlen/2 - 100})$ OR $(|X_p - X_q| \le 2^{nlen/2 - 100}))$, then go to step 6.

8. Zeroize the internally generated that are not returned:

    8.1 $X_p = 0$.

    8.2 $X_q = 0$.

    8.3   *prime_seed* = 0.

    8.4 $p_1 = 0$.

    8.5 $p_2 = 0$.

    8.6 $q_1 = 0$.

    8.7 $q_2 = 0$.

9. Return (**SUCCESS**, p, q).

B.3.6 Generation of Probable Primes with Conditions Based on Auxiliary Probable Primes

An approved method that satisfies the constraints of Appendix B.3.1 **shall** be used for the generation of IFC primes p and q that are probably prime and meet the additional constraints of Appendix B.3.1 (see case B.3). For this case, the prime factors p_1, p_2, q_1 and q_2 are also probably prime.

Four random numbers X_{p1}, X_{p2}, X_{q1} and X_{q2} are generated, from which the prime factors p_1, p_2, q_1 and q_2 are determined. p_1 and p_2, and an additional random number X_p are then used to determine p, and q_1 and q_2 and a random number X_q are used to obtain q. Let $bitlen_1$, $bitlen_2$, $bitlen_3$, and $bitlen_4$ be the bit lengths for p_1, p_2, q_1 and q_2, respectively chosen in accordance with Table B.1.

The following process or its equivalent **shall** be used to generate p and q:

Input:

nlen	The intended bit length of the modulus n.
e	The public verification exponent.

Output:

status	The status of the generation process, where *status* is either **SUCCESS** or **FAILURE**. If **FAILURE** is returned then zeros **shall** be returned as the values for p and q.
p and *q*	The private prime factors of n.

Process:

1. If *nlen* is neither 1024, 2048, nor 3072, then return (**FAILURE**, 0, 0).

2. If $((e \leq 2^{16})$ OR $(e \geq 2^{256})$ OR (e is not odd)), then return (**FAILURE**, 0, 0).

3. Set the value of *security_strength* in accordance with the value of *nlen*, as specified in SP 800-57, Part 1.

4. Generate p:

   4.1 Generate an odd integer X_{p1} of length $bitlen_1$ bits, and a second odd integer X_{p2} of length $bitlen_2$ bits, using an approved random number generator that supports the *security_strength*.

   4.2 Sequentially search successive odd integers, starting at X_{p1} until the first probable prime p_1 is found. Candidate integers **shall** be tested for primality as specified in Appendix C.3. Repeat the process to find p_2, starting at X_{p2}. The probable primes p_1 and p_2 **shall** be the first integers that pass the primality test.

4.3 Generate a prime p using the routine in Appendix C.9 with inputs of $p_1, p_2,$ *nlen, e* and *security_ strength*, also obtaining X_p. If **FAILURE** is returned, return (**FAILURE**, 0, 0).

5. Generate q:

5.1 Generate an odd integer X_{q1} of length *bitlen*$_3$ bits, and a second odd integer X_{q2} of length *bitlen*$_4$ bits, using an approved random number generator that supports the *security_strength*.

5.2 Sequentially search successive odd integers, starting at X_{q1} until the first probable prime q_1 is found. Candidate integers **shall** be tested for primality as specified in Appendix C.3. Repeat the process to find q_2, starting at X_{q2}. The probable primes q_1 and q_2 **shall** be the first integers that pass the primality test.

5.3 Generate a prime q using the routine in Appendix C.9 with inputs of $q_1, q_2,$ *nlen, e* and *security_ strength*, also obtaining X_q. If **FAILURE** is returned, return (**FAILURE**, 0, 0).

6. If $((|X_p - X_q| \le 2^{nlen/2 - 100})$ OR $(|p - q| \le 2^{nlen/2 - 100}))$, then go to step 5.

7. Zeroize the internally generated values that are not returned:

7.1 $X_p = 0$.

7.2 $X_q = 0$.

7.3 $X_{p1} = 0$.

7.4 $X_{p2} = 0$.

7.5 $X_{q1} = 0$.

7.6 $X_{q2} = 0$.

7.7 $p_1 = 0$.

7.8 $p_2 = 0$.

7.9 $q_1 = 0$.

7.10 $q_2 = 0$.

8. Return (**SUCCESS**, p, q).

B.4 ECC Key Pair Generation

An ECC key pair d and Q is generated for a set of domain parameters (q, *FR, a, b* {, *domain_parameter_seed*}, *G, n, h*). Two methods are provided for the generation of the ECC private key d and public key Q; one of these two methods **shall** be used to generate d and Q.

Prior to generating ECDSA key pairs, assurance of the validity of the domain parameters (*q*, *FR*, *a*, *b* {, *domain_parameter_seed*}, *G*, *n*, *h*) **shall** have been obtained as specified in Section 3.1.

For ECDSA, the valid bit-lengths of *n* are provided in Section 6.1.1. See ANS X9.62 for definitions of the elliptic curve math and the conversion routines.

B.4.1 Key Pair Generation Using Extra Random Bits

In this method, 64 more bits are requested from the RBG than are needed for *d* so that bias produced by the mod function in step 6 is negligible.

The following process or its equivalent may be used to generate an ECC key pair.

Input:

1. (*q*, *FR*, *a*, *b* {, *domain_parameter_seed*}, *G*, *n*, *h*)

   > The domain parameters that are used for this process. *n* is a prime number, and *G* is a point on the elliptic curve.

Output:

1. *status*   The status returned from the key pair generation procedure. The status will indicate **SUCCESS** or an **ERROR**.

2. (*d*, *Q*)   The generated private and public keys. If an error is encountered during the generation process, invalid values for *d* and *Q* **should** be returned, as represented by *Invalid_d* and *Invalid_Q* in the following specification. *d* is an integer, and *Q* is an elliptic curve point. The generated private key *d* is in the range [1, *n*–1].

Process:

1. $N = \textbf{len}(n)$.

   > Comment: Check that *N* is included in Table 1 of Section 6.1.1.

2. If *N* is invalid, then return an **ERROR** indication, *Invalid_d*, and *Invalid_Q*.

3. *requested_security_strength* = the security strength associated with *N*; see SP 800-57, Part 1.

4. Obtain a string of *N*+64 *returned_bits* from an **RBG** with a security strength of *requested_security_strength* or more. If an **ERROR** indication is returned, then return an **ERROR** indication, *Invalid_d*, and *Invalid_Q*.

5. Convert *returned_bits* to the (non-negative) integer *c* (see Appendix C.2.1).

6. $d = (c \bmod (n-1)) + 1$.

7. $Q = dG$.

8. Return **SUCCESS**, d, and Q.

B.4.2 Key Pair Generation by Testing Candidates

In this method, a random number is obtained and tested to determine that it will produce a value of d in the correct range. If d is out-of-range, another random number is obtained (i.e., the process is iterated until an acceptable value of d is obtained.

The following process or its equivalent may be used to generate an ECC key pair.

Input:

1. $(q, FR, a, b \{, domain\_parameter\_seed\}, G, n, h)$

   The domain parameters that are used for this process. n is a prime number, and G is a point on the elliptic curve.

Output:

1. *status*   The status returned from the key pair generation procedure. The status will indicate **SUCCESS** or an **ERROR**.

2. (d, Q) The generated private and public keys. If an error is encountered during the generation process, invalid values for d and Q **should** be returned, as represented by *Invalid_d* and *Invalid_Q* in the following specification. d is an integer, and Q is an elliptic curve point. The generated private key d is in the range $[1, n–1]$.

Process:

1. $N = \textbf{len}(n)$.

   Comment: Check that N is included in Table 1 of Section 6.1.1.

2. If N is invalid, then return an **ERROR** indication, *Invalid_d*, and *Invalid_Q*.

3. *requested_security_strength* = the security strength associated with N; see SP 800-57, Part 1.

4. Obtain a string of N *returned_bits* from an **RBG** with a security strength of *requested_security_strength* or more. If an **ERROR** indication is returned, then return an **ERROR** indication, *Invalid_d*, and *Invalid_Q*.

5. Convert *returned_bits* to the (non-negative) integer c (see Appendix C.2.1).

6. If $(c > n–2)$, then go to step 4.

7. $d = c + 1$.

8. $Q = dG$.

9. Return **SUCCESS**, d, and Q.

B.5   ECC Per-Message Secret Number Generation

ECDSA requires the generation of a new random number k for each message to be signed. Two methods are provided for the generation of k; one of these two methods or another approved method **shall** be used.

The valid values of n are provided in Section 6.1.1. See ANS X9.62 for definitions of the elliptic curve math and the conversion routines.

Let **inverse**(k, n) be a function that computes the inverse of a (non-negative) integer k with respect to multiplication modulo the prime number n. A technique for computing the inverse is provided in Appendix C.1.

B.5.1 Per-Message Secret Number Generation Using Extra Random Bits

In this method, 64 more bits are requested from the RBG than are needed for k so that bias produced by the mod function in step 6 is not readily apparent.

The following process or its equivalent may be used to generate a per-message secret number.

Input:

1. $(q, FR, a, b \{, domain\_parameter\_seed\}, G, n, h)$

    The domain parameters that are used for this process. n is a prime number, and G is a point on the elliptic curve.

Output:

1. *status*   The status returned from the key pair generation procedure. The status will indicate **SUCCESS** or an **ERROR**.

2. (k, k^{-1}) The generated secret number k and its inverse k^{-1}. If an error is encountered during the generation process, invalid values for k and k^{-1} **should** be returned, as represented by *Invalid_k* and *Invalid_k_inverse* in the following specification. k and k^{-1} are integers in the range $[1, n-1]$.

Process:

1. $N = \mathbf{len}(n)$.

    Comment: Check that N is included in Table 1 of Section 6.1.1.

2. If N is invalid, then return an **ERROR** indication, *Invalid_k*, and *Invalid_k_inverse*.

64

3. *requested_security_strength* = the security strength associated with N; see SP 800-57, Part 1.

4. Obtain a string of $N+64$ *returned_bits* from an **RBG** with a security strength of *requested_security_strength* or more. If an **ERROR** indication is returned, then return an **ERROR** indication, *Invalid_k*, and *Invalid_k_inverse*.

5. Convert *returned_bits* to the non-negative integer c (see Appendix C.2.1).

6. $k = (c \bmod (n-1)) + 1$.

7. $(status,\ k^{-1}) = \textbf{inverse}(k, n)$.

8. Return *status*, k, and k^{-1}.

B.5.2 Per-Message Secret Number Generation by Testing Candidates

In this method, a random number is obtained and tested to determine that it will produce a value of k in the correct range. If k is out-of-range, another random number is obtained (i.e., the process is iterated until an acceptable value of k is obtained).

The following process or its equivalent may b used to generate a per-message secret number.

Input:

    1. $(q, FR, a, b \{, domain\_parameter\_seed\}, G, n, h)$

                The domain parameters that are used for this process. n is a prime number, and G is a point on the elliptic curve.

Output:

    1.   *status*   The status returned from the key pair generation procedure. The status will indicate **SUCCESS** or an **ERROR**.

    2. (k, k^{-1}) The generated secret number k and its inverse k^{-1}. If an error is encountered during the generation process, invalid values for k and k^{-1} **should** be returned, as represented by *Invalid_k* and *Invalid_k_inverse* in the following specification. k and k^{-1} are integers in the range $[1, n-1]$.

Process:

    1. $N = \textbf{len}(n)$.

                                Comment: Check that N is included in Table 1 of Section 6.1.1.

    2.   If N is not included in Table 1, then return an **ERROR** indication, *Invalid_k*, and *Invalid_k_inverse*.

3. *requested_security_strength* = the security strength associated with N; see SP 800-57, Part 1.

4. Obtain a string of N *returned_bits* from an **RBG** with a security strength of *requested_security_strength* or more. If an **ERROR** indication is returned, then return an **ERROR** indication, *Invalid_k*, and *Invalid_k_inverse*.

5. Convert *returned_bits* to the (non-negative) integer c (see Appendix C.2.1).

6. If $(c > n–2)$, then go to step 4.

7. $k = c + 1$.

8. $(status, k^{-1})$ = **inverse**(k, n).

9. Return *status*, k, and k^{-1}.

Appendix C: Generation of Other Quantities

This appendix contains routines for supplementary processes required for the implementation of this Standard. Appendix C.1 is needed to produce the inverse of the per-message secret k (see Section 4.5, and Appendices B.2.1, B.2.2, B.5.1 and B.5.2) and the inverse of the signature portion s that is used during signature verification (see Section 4.7). The routines in Appendix C.2 are required to convert between bit strings and integers where required in implementing this Standard. Appendix C.3 contains probabilistic primality tests to be used during the generation of DSA domain parameters and RSA key pairs. Appendices C.4 and C.5 contain algorithms required during the Lucas probabilistic primality test of Appendix C.3.3 to check for a perfect square and to compute the Jacobi symbol. Appendix C.6 contains the Shawe-Taylor algorithm for the construction of primes. Appendix C.7 provides a process to perform trial division, as required by the random prime generation routine in Appendix C.6. The sieve procedure in Appendix C.8 is needed by the trial division routine in Appendix C.7. The trial division process in Appendix C.7 and the sieve procedure in Appendix C.8 have been extracted from ANS X9.80, *Prime Number Generation, Primality Testing, and Primality Certificates*. Appendix C.9 is required during the generation of RSA key pairs. Appendix C.10 provides a method for constructing provable primes for RSA (see Appendix B.3.2.2 and B.3.4).

C.1   Computation of the Inverse Value

This algorithm or an algorithm that produces an equivalent result **shall** be used to compute the multiplicative inverse $z^{-1} \bmod a$, where $0 < z < a$, $0 < z^{-1} < a$, and a is a prime number. In this Standard, z is either k or s, and a is either q or n.

Input:

    1. z The value to be inverted mod a (i.e., either k or s).

    2. a The domain parameter and (prime) modulus (i.e., either q or n).

Output:

    1. *status*   The status returned from this function, where the *status* is either **SUCCESS** or **ERROR**.

    2. z^{-1} The multiplicative inverse of $z \bmod a$, if it exists.

Process:

    1. Verify that a and z are positive integers such that $z < a$; if not, return an **ERROR** indication.

    2. Set $i = a$, $j = z$, $y_2 = 0$, and $y_1 = 1$.

    3. *quotient* $= \lfloor i/j \rfloor$.

4. $remainder = i - (j * quotient)$.

5. $y = y_2 - (y_1 * quotient)$.

6. Set $i = j$, $j = remainder$, $y_2 = y_1$, and $y_1 = y$.

7. If ($j > 0$), then go to step 3.

8. If ($i \neq 1$), then return an **ERROR** indication.

9. Return **SUCCESS** and $y_2 \bmod a$.

C.2   Conversion Between Bit Strings and Integers

C.2.1   Conversion of a Bit String to an Integer

An n-long sequence of bits $\{ x_1, \ldots, x_n \}$ is converted to an integer by the rule

$$\{ x_1, \ldots, x_n \} \rightarrow (x_1 * 2^{n-1}) + (x_2 * 2^{n-2}) + \ldots + (n_1 * 2) + x_n .$$

Note that the first bit of a sequence corresponds to the most significant bit of the corresponding integer, and the last bit corresponds to the least significant bit.

Input:

     1. $b_1, b_2, \ldots, b_n$ The bit string to be converted.

Output:

     1. C The requested integer representation of the bit string.

Process:

     1.   Let $(b_1, b_2, \ldots, b_n)$ be the bits of b from leftmost to rightmost.

     2. $C = \sum_{i=1}^{n} 2^{(n-i)} b_i$

     3.   Return C.

In this Standard, the binary length of an integer C is defined as the smallest integer n satisfying $C < 2^n$.

C.2.2   Conversion of an Integer to a Bit String

An integer x in the range $0 \leq x < 2^n$ may be converted to an n-long sequence of bits by using its binary expansion as shown below:

$$x = (x_1 * 2^{n-1}) + (x_2 * 2^{n-2}) + \ldots + (x_{n-1} * 2) + x_n \rightarrow \{x_1, \ldots, x_n\}$$

Note that the first bit of a sequence corresponds to the most significant bit of the corresponding integer, and the last bit corresponds to the least significant bit.

Input:

    1. C The non-negative integer to be converted.

Output:

    1. $b_1, b_2, \ldots, b_n$ The bit string representation of the integer C.

Process:

    1. Let $(b_1, b_2, \ldots, b_n)$ represent the bit string, where $b_i = 0$ or 1, and b_1 is the most significant bit, while b_n is the least significant bit.

    2. For any integer n that satisfies $C < 2^n$, the bits b_i **shall** satisfy:

$$C = \sum_{i=1}^{n} 2^{(n-i)} b_i$$

    3. Return $b_1, b_2, \ldots, b_n$.

In this Standard, the binary length of the integer C is defined as the smallest integer n that satisfies $C < 2^n$.

C.3 Probabilistic Primality Tests

A probabilistic primality test may be required during the generation and validation of prime numbers. An approved robust probabilistic primality test **shall** be selected and used.

There are several probabilistic algorithms available. The Miller-Rabin probabilistic primality tests described in Appendices C.3.1 and C.3.2 are versions of a procedure due to M.O. Rabin, based in part on ideas of Gary L. Miller; one of these versions **shall** be used as the Miller-Rabin test discussed below. For more information, see [4]. For these tests, let **RBG** be an approved random bit generator.

There are several Lucas probabilistic primality tests available; the version provided in [5] is specified in Appendix C.3.3.

This Standard allows two alternatives for testing primality: either using several iterations of only the Miller-Rabin test, or using the iterated Miller-Rabin test, followed by a single Lucas test. The value of *iterations* (as used in Appendices C.3.1 and C.3.2) depends on the algorithm being used, the security strength, the error probability used, the length (in bits) of the candidate prime and the type of tests to be performed. Tables C.1, C.2 and C.3 list the minimum number of *iterations* of the Miller-Rabin tests that **shall** be performed.

As stated in Appendix F, if the definition of the error probability that led to the values of the number of Miller-Rabin tests for p and q in Tables C.1, C.2 and C.3 is not conservative enough, the prescribed number of Miller-Rabin tests can be followed by a single Lucas test. Since there are no known non-prime values that pass the two test combination (i.e., the indicated number of rounds of the Miller-Rabin test with randomly selected bases, followed by one round of the Lucas test), the two test combination may provide additional assurance of primality over the use of only the Miller-Rabin test. For DSA, the two-test combination may provide better performance. However, the Lucas test is not required when testing the p_1, p_2, q_1 and q_2 values for primality when generating RSA primes. See Appendix F for further information.

Table C.1. Minimum number of Miller-Rabin iterations for DSA

Parameters	M-R Tests Only	M-R Tests when followed by One Lucas test
p: 1024 bits q: 160 bits Error probability = 2^{-80}	For p and q: 40	For p: 3 For q: 19
p: 2048 bits q: 224 bits Error probability = 2^{-112}	For p and q: 56	For p: 3 For q: 24
p: 2048 bits q: 256 bits Error probability = 2^{-112}	For p and q: 56	For p: 3 For q: 27
p: 3072 bits q: 256 bits Error probability = 2^{-128}	For p and q: 64	For p: 2 For q: 27

Table C.2. Minimum number of rounds of M-R testing when generating primes for use in RSA Digital Signatures

Parameters	M-R Tests Only
p_1, p_2, q_1 and $q_2 > 100$ bits p and q: 512 bits Error probability $= 2^{-80}$	For p_1, p_2, q_1 and q_2: 28 For p and q: 5
p_1, p_2, q_1 and $q_2 > 140$ bits p and q: 1024 bits Error probability $= 2^{-112}$	For p_1, p_2, q_1 and q_2: 38 For p and q: 5
p_1, p_2, q_1 and $q_2 > 170$ bits p and q: 1536 bits Error probability $= 2^{-128}$	For p_1, p_2, q_1 and, q_2: 41 For p and q: 4

Table C.3. Minimum number of rounds of M-R testing when generating primes for use in RSA Digital Signatures using an error probability of 2^{-100}

Parameters	M-R Tests Only
p_1, p_2, q_1 and $q_2 > 100$ bits p and q: 512	For p_1, p_2, q_1 and q_2: 38 For p and q: 7
p_1, p_2, q_1 and $q_2 > 140$ bits p and q: 1024 bits	For p_1, p_2, q_1 and q_2: 32 For p and q: 4
p_1, p_2, q_1 and $q_2 > 170$ bits p and q: 1536 bits	For p_1, p_2, q_1 and q_2: 27 For p and q: 3

C.3.1 Miller-Rabin Probabilistic Primality Test

Let **RBG** be an approved random bit generator.

Input:

1. w The odd integer to be tested for primality. This will be either p or q, or one of the auxiliary primes p_1, p_2, q_1 or q_2.

71

Output:

1. *status* The status returned from the validation procedure, where *status* is either **PROBABLY PRIME** or **COMPOSITE**.

Process:

1. Let a be the largest integer such that 2^a divides $w-1$.

2. $m = (w-1) / 2^a$.

3. $wlen = \textbf{len}\,(w)$.

4. For $i = 1$ to *iterations* do

    4.1   Obtain a string b of *wlen* bits from an RBG.

                  Comment: Ensure that $1 < b < w-1$.

    4.2   If $((b \leq 1)$ or $(b \geq w-1))$, then go to step 4.1.

    4.3 $z = b^m \bmod w$.

    4.4   If $((z = 1)$ or $(z = w - 1))$, then go to step 4.7.

    4.5   For $j = 1$ to $a - 1$ do.

        4.5.1 $z = z^2 \bmod w$.

        4.5.2   If $(z = w-1)$, then go to step 4.7.

        4.5.3   If $(z = 1)$, then go to step 4.6.

    4.6 Return **COMPOSITE.**

    4.7 Continue.   Comment: Increment i for the do-loop in step 4.

5. Return **PROBABLY PRIME.**

C.3.2 Enhanced Miller-Rabin Probabilistic Primality Test

This method provides additional information when an error is encountered that may be useful when generating or validating RSA moduli. Let **RBG** be an approved random bit generator.

Input:

1. w The odd integer to be tested for primality. This will be either p or q, or one of the auxiliary primes p_1, p_2, q_1 or q_2.

| 2. | *iterations* | The number of iterations of the test to be performed; the value **shall** be consistent with Table C.1, C.2 or C.3. |

Output:

| 1. | *status* | The status returned from the validation procedure, where *status* is either **PROBABLY PRIME**, **PROVABLY COMPOSITE WITH FACTOR** (returned with the factor), and **PROVABLY COMPOSITE AND NOT A POWER OF A PRIME**. |

Process:

1. Let a be the largest integer such that 2^a divides $w-1$.

2. $m = (w-1) / 2^a$.

3. $wlen = \mathbf{len}\,(w)$.

4. For $i = 1$ to *iterations* do

    4.1   Obtain a string b of $wlen$ bits from an RBG.

                      Comment: Ensure that $1 < b < w-1$.

    4.2   If $((b \le 1)$ or $(b \ge w-1))$, then go to step 4.1.

    4.3 $g = \mathbf{GCD}(b, w)$.

    4.4   If $(g > 1)$, then return **PROVABLY COMPOSITE WITH FACTOR** and the value of g.

    4.5 $z = b^m \bmod w$.

    4.6   If $((z = 1)$ or $(z = w - 1))$, then go to step 4.15.

    4.7   For $j = 1$ to $a - 1$ do.

         4.7.1 $x = z$.   Comment: $x \ne 1$ and $x \ne w-1$.

         4.7.2 $z = x^2 \bmod w$.

         4.7.3 If $(z = w-1)$, then go to step 4.15.

         4.7.4 If $(z = 1)$, then go to step 4.12.

    4.8 $x = z$.   Comment: $x = b^{(w-1)/2} \bmod w$ and $x \ne w-1$.

    4.9 $z = x^2 \bmod w$.

    4.10 If $(z = 1)$, then go to step 4.12.

    4.11 $x = z$.   Comment: $x = b^{(w-1)} \bmod w$ and $x \ne 1$.

4.12 $g = \mathbf{GCD}(x–1, w)$.

4.13 If $(g > 1)$, then return **PROVABLY COMPOSITE WITH FACTOR** and the value of g.

4.14 Return **PROVABLY COMPOSITE AND NOT A POWER OF A PRIME.**

4.15 Continue.   Comment: Increment i for the do-loop in step 4.

5. Return **PROBABLY PRIME.**

C.3.3 (General) Lucas Probabilistic Primality Test

The following process or its equivalent **shall** be used as the Lucas test.

Input:

C The candidate odd integer to be tested for primality.

Output:

status Where *status* is either **PROBABLY PRIME** or **COMPOSITE**.

Process:

1. Test whether C is a perfect square (see Appendix C.4). If so, return (**COMPOSITE**).

2. Find the first D in the sequence $\{5, –7, 9, –11, 13, –15, 17, \dots\}$ for which the Jacobi symbol $\left(\frac{D}{C}\right) = –1$. See Appendix C.5 for an approved method to compute the Jacobi Symbol. If $\left(\frac{D}{C}\right) = 0$ for any D in the sequence, return (**COMPOSITE**).

3. $K = C+1$.

4. Let $K_r\, K_{r-1} \dots K_0$ be the binary expansion of K, with $K_r = 1$.

5. Set $U_r = 1$ and $V_r = 1$.

6. For $i = r–1$ to 0, do

    6.1 $U_{temp} = U_{i+1}\, V_{i+1} \bmod C$.

    6.2 $V_{temp} = \dfrac{V_{i+1}{}^2 + DU_{i+1}{}^2}{2} \bmod C$.

    6.3   If $(K_i = 1)$, then   Comment: If $K_i = 1$, then do steps 6.3.1 and 6.3.2; otherwise, do steps 6.3.3 and 6.3.4.

          6.3.1 $U_i = \dfrac{U_{temp} + V_{temp}}{2} \bmod C$.

74

$$6.3.2 \quad V_i = \frac{V_{temp} + DU_{temp}}{2} \bmod C.$$

Else

$$6.3.3 \quad U_i = U_{temp}.$$

$$6.3.4 \quad V_i = V_{temp}.$$

7. If $(U_0 = 0)$, then return (**PROBABLY PRIME**). Otherwise, return (**COMPOSITE**).

Steps 6.2, 6.3.1 and 6.3.2 contain expressions of the form $A/2 \bmod C$, where A is an integer, and C is an odd integer. If $A/2$ is not an integer (i.e., A is odd), then $A/2 \bmod C$ may be calculated as $(A+C)/2 \bmod C$. Alternatively, $A/2 \bmod C = A \cdot (C+1)/2 \bmod C$, for any integer A, without regard to A being odd or even.

C.4 Checking for a Perfect Square

The following algorithm may be used to determine whether an n-bit positive integer C is a perfect square:

Input:

    C The integer to be checked.

Output:

    status Where *status* is either **PERFECT SQUARE** or **NOT A PERFECT SQUARE**.

Process:

1. Set n, such that $2^n > C \geq 2^{(n-1)}$.

2. $m = \lceil n/2 \rceil$.

3. $i = 0$.

4. Select X_0, such that $2^m > X_0 \geq 2^{(m-1)}$.

5. Repeat

      5.1 $i = i + 1$.

      5.2 $X_i = ((X_{i-1})^2 + C)/(2X_{i-1})$.

    Until $(X_i)^2 < 2^m + C$.

6. If $C = \lfloor X_i \rfloor^2$, then

    status = **PERFECT SQUARE**.

Else

    status = **NOT A PERFECT SQUARE**.

75

7. **Return** *status*.

Notes:

1. By starting with $X_0 > (1/2)\,\textbf{Sqrt}(C)$, $|X_0 - \textbf{Sqrt}(C)|$ is guaranteed to be less than X_0. This inequality is maintained in step 5; i.e., $|X_i - \textbf{Sqrt}(C)| < X_i$ for all i.

2. For $i \geq 1$, $0 \leq X_i - \textbf{Sqrt}(C) = (X_{i-1} - \textbf{Sqrt}(C))^2 / (2\,X_{i-1}) < X_0/2^i$.

   In particular, $0 \leq X_m - \textbf{Sqrt}(C) < 1$. If $\textbf{Sqrt}(C)$ were an integer, then it would be equal to the floor of X_m.

3. In general, the inequality $X_i - \textbf{Sqrt}(C) < 1$ will occur for values of i that are much less than m. To detect this, the fact that $2^{(m-1)} \leq \textbf{Sqrt}(C) < X_i$ for all $i \geq 1$ can be used,

$$X_i - \textbf{Sqrt}(C) = ((X_i)^2 - C)/(X_i + \textbf{Sqrt}(C))$$

$$\leq ((X_i)^2 - C)/(2\,\textbf{Sqrt}(C))$$

$$\leq ((X_i)^2 - C)/(2^m)$$

Thus, the condition $(X_i)^2 < 2^m + C$ implies that $X_i - \textbf{Sqrt}(C) < 1$.

C.5 Jacobi Symbol Algorithm

This routine computes the Jacobi symbol $\left(\dfrac{a}{n}\right)$.

Jacobi( ):

  Input:

    a Any integer. For this Standard, the initial value is in the sequence $\{5, -7, 9, -11, 13, -15, 17, \ldots\}$, as determined by Appendix C.3.3.

    n Any integer. For this Standard, the initial value is the candidate being tested, as determined by Appendix C.3.3.

  Output:

    result   The calculated Jacobi symbol.

  Process:

    1. $a = a \bmod n$.   Comment: a will be in the range $0 \leq a < n$.

    2. If $a = 1$, or $n = 1$, then return (1).

    3. If $a = 0$, then return (0).

    4. Define e and a_1 such that $a = 2^e\,a_1$, where a_1 is odd.

5. If e is even, then $s = 1$.

   Else if (($n \equiv 1$ (mod 8)) or ($n \equiv 7$ (mod 8))), then $s = 1$.

   Else if (($n \equiv 3$ (mod 8)) or ($n \equiv 5$ (mod 8))), then $s = -1$.

6. If (($n \equiv 3$ (mod 4)) and ($a_1 \equiv 3$ (mod 4))), then $s = -s$.

7. $n_1 = n \bmod a_1$.

8. Return (s * Jacobi (n_1, a_1)).   Comment: Call this routine recursively.

Example: Compute the Jacobi symbol for $a = 5$ and $n = 3439601197$:

1. n is not 1, and a is not 1, so proceed to Step 2.

2. a is not 0, so proceed to Step 3.

3. $5 = 2^0 * 5$, so $e = 0$, and $a_1 = 5$.

4. e is even, so $s = 1$.

5. a_1 is not congruent to 3 mod 4, so do not change s.

6. $n_1 = 2 = n \bmod 5$.

7. Compute and return (1 * Jacobi(2, 5)). This calls Jacobi recursively. Compute the Jacobi symbol for $a = 2$ and $n = 5$:

   7.1 n is not 1, and a is not 1, so proceed to Step 7.2.

   7.2 a is not 0, so proceed to Step 7.3.

   7.3 $2 = 2^1 * 1$, so $e = 1$, and $a_1 = 1$.

   7.4 e is odd, and $n \equiv 5$ (mod 8), so set $s = -1$.

   7.5 n is not 3 mod 4, and a_1 is not 3 mod 4, so proceed to step 7.6.

   7.6 $n_1 = 0 = n \bmod 1$.

   7.7 Return (-1 * Jacobi(0, 1) $= -1$). This calls Jacobi recursively. Compute the Jacobi symbol for $a = 0$ and $n = 1$:

      7.7.1 $n = 1$, so return 1.

Thus, Jacobi (0,1) = 1, so Jacobi (2,5) = $-1*(1) = -1$, and Jacobi (5, 3439601197) = $1* (-1) = -1$.

C.6   Shawe-Taylor Random_Prime Routine

This routine is recursive and may be used to construct a provable prime number using a hash function.

Let **Hash( )** be the selected hash function, and let *outlen* be the bit length of the hash function output block. The following process or its equivalent **shall** be used to generate a prime number for this constructive method.

ST_Random_Prime ( ):

    Input:

        1. *length*   The length of the prime to be generated.

        2. *input_seed*   The seed to be used for the generation of the requested prime.

    Output:

        1. *status*   The status returned from the generation routine, where *status* is either **SUCCESS** or **FAILURE**. If **FAILURE** is returned, then zeros are returned as the other output values.

        2. *prime*   The requested prime.

        3 *prime_seed*   A seed determined during generation.

        4. *prime_gen_counter*   (Optional) A counter determined during the generation of the prime.

    Process:

        1. If (*length* < 2), then return (**FAILURE**, 0, 0 {, 0}).

        2. If (*length* $\geq$ 33), then go to step 14.

        3. *prime_seed* = *input_seed*.

        4. *prime_gen_counter* = 0.

                                               Comment: Generate a pseudorandom integer *c* of *length* bits.

        5. $c = \textbf{Hash}(prime\_seed) \oplus \textbf{Hash}(prime\_seed + 1)$.

        6. $c = 2^{length-1} + (c \bmod 2^{length-1})$.

        7. $c = (2 * \lfloor c/2 \rfloor) + 1$.

                                               Comment: Set *prime* to the least odd integer greater than or equal to *c*.

        8. *prime_gen_counter* = *prime_gen_counter* + 1.

        9. *prime_seed* = *prime_seed* + 2.

10. Perform a deterministic primality test on c. For example, since c is small, its primality can be tested by trial division. See Appendix C.7.

11. If (c is a prime number), then

    11.1   *prime* = c.

    11.2   Return (**SUCCESS**, *prime*, *prime_seed* {, *prime_gen_counter*}).

12. If (*prime_gen_counter* > (4 * *length*)), then return (**FAILURE**, 0, 0 {, 0}).

13. Go to step 5.

14. (*status*, c_0, *prime_seed*, *prime_gen_counter*) = (**ST_Random_Prime** (($\lceil length / 2 \rceil$ + 1), *input_seed*).

15. If **FAILURE** is returned, return (**FAILURE**, 0, 0 {, 0}).

16. *iterations* = $\lceil length / outlen \rceil - 1$.

17. *old_counter* = *prime_gen_counter*.

Comment: Generate a pseudorandom integer
x in the interval $[2^{length-1}, 2^{length}]$.

18. $x = 0$.

19. For $i = 0$ to *iterations* do

    $x = x + (\textbf{Hash}(prime\_seed + i) * 2^{i \times outlen})$.

20. *prime_seed* = *prime_seed* + *iterations* + 1.

21. $x = 2^{length-1} + (x \bmod 2^{length-1})$.

Comment: Generate a candidate prime c in
the interval $[2^{length-1}, 2^{length}]$.

22. $t = \lceil x / (2c_0) \rceil$.

23. If ($2tc_0 + 1 > 2^{length}$), then $t = \lceil 2^{length-1} / (2c_0) \rceil$.

24. $c = 2tc_0 + 1$.

25. *prime_gen_counter* = *prime_gen_counter* + 1.

Comment: Test the candidate prime c for
primality; first pick an integer a between 2
and $c - 2$.

26. $a = 0$.

27. For $i = 0$ to *iterations* do

    $a = a + (\textbf{Hash}(prime\_seed + i) * 2^{i * outlen})$.

28. *prime_seed* = *prime_seed* + *iterations* + 1.

29. $a = 2 + (a \bmod (c - 3))$.

30. $z = a^{2t} \bmod c$.

31. If $((1 = \textbf{GCD}(z - 1, c))$ and $(1 = z^{c_0} \bmod c))$, then

    31.1   *prime* = *c*.

    31.2   Return (**SUCCESS**, *prime*, *prime_seed* {, *prime_gen_counter*}).

32. If $(prime\_gen\_counter \geq ((4 * length) + old\_counter))$, then return (**FAILURE**, 0, 0 {, 0}).

33. $t = t + 1$.

34. Go to step 23.

C.7   Trial Division

An integer is proven to be prime by showing that it has no prime factors less than or equal to its square root. This procedure is not recommended for testing any integers longer than 10 digits.

To prove that *c* is prime:

1. Prepare a table of primes less than $\sqrt{c}$. This can be done by applying the sieve procedure in Appendix C.8.

2. Divide *c* by every prime in the table. If *c* is divisible by one of the primes, then declare that *c* is composite and exit. If convenient, *c* may be divided by composite numbers. For example, rather than preparing a table of primes, it might be more convenient to divide by all integers except those divisible by 3 or 5.

3. Otherwise, declare that *c* is prime and exit.

C.8   Sieve Procedure

A *sieve procedure* is described as follows: Given a sequence of integers $Y_0, Y_0 + 1, \ldots, Y_0 + J$, a sieve will identify the integers in the sequence that are divisible by primes up to some selected limit.

Note that the definitions of the mathematical symbols in this process (e.g., *h*, *L*, *M*, *p*) are internal to this process only, and should not be confused with their use elsewhere in this Standard.

Start by selecting a *factor base* of all the primes p_j, from 2 up to some selected limit *L*. The value of *L* is arbitrary and may be determined by computer limitations. A good, typical value of *L* would be anywhere from 10^3 to 10^5.

1. Compute $S_j = Y_0 \bmod p_j$ for all p_j in the factor base.

2. Initialize an array of length $J + 1$ to zero.

3. Starting at $Y_0 - S_j + p_j$, let every $p_j{}^{th}$ element of the array be set to 1. Do this for the entire length of the array and for every j.

4. When finished, every location in the array that has the value 1 is divisible by some small prime, and is therefore a composite.

The array can be either a bit array for compactness when memory is small, or a byte array for speed when memory is readily available. There is no need to sieve the entire sieve interval at once. The array can be partitioned into suitably small pieces, sieving each piece before going on to the next piece. When finished, every location with the value 0 is a candidate for prime testing.

The amount of work for this procedure is approximately $M \log \log L$, where M is the length of the sieve interval; this is a very efficient procedure for removing composite candidates for primality testing. If $L = 10^5$, the sieve will remove about 96% of all composites.

In some cases, rather than having a set of consecutive integers to sieve, the set of integers to be tested consists of integers lying in an arithmetic progression Y_0, $Y_0 + h$, $Y_0 + 2h$, ..., $Y_0 + Jh$, where h is large and not divisible by any primes in the factor base.

1. Select a factor base and initialize an array of length $J + 1$ to 0.

2. Compute $S_j = Y_0 \bmod p_j$ for all p_j in the factor base.

3. Compute $T_j = h \bmod p_j$ and $r = -S_j T_j{}^{-1} \bmod p_j$.

4. Starting at $Y_0 + r$, let every $p_j{}^{th}$ element of the array be set to 1. Do this for the entire length of the array and for every j. Note that the position $Y_0 + r$ in the array actually denotes the number $Y_0 + rh$.

5. When finished, every location in the array that has the value 1 is divisible by some small prime and is therefore composite.

Note: The prime "2" takes the longest amount of time ($M/2$) to sieve, since it touches the most locations in the sieve array. An easy optimization is to combine the initialization of the sieve array with the sieving of the prime "2". It is also possible to sieve the prime "3" during initialization. These optimizations can save about 1/3 of the total sieve time.

C.9 Compute a Probable Prime Factor Based on Auxiliary Primes

This routine constructs a probable prime (a candidate for p or q) using two auxiliary prime numbers and the Chinese Remainder Theorem (CRT).

Input:

r_1 and r_2 Two odd prime numbers satisfying
$\log_2(r_1 r_2) \le (nlen/2) - \log_2(nlen/2) - 6$.

nlen	The desired length of *n*, the RSA modulus.
e	The public verification exponent.
security_strength	The minimum security strength required for random number generation.

Output:

status	The status returned from the generation procedure, where *status* is either **SUCCESS** or **FAILURE**. If **FAILURE** is returned, then zeros are returned as the other output values.
private_prime_factor	The prime factor of *n*.
X	The random number used during the generation of the *private_prime_factor*.

Process:

1. If $(\textbf{GCD}(2r_1, r_2) \neq 1)$, then return (**FAILURE**, 0, 0).

2. $R = ((r_2^{-1} \bmod 2r_1) * r_2) - (((2r_1)^{-1} \bmod r_2) * 2r_1)$.

   > Comment: Apply the CRT, so that $R \equiv 1 \pmod{2r_1}$ and $R \equiv -1 \pmod{r_2}$.

3. Generate a random number *X* using an approved random number generator that supports the *security_ strength*, such that $\left(\sqrt{2}\right)\left(2^{nlen/2-1}\right) \le X \le \left(2^{nlen/2} - 1\right)$.

4. $Y = X + ((R - X) \bmod 2r_1r_2)$.

   > Comment: *Y* is the first odd integer $\ge X$, such that r_1 is a prime factor of *Y*–1, and r_2 is a prime factor of *Y*+1.

   > Comment: Determine the requested prime number by constructing candidates from a sequence and performing primality tests.

5. $i = 0$.

6. If $(Y \ge 2^{nlen/2})$, then go to step 3.

7. If $(\textbf{GCD}(Y{-}1, e) = 1)$, then

   7.1 Check the primality of *Y* as specified in Appendix C.3. If **PROBABLY PRIME** is ***not*** returned, go to step 8.

   7.2 *private_prime_factor* = *Y*.

   7.3 Return (**SUCCESS**, *private_prime_factor*, *X*).

8. $i = i + 1$.

9. If ($i \geq 5(nlen/2)$), then return (**FAILURE**, 0, 0).

10. $Y = Y + (2r_1r_2)$.

11. Go to step 6.

C.10 Construct a Provable Prime (possibly with Conditions), Based on Contemporaneously Constructed Auxiliary Provable Primes

The following process (or its equivalent) **shall** be used to generate an L-bit provable prime p (a candidate for one of the prime factors of an RSA modulus). Note that the use of p in this specification is used generically; both RSA prime factors p and q may be generated using this method.

If a so-called "strong prime" is required, this process can generate primes p_1 and p_2 (of specified bit-lengths N_1 and N_2) that divide $p-1$ and $p+1$, respectively. The resulting prime p will satisfy the conditions traditionally required of a strong prime, provided that the requested bit-lengths for p_1 and p_2 have appropriate sizes.

Regardless of the bit-lengths selected for p_1 and p_2, the quantity $p-1$ will have a prime divisor p_0 whose bit-length is slightly more than half that of p. In addition, the quantity $p_0 -1$ will have a prime divisor whose bit-length is slightly more than half that of p_0.

This algorithm requires that $N_1 + N_2 \leq L - \lceil L/2 \rceil - 4$. Values for N_1 and N_2 **should** be chosen such that $N_1 + N_2 \leq (L/2) - \log_2(L) - 7$, to ensure that the algorithm can generate as many as $5L$ distinct candidates for p.

Let **Hash** be the selected hash function to be used, and let *outlen* be the bit length of the hash function output block.

Provable_Prime_Construction():

> **Input:**

1.	L	A positive integer equal to the requested bit-length for p. Note that acceptable values for $L = nlen/2$ are computed as specified in Appendix B.3.1, criteria 2(b) and (c), with *nlen* assuming a value specified in Table B.1.
2.	N_1	A positive integer equal to the requested bit-length for p_1. If $N_1 \geq 2$, then p_1 is an odd prime of N_1 bits; otherwise, $p_1 = 1$. Acceptable values for $N_1 \geq 2$ are provided in Table B.1
3.	N_2	A positive integer equal to the requested bit-length for p_2. If $N_2 \geq 2$, then p_2 is an odd prime of N_2 bits; otherwise, $p_2 = 1$. Acceptable values for $N_2 \geq 2$ are provided in Table B.1
4.	*firstseed*	A bit string equal to the first seed to be used.

5. *e*   The public verification exponent.

Output:

1. *status*   The status returned from the generation procedure, where *status* is either **SUCCESS** or **FAILURE**. If **FAILURE** is returned, then zeros are returned as the other output values.

2. p, p_1, p_2 The required prime p, along with p_1 and p_2 having the property that p_1 divides $p-1$ and p_2 divides $p+1$.

3. *pseed*   A seed determined during generation.

Process:

1. If L, N_1, and N_2 are not acceptable, then, return (**FAILURE**, 0, 0, 0, 0).

    > Comment: Generate p_1 and p_2, as well as the prime p_0.

2. If $N_1 = 1$, then

    2.1 $p_1 = 1$.

    2.2 *p₂seed = firstseed.*

3. If $N_1 \geq 2$, then

    3.1 Using N_1 as the length and *firstseed* as the *input_seed*, use the random prime generation routine in Appendix C.6 to obtain p_1 and *p₂seed*.

    3.2 If **FAILURE** is returned, then return (**FAILURE**, 0, 0, 0, 0).

4. If $N_2 = 1$, then

    4.1 $p_2 = 1$.

    4.2 *p₀seed = p₂seed.*

5. If $N_2 \geq 2$, then

    5.1 Using N_2 as the length and *p₂seed* as the *input_seed*, use the random prime generation routine in Appendix C.6 to obtain p_2 and *p₀seed*.

    5.2 If **FAILURE** is returned, then return (**FAILURE**, 0, 0, 0, 0).

6. Using $\lceil L/2 \rceil + 1$ as the length and *p₀seed* as the *input_seed*, use the random prime generation routine in Appendix C.6 to obtain p_0 and *pseed*. If **FAILURE** is returned, then return (**FAILURE**, 0, 0, 0, 0).

    > Comment: Generate a (strong) prime p in the interval $[(\sqrt{2})(2^{L-1}), 2^L - 1]$.

84

7. $iterations = \lceil L / outlen \rceil - 1$.

8. $pgen\_counter = 0$.

> Comment: Generate pseudo-random x in the interval $[(\sqrt{2})(2^{L-1})-1, 2^L -1]$.

9. $x = 0$.

10. For $i = 0$ to $iterations$ do

$$x = x + (\textbf{Hash}(pseed + i)) * 2^{i * outlen}.$$

11. $pseed = pseed + iterations + 1$.

12. $x = \lfloor (\sqrt{2})(2^{L-1}) \rfloor + (x \bmod (2^L - \lfloor (\sqrt{2})(2^{L-1}) \rfloor))$.

> Comment: Generate a candidate for the prime p.

13. If $(\textbf{GCD}(p_0 p_1, p_2) \neq 1)$, then return $(\textbf{FAILURE}, 0, 0, 0, 0)$.

14. Compute y in the interval $[1, p_2]$ such that $0 = (y p_0 p_1 - 1) \bmod p_2$.

15. $t = \lceil ((2 y p_0 p_1) + x)/(2 p_0 p_1 p_2) \rceil$.

16. If $((2(t p_2 - y) p_0 p_1 + 1) > 2^L)$, then

$$t = \lceil ((2 y p_0 p_1) + \lfloor (\sqrt{2})(2^{L-1}) \rfloor) / (2 p_0 p_1 p_2) \rceil.$$

> Comment: p satisfies
> $0 = (p-1) \bmod (2p_0 p_1)$ and
> $0 = (p+1) \bmod p_2$.

17. $p = 2(t p_2 - y) p_0 p_1 + 1$.

18. $pgen\_counter = pgen\_counter + 1$.

19. If $(\textbf{GCD}(p-1, e) = 1)$, then

> Comment: Choose an integer a in the interval $[2, p-2]$.

19.1 $a = 0$

19.2   For $i = 0$ to $iterations$ do

$$a = a + (\textbf{Hash}(pseed + i)) * 2^{i * outlen}.$$

19.3 $pseed = pseed + iterations + 1$.

19.4 $a = 2 + (a \bmod (p-3))$.

> Comment: Test p for primality:

19.5 $z = a^{2(t p_2 - y) p_1} \bmod p$.

85

19.6   If $((1 = \mathbf{GCD}(z-1, p))$ and $(1 = (z^{p_0} \bmod p))$, then return (**SUCCESS**, p, p_1, p_2, *pseed*).

20. If (*pgen_counter* $\geq 5L$), then return (**FAILURE**, 0, 0, 0, 0).

21. $t = t + 1$.

22. Go to step 16.

Appendix D: Recommended Elliptic Curves for Federal Government Use

This collection of elliptic curves is recommended for Federal government use and contains choices for the private key length and underlying fields. These curves were generated using SHA-1 and the method given in the ANS X9.62 and IEEE Standard 1363-2000 standards. This appendix describes the process that was used. Note that these curves are the same as those included in the previous version of this Standard.

D.1   NIST Recommended Elliptic Curves

D.1.1 Choices

D.1.1.1   Choice of Key Lengths

The principal parameters for elliptic curve cryptography are the elliptic curve E and a designated point G on E called the *base point*. The base point has order n, which is a large prime. The number of points on the curve is hn for some integer h (the *cofactor*), which is not divisible by n. For efficiency reasons, it is desirable to have the cofactor be as small as possible.

All of the curves given below have cofactors 1, 2, or 4. As a result, the private and public keys for a curve are approximately the same length.

D.1.1.2 Choice of Underlying Fields

For each key length, two kinds of fields are provided.

- A *prime field* is the field $GF(p)$, which contains a prime number p of elements. The elements of this field are the integers modulo p, and the field arithmetic is implemented in terms of the arithmetic of integers modulo p.

- A *binary field* is the field $GF(2^m)$, which contains 2^m elements for some m (called the *degree* of the field). The elements of this field are the bit strings of length m, and the field arithmetic is implemented in terms of operations on the bits.

The security strengths for five ranges of the bit length of n is provided in SP 800-57. For the field $GF(p)$, the security strength is dependent on the length of the binary expansion of p. For the field $GF(2^m)$, the security strength is dependent on the value of m. Table E-1 provides the bit lengths of the various underlying fields of the curves provided in this appendix. Column 1 lists the ranges for the bit length of n (also see Table 1 in Section 6.1.1). Column 2 identifies the value of p used for the curves over prime fields, where **len**(p) is the length of the binary expansion of the integer p. Column 3 provides the value of m for the curves over binary fields.

Table D-1: Bit Lengths of the Underlying Fields of the Recommended Curves

Bit Length of n	Prime Field	Binary Field
161 – 223	$\mathbf{len}(p) = 192$	$m = 163$
224 – 255	$\mathbf{len}(p) = 224$	$m = 233$
256 – 383	$\mathbf{len}(p) = 256$	$m = 283$
384 – 511	$\mathbf{len}(p) = 384$	$m = 409$
≥ 512	$\mathbf{len}(p) = 521$	$m = 571$

D.1.1.3 Choice of Basis for Binary Fields

To describe the arithmetic of a binary field, it is first necessary to specify how a bit string is to be interpreted. This is referred to as choosing a *basis* for the field. There are two common types of bases: a *polynomial basis* and a *normal basis*.

- A polynomial basis is specified by an irreducible polynomial modulo 2, called the *field polynomial*. The bit string $(a_{m-1} \ldots a_2\ a_1\ a_0)$ is taken to represent the polynomial

$$a_{m-1}\, t^{m-1} + \ldots + a_2\, t^2 + a_1\, t + a_0$$

  over $GF(2)$. The field arithmetic is implemented as polynomial arithmetic modulo $p(t)$, where $p(t)$ is the field polynomial.

- A normal basis is specified by an element θ of a particular kind. The bit string $(a_0\ a_1\ a_2 \ldots a_{m-1})$ is taken to represent the element

$$a_0\, \theta + a_1\, \theta^2 + a_2\, \theta^{2^2} + \ldots + a_{m-1}\, \theta^{2^{m-1}}.$$

  Normal basis field arithmetic is not easy to describe or efficient to implement in general, except for a special class called *Type T low-complexity* normal bases. For a given field degree m, the choice of T specifies the basis and the field arithmetic (see Appendix D.3).

There are many polynomial bases and normal bases from which to choose. The following procedures are commonly used to select a basis representation.

- *Polynomial Basis*: If an irreducible *trinomial* $t^m + t^k + 1$ exists over $GF(2)$, then the field polynomial $p(t)$ is chosen to be the irreducible trinomial with the lowest-degree middle term t^k. If no irreducible trinomial exists, then a *pentanomial* $t^m + t^a + t^b + t^c + 1$ is selected. The particular pentanomial chosen has the following properties: the second term t^a has the lowest degree m; the third term t^b has the lowest degree among all irreducible pentanomials of degree m and second term t^a; and the fourth term t^c has the lowest degree among all irreducible pentanomials of degree m, second term t^a, and third term t^b.

- *Normal Basis*: Choose the Type T low-complexity normal basis with the smallest *T*.

For each binary field, the parameters are given for the above basis representations.

D.1.1.4 Choice of Curves

Two kinds of curves are given:

- *Pseudo-random* curves are those whose coefficients are generated from the output of a seeded cryptographic hash function. If the domain parameter seed value is given along with the coefficients, it can be easily verified that the coefficients were generated by that method.

- *Special curves* are those whose coefficients and underlying field have been selected to optimize the efficiency of the elliptic curve operations.

For each curve size range, the following curves are given:

→ A pseudo-random curve over $GF(p)$.

→ A pseudo-random curve over $GF(2^m)$.

→ A special curve over $GF(2^m)$ called a *Koblitz curve* or *anomalous binary curve*.

The pseudo-random curves were generated as specified in ANS X9.62 using SHA-1.

D.1.1.5 Choice of Base Points

Any point of order *n* can serve as the base point. Each curve is supplied with a sample base point $G = (G_x, G_y)$. Users may want to generate their own base points to ensure cryptographic separation of networks. See ANS X9.62 or IEEE Standard 1363-2000.

D.1.2 Curves over Prime Fields

For each prime *p*, a pseudo-random curve

$$E : y^2 \equiv x^3 - 3x + b \pmod{p}$$

of prime order *n* is listed[4]. (Thus, for these curves, the cofactor is always $h = 1$.) The following parameters are given:

- The prime modulus *p*

- The order *n*

- The 160-bit input seed *SEED* to the SHA-1 based algorithm (i.e., the domain parameter seed)

- The output *c* of the SHA-1 based algorithm

---

[4] The selection $a \equiv -3$ for the coefficient of *x* was made for reasons of efficiency; see IEEE Std 1363-2000.

- The coefficient b (satisfying $b^2 c \equiv -27 \pmod{p}$)
- The base point x coordinate G_x
- The base point y coordinate G_y

The integers p and n are given in decimal form; bit strings and field elements are given in hexadecimal.

D.1.2.1 Curve P-192

$p =$ 6277101735386680763835789423207666416083908700390324961279

$n =$ 6277101735386680763835789423176059013767194773182842284081

$SEED =$ 3045ae6f c8422f64 ed579528 d38120ea e12196d5

$c =$ 3099d2bb bfcb2538 542dcd5f b078b6ef 5f3d6fe2 c745de65

$b =$ 64210519 e59c80e7 0fa7e9ab 72243049 feb8deec c146b9b1

$G_x =$ 188da80e b03090f6 7cbf20eb 43a18800 f4ff0afd 82ff1012

$G_y =$ 07192b95 ffc8da78 631011ed 6b24cdd5 73f977a1 1e794811

D.1.2.2 Curve P-224

$p =$ 2695994666715063979466701508701963067355791626002630814351
0066298881

$n =$ 2695994666715063979466701508701962594045780771442439172168
2722368061

$SEED =$ bd713447 99d5c7fc dc45b59f a3b9ab8f 6a948bc5

$c =$ 5b056c7e 11dd68f4 0469ee7f 3c7a7d74 f7d12111 6506d031
218291fb

$b =$ b4050a85 0c04b3ab f5413256 5044b0b7 d7bfd8ba 270b3943
2355ffb4

$G_x =$ b70e0cbd 6bb4bf7f 321390b9 4a03c1d3 56c21122 343280d6
115c1d21

$G_y =$ bd376388 b5f723fb 4c22dfe6 cd4375a0 5a074764 44d58199
85007e34

D.1.2.3 Curve P-256

$p =$ 115792089210356248762697446949407573530086143415290314195533631308867097853951

$n =$ 115792089210356248762697446949407573529996955224135760342422259061068512044369

$SEED =$ c49d3608 86e70493 6a6678e1 139d26b7 819f7e90

$c =$ 7efba166 2985be94 03cb055c 75d4f7e0 ce8d84a9 c5114abc af317768 0104fa0d

$b =$ 5ac635d8 aa3a93e7 b3ebbd55 769886bc 651d06b0 cc53b0f6 3bce3c3e 27d2604b

$G_x =$ 6b17d1f2 e12c4247 f8bce6e5 63a440f2 77037d81 2deb33a0 f4a13945 d898c296

$G_y =$ 4fe342e2 fe1a7f9b 8ee7eb4a 7c0f9e16 2bce3357 6b315ece cbb64068 37bf51f5

D.1.2.4 Curve P-384

$p =$ 39402006196394479212279040100143613805079739270465446667948293404245721771496870329047266088258938001861606973112319

$n =$ 39402006196394479212279040100143613805079739270465446667946905279627659399113263569398956308152294913554433653942643

$SEED =$ a335926a a319a27a 1d00896a 6773a482 7acdac73

$c =$ 79d1e655 f868f02f ff48dcde e14151dd b80643c1 406d0ca1 0dfe6fc5 2009540a 495e8042 ea5f744f 6e184667 cc722483

$b =$ b3312fa7 e23ee7e4 988e056b e3f82d19 181d9c6e fe814112 0314088f 5013875a c656398d 8a2ed19d 2a85c8ed d3ec2aef

$G_x =$ aa87ca22 be8b0537 8eb1c71e f320ad74 6e1d3b62 8ba79b98 59f741e0 82542a38 5502f25d bf55296c 3a545e38 72760ab7

$G_y =$ 3617de4a 96262c6f 5d9e98bf 9292dc29 f8f41dbd 289a147c e9da3113 b5f0b8c0 0a60b1ce 1d7e819d 7a431d7c 90ea0e5f

91

D.1.2.5 Curve P-521

p = 686479766013060971498190079908139321726943530014330540939 44634591855431833976560521225596406614545549772963113914 808580371219879997166438125740282911150571511

n = 686479766013060971498190079908139321726943530014330540939 44634591855431833976553942450577463332171975329639963713 33211138647686124403803403728088927070005449

$SEED$ = d09e8800 291cb853 96cc6717 393284aa a0da64ba

c = 0b4 8bfa5f42 0a349495 39d2bdfc 264eeeeb 077688e4 4fbf0ad8 f6d0edb3 7bd6b533 28100051 8e19f1b9 ffbe0fe9 ed8a3c22 00b8f875 e523868c 70c1e5bf 55bad637

b = 051 953eb961 8e1c9a1f 929a21a0 b68540ee a2da725b 99b315f3 b8b48991 8ef109e1 56193951 ec7e937b 1652c0bd 3bb1bf07 3573df88 3d2c34f1 ef451fd4 6b503f00

G_x = c6 858e06b7 0404e9cd 9e3ecb66 2395b442 9c648139 053fb521 f828af60 6b4d3dba a14b5e77 efe75928 fe1dc127 a2ffa8de 3348b3c1 856a429b f97e7e31 c2e5bd66

G_y = 118 39296a78 9a3bc004 5c8a5fb4 2c7d1bd9 98f54449 579b4468 17afbd17 273e662c 97ee7299 5ef42640 c550b901 3fad0761 353c7086 a272c240 88be9476 9fd16650

D.1.3 Curves over Binary Fields

For each field degree m, a pseudo-random curve is given, along with a Koblitz curve. The pseudo-random curve has the form

$$E: y^2 + xy = x^3 + x^2 + b,$$

and the Koblitz curve has the form

$$E_a: y^2 + xy = x^3 + ax^2 + 1,$$

where $a = 0$ or 1.

For each pseudorandom curve, the cofactor is $h = 2$. The cofactor of each Koblitz curve is $h = 2$ if $a = 1$, and $h = 4$ if $a = 0$.

The coefficients of the pseudo-random curves, and the coordinates of the base points of both kinds of curves, are given in terms of both the polynomial and normal basis representations discussed in Appendix D.1.1.3.

For each m, the following parameters are given:

Field Representation:

- The normal basis type T
- The field polynomial (a trinomial or pentanomial)

Koblitz Curve:

- The coefficient a
- The base point order n
- The base point x coordinate G_x
- The base point y coordinate G_y

Pseudo-random curve:

- The base point order n

Pseudo-random curve (Polynomial Basis representation):

- The coefficient b
- The base point x coordinate G_x
- The base point y coordinate G_y

Pseudo-random curve (Normal Basis representation):

- The 160-bit input seed *SEED* to the SHA-1 based algorithm (i.e., the domain parameter seed)
- The coefficient b (i.e., the output of the SHA-1 based algorithm)
- The base point x coordinate G_x
- The base point y coordinate G_y

Integers (such as T, m, and n) are given in decimal form; bit strings and field elements are given in hexadecimal.

D.1.3.1 Degree 163 Binary Field

$T = \quad 4$

$p(t) = \ t^{163} + t^7 + t^6 + t^3 + 1$

D.1.3.1.1 Curve K-163

$a =$ 1

$n =$ 5846006549323611672814741753598448348329118574063

Polynomial Basis:

$G_x =$ 2 fe13c053 7bbc11ac aa07d793 de4e6d5e 5c94eee8

$G_y =$ 2 89070fb0 5d38ff58 321f2e80 0536d538 ccdaa3d9

Normal Basis:

$G_x =$ 0 5679b353 caa46825 fea2d371 3ba450da 0c2a4541

$G_y =$ 2 35b7c671 00506899 06bac3d9 dec76a83 5591edb2

D.1.3.1.2 Curve B-163

$n =$ 5846006549323611672814742442876390689256843201587

Polynomial Basis:

$b =$ 2 0a601907 b8c953ca 1481eb10 512f7874 4a3205fd

$G_x =$ 3 f0eba162 86a2d57e a0991168 d4994637 e8343e36

$G_y =$ 0 d51fbc6c 71a0094f a2cdd545 b11c5c0c 797324f1

Normal Basis:

$SEED =$ 85e25bfe 5c86226c db12016f 7553f9d0 e693a268

$b =$ 6 645f3cac f1638e13 9c6cd13e f61734fb c9e3d9fb

$G_x =$ 0 311103c1 7167564a ce77ccb0 9c681f88 6ba54ee8

$G_y =$ 3 33ac13c6 447f2e67 613bf700 9daf98c8 7bb50c7f

D.1.3.2 Degree 233 Binary Field

$T =$ 2

$p(t) =$ $t^{233} + t^{74} + 1$

D.1.3.2.1 Curve K-233

$a =$ 0

$n =$ 34508731733952818937173779311385127605709409888622521\
63280870247413433

Polynomial Basis:

$G_x =$ 172 32ba853a 7e731af1 29f22ff4 149563a4 19c26bf5
0a4c9d6e efad6126

$G_y =$ 1db 537dece8 19b7f70f 555a67c4 27a8cd9b f18aeb9b
56e0c110 56fae6a3

Normal Basis:

$G_x =$ 0fd e76d9dcd 26e643ac 26f1aa90 1aa12978 4b71fc07
22b2d056 14d650b3

$G_y =$ 064 3e317633 155c9e04 47ba8020 a3c43177 450ee036
d6335014 34cac978

D.1.3.2.2 Curve B-233

$n =$ 69017463467905637874347558622770255583981273734501355\
5379383634485463

Polynomial Basis:

$b =$ 066 647ede6c 332c7f8c 0923bb58 213b333b 20e9ce42
81fe115f 7d8f90ad

$G_x =$ 0fa c9dfcbac 8313bb21 39f1bb75 5fef65bc 391f8b36
f8f8eb73 71fd558b

$G_y =$ 100 6a08a419 03350678 e58528be bf8a0bef f867a7ca
36716f7e 01f81052

Normal Basis:

$SEED =$ 74d59ff0 7f6b413d 0ea14b34 4b20a2db 049b50c3

$b =$ 1a0 03e0962d 4f9a8e40 7c904a95 38163adb 82521260 0c7752ad 52233279

$G_x =$ 18b 863524b3 cdfefb94 f2784e0b 116faac5 4404bc91 62a363ba b84a14c5

$G_y =$ 049 25df77bd 8b8ff1a5 ff519417 822bfedf 2bbd7526 44292c98 c7af6e02

D.1.3.3   Degree 283 Binary Field

$T =$ 6

$p(t) =$ $t^{283} + t^{12} + t^7 + t^5 + 1$

D.1.3.3.1   Curve K-283

$a =$ 0

$n =$ 3885337784451458141838923813647037813284811733793061324 295874997529815829704422603873

Polynomial Basis:

$G_x =$ 503213f 78ca4488 3f1a3b81 62f188e5 53cd265f 23c1567a 16876913 b0c2ac24 58492836

$G_y =$ 1ccda38 0f1c9e31 8d90f95d 07e5426f e87e45c0 e8184698 e4596236 4e341161 77dd2259

Normal Basis:

$G_x =$ 3ab9593 f8db09fc 188f1d7c 4ac9fcc3 e57fcd3b db15024b 212c7022 9de5fcd9 2eb0ea60

$G_y =$ 2118c47 55e7345c d8f603ef 93b98b10 6fe8854f feb9a3b3 04634cc8 3a0e759f 0c2686b1

D.1.3.3.2 Curve B-283

$n =$ 7770675568902916283677847627294075626569625924376904889

         10919652677004427778737869287 1

Polynomial Basis:

$b =$ 27b680a c8b8596d a5a4af8a 19a0303f ca97fd76 45309fa2

         a581485a f6263e31 3b79a2f5

$G_x =$ 5f93925 8db7dd90 e1934f8c 70b0dfec 2eed25b8 557eac9c

         80e2e198 f8cdbecd 86b12053

$G_y =$ 3676854 fe24141c b98fe6d4 b20d02b4 516ff702 350eddb0

         826779c8 13f0df45 be8112f4

Normal Basis:

$SEED =$ 77e2b073 70eb0f83 2a6dd5b6 2dfc88cd 06bb84be

$b =$ 157261b 894739fb 5a13503f 55f0b3f1 0c560116 66331022

         01138cc1 80c0206b dafbc951

$G_x =$ 749468e 464ee468 634b21f7 f61cb700 701817e6 bc36a236

         4cb8906e 940948ea a463c35d

$G_y =$ 62968bd 3b489ac5 c9b859da 68475c31 5bafcdc4 ccd0dc90

         5b70f624 46f49c05 2f49c08c

D.1.3.4 Degree 409 Binary Field

$T =$ 4

$p(t) =$ $t^{409} + t^{87} + 1$

D.1.3.4.1 Curve K-409

$a =$ 0

$n =$ 330527984395124299475957654016385519914202341482140 60964\

         23243950228807112892491910506732584577774580140963665906 1

         7731358671

Polynomial Basis:

G_x =   060f05f 658f49c1 ad3ab189 0f718421 0efd0987 e307c84c
          27accfb8 f9f67cc2 c460189e b5aaaa62 ee222eb1 b35540cf
          e9023746

G_y = 1e36905 0b7c4e42 acba1dac bf04299c 3460782f 918ea427
          e6325165 e9ea10e3 da5f6c42 e9c55215 aa9ca27a 5863ec48
          d8e0286b

Normal Basis:

G_x =   1b559c7 cba2422e 3affe133 43e808b5 5e012d72 6ca0b7e6
          a63aeafb c1e3a98e 10ca0fcf 98350c3b 7f89a975 4a8e1dc0
          713cec4a

G_y =   16d8c42 052f07e7 713e7490 eff318ba 1abd6fef 8a5433c8
          94b24f5c 817aeb79 852496fb ee803a47 bc8a2038 78ebf1c4
          99afd7d6

D.1.3.4.2 Curve B-409

n =   6610559687902485989519153080327710398284046829642812192
          8464879830415777482737480520814372376217911096597986728 8
          366567526771

Polynomial Basis:

b =   021a5c2 c8ee9feb 5c4b9a75 3b7b476b 7fd6422e f1f3dd67
          4761fa99 d6ac27c8 a9a197b2 72822f6c d57a55aa 4f50ae31
          7b13545f

G_x =   15d4860 d088ddb3 496b0c60 64756260 441cde4a f1771d4d
          b01ffe5b 34e59703 dc255a86 8a118051 5603aeab 60794e54
          bb7996a7

98

$G_y =$ 061b1cf ab6be5f3 2bbfa783 24ed106a 7636b9c5 a7bd198d
0158aa4f 5488d08f 38514f1f df4b4f40 d2181b36 81c364ba
0273c706

Normal Basis:

$SEED =$ 4099b5a4 57f9d69f 79213d09 4c4bcd4d 4262210b

$b =$ 124d065 1c3d3772 f7f5a1fe 6e715559 e2129bdf a04d52f7
b6ac7c53 2cf0ed06 f610072d 88ad2fdc c50c6fde 72843670
f8b3742a

$G_x =$ 0ceacbc 9f475767 d8e69f3b 5dfab398 13685262 bcacf22b
84c7b6dd 981899e7 318c96f0 761f77c6 02c016ce d7c548de
830d708f

$G_y =$ 199d64b a8f089c6 db0e0b61 e80bb959 34afd0ca f2e8be76
d1c5e9af fc7476df 49142691 ad303902 88aa09bc c59c1573
aa3c009a

D.1.3.5 Degree 571 Binary Field

$T =$ 10

$p(t) =$ $t^{571} + t^{10} + t^5 + t^2 + 1$

D.1.3.5.1 Curve K-571

$a =$ 0

$n =$ 1932268761508629172347675945465993672149463664853217499
3286176257257595711447802122681339785227067118347067128
0082535146127367497406661731192968242161709250355573368527
6673

Polynomial Basis:

$G_x =$ 26eb7a8 59923fbc 82189631 f8103fe4 ac9ca297 0012d5d4
60248048 01841ca4 43709584 93b205e6 47da304d b4ceb08c

99

$$G_y = \begin{array}{llllll} & \text{bbd1ba39} & \text{494776fb} & \text{988b4717} & \text{4dca88c7} & \text{e2945283} & \text{a01c8972} \\ & \text{349dc80} & \text{7f4fbf37} & \text{4f4aeade} & \text{3bca9531} & \text{4dd58cec} & \text{9f307a54} \\ & \text{ffc61efc} & \text{006d8a2c} & \text{9d4979c0} & \text{ac44aea7} & \text{4fbebbb9} & \text{f772aedc} \\ & \text{b620b01a} & \text{7ba7af1b} & \text{320430c8} & \text{591984f6} & \text{01cd4c14} & \text{3ef1c7a3} \end{array}$$

Normal Basis:

$$G_x = \begin{array}{llllll} & \text{04bb2db} & \text{a418d0db} & \text{107adae0} & \text{03427e5d} & \text{7cc139ac} & \text{b465e593} \\ & \text{4f0bea2a} & \text{b2f3622b} & \text{c29b3d5b} & \text{9aa7a1fd} & \text{fd5d8be6} & \text{6057c100} \\ & \text{8e71e484} & \text{bcd98f22} & \text{bf847642} & \text{37673674} & \text{29ef2ec5} & \text{bc3ebcf7} \end{array}$$

$$G_y = \begin{array}{llllll} & \text{44cbb57} & \text{de20788d} & \text{2c952d7b} & \text{56cf39bd} & \text{3e89b189} & \text{84bd124e} \\ & \text{751ceff4} & \text{369dd8da} & \text{c6a59e6e} & \text{745df44d} & \text{8220ce22} & \text{aa2c852c} \\ & \text{fcbbef49} & \text{ebaa98bd} & \text{2483e331} & \text{80e04286} & \text{feaa2530} & \text{50caff60} \end{array}$$

D.1.3.5.2 Curve B-571

$n =$ 38645375230172583446953518909319873442989273297064349986572352514515191422895604245361439993894157730831338811219269444862468724628168130702345282883033324113931911052 85703

Polynomial Basis:

$$b = \begin{array}{llllll} & \text{2f40e7e} & \text{2221f295} & \text{de297117} & \text{b7f3d62f} & \text{5c6a97ff} & \text{cb8ceff1} \\ & \text{cd6ba8ce} & \text{4a9a18ad} & \text{84ffabbd} & \text{8efa5933} & \text{2be7ad67} & \text{56a66e29} \\ & \text{4afd185a} & \text{78ff12aa} & \text{520e4de7} & \text{39baca0c} & \text{7ffeff7f} & \text{2955727a} \end{array}$$

$$G_x = \begin{array}{llllll} & \text{303001d} & \text{34b85629} & \text{6c16c0d4} & \text{0d3cd775} & \text{0a93d1d2} & \text{955fa80a} \\ & \text{a5f40fc8} & \text{db7b2abd} & \text{bde53950} & \text{f4c0d293} & \text{cdd711a3} & \text{5b67fb14} \\ & \text{99ae6003} & \text{8614f139} & \text{4abfa3b4} & \text{c850d927} & \text{e1e7769c} & \text{8eec2d19} \end{array}$$

$$G_y = \begin{array}{llllll} & \text{37bf273} & \text{42da639b} & \text{6dccfffe} & \text{b73d69d7} & \text{8c6c27a6} & \text{009cbbca} \\ & \text{1980f853} & \text{3921e8a6} & \text{84423e43} & \text{bab08a57} & \text{6291af8f} & \text{461bb2a8} \\ & \text{b3531d2f} & \text{0485c19b} & \text{16e2f151} & \text{6e23dd3c} & \text{1a4827af} & \text{1b8ac15b} \end{array}$$

Normal Basis:

$SEED =$ 2aa058f7 3a0e33ab 486b0f61 0410c53a 7f132310

$b =$ 3762d0d 47116006 179da356 88eeaccf 591a5cde a7500011
  8d9608c5 9132d434 26101a1d fb377411 5f586623 f75f0000
  1ce61198 3c1275fa 31f5bc9f 4be1a0f4 67f01ca8 85c74777

$G_x =$ 0735e03 5def5925 cc33173e b2a8ce77 67522b46 6d278b65
  0a291612 7dfea9d2 d361089f 0a7a0247 a184e1c7 0d417866
  e0fe0feb 0ff8f2f3 f9176418 f97d117e 624e2015 df1662a8

$G_y =$ 04a3642 0572616c df7e606f ccadaecf c3b76dab 0eb1248d
  d03fbdfc 9cd3242c 4726be57 9855e812 de7ec5c5 00b4576a
  24628048 b6a72d88 0062eed0 dd34b109 6d3acbb6 b01a4a97

D.2   Implementation of Modular Arithmetic

The prime moduli in the above examples are of a special type (called *generalized Mersenne numbers*) for which modular multiplication can be carried out more efficiently than in general. This section provides the rules for implementing this faster arithmetic for each of the prime moduli appearing in the examples.

The usual way to multiply two integers (mod m) is to take the integer product and reduce it (mod m). One therefore has the following problem: given an integer A less than m^2, compute

$$B = A \bmod m.$$

In general, one must obtain B as the remainder of an integer division. If m is a generalized Mersenne number, however, then B can be expressed as a sum or difference (mod m) of a small number of terms. To compute this expression, the integer sum or difference can be evaluated and the result reduced modulo m. The latter reduction can be accomplished by adding or subtracting a few copies of m.

The prime modulus p for each of the five example curves is a generalized Mersenne number.

D.2.1 Curve P-192

The modulus for this curve is $p = 2^{192} - 2^{64} - 1$. Every integer A less than p^2 can be written as

$$A = A_5 \cdot 2^{320} + A_4 \cdot 2^{256} + A_3 \cdot 2^{192} + A_2 \cdot 2^{128} + A_1 \cdot 2^{64} + A_0,$$

where each A_i is a 64-bit integer. As a concatenation of 64-bit words, this can be denoted by

$$A = (A_5 \parallel A_4 \parallel A_3 \parallel A_2 \parallel A_0).$$

The expression for B is

$$B = T + S_1 + S_2 + S_3 \bmod p,$$

101

where the 192-bit terms are given by

$$T = (A_2 \| A_1 \| A_0)$$
$$S_1 = (A_3 \| A_3)$$
$$S_2 = (A_4 \| A_4 \| 0)$$
$$S_3 = (A_5 \| A_5 \| A_5).$$

D.2.2 Curve P-224

The modulus for this curve is $p = 2^{224} - 2^{96} + 1$. Every integer A less than $p^{2\Box}$ can be written as:

$$A = A_{13} \cdot 2^{416} + A_{12} \cdot 2^{384} + A_{11} \cdot 2^{352} + A_{10} \cdot 2^{320} + A_9 \cdot 2^{288} + A_8 \cdot 2^{256} + A_7 \cdot 2^{224} + A_6 \cdot 2^{192} +$$
$$A_5 \cdot 2^{160} + A_4 \cdot 2^{128} + A_3 \cdot 2^{96} + A_2 \cdot 2^{64} + A_1 \cdot 2^{32} + A_0,$$

where each A_i is a 32-bit integer. As a concatenation of 32-bit words, this can be denoted by:

$$A = (A_{13} \| A_{12} \| \ldots \| A_0).$$

The expression for B is:

$$B = T + S_1 + S_2 - D_1 - D_2 \bmod p,$$

where the 224-bit terms are given by:

$$T = (A_6 \| A_5 \| A_4 \| A_3 \| A_2 \| A_1 \| A_0)$$
$$S_1 = (A_{10} \| A_9 \| A_8 \| A_7 \| 0 \| 0 \| 0)$$
$$S_2 = (0 \| A_{13} \| A_{12} \| A_{11} \| 0 \| 0 \| 0)$$
$$D_1 = (A_{13} \| A_{12} \| A_{11} \| A_{10} \| A_9 \| A_8 \| A_7)$$
$$D_2 = (0 \| 0 \| 0 \| 0 \| A_{13} \| A_{12} \| A_{11}).$$

D.2.3 Curve P-256

The modulus for this curve is $p = 2^{256} - 2^{224} + 2^{192} + 2^{96} - 1$. Every integer A less than p^2 can be written as:

$$A = A_{15} \cdot 2^{480} + A_{14} \cdot 2^{448} + A_{13} \cdot 2^{416} + A_{12} \cdot 2^{384} + A_{11} \cdot 2^{352} + A_{10} \cdot 2^{320} + A_9 \cdot 2^{288} + A_8 \cdot 2^{256} +$$
$$A_7 \cdot 2^{224} + A_6 \cdot 2^{192} + A_5 \cdot 2^{160} + A_4 \cdot 2^{128} + A_3 \cdot 2^{96} + A_2 \cdot 2^{64} + A_1 \cdot 2^{32} + A_0,$$

where each A_i is a 32-bit integer. As a concatenation of 32-bit words, this can be denoted by

$$A = (A_{15} \| A_{14} \| \cdots \| A_0).$$

The expression for B is:

$$B = T + 2S_1 + 2S_2 + S_3 + S_4 - D_1 - D_2 - D_3 - D_4 \bmod p,$$

where the 256-bit terms are given by:

$T = (\ A_7 \parallel A_6 \parallel\ A_5\ \square\ \parallel A_4 \parallel A_3 \parallel A_2 \parallel A_1 \parallel A_0\ )$

$S_1 = (\ A_{15} \parallel A_{14}\square\ \parallel A_{13} \parallel A_{12} \parallel A_{11} \parallel 0 \parallel 0 \parallel 0\ )$

$S_2 = (\ 0 \parallel A_{15} \parallel A_{14}\square\ \parallel A_{13} \parallel A_{12} \parallel 0 \parallel 0 \parallel 0\ )$

$S_3 = (\ A_{15} \parallel A_{14}\square\ \parallel 0 \parallel 0 \parallel 0 \parallel A_{10} \parallel A_9 \parallel A_8\ )$

$S_4 = (\ A_8 \parallel A_{13} \parallel A_{15} \parallel A_{14} \parallel A_{13} \parallel A_{11} \parallel A_{10} \parallel A_9\ )$

$D_1 = (\ A_{10} \parallel\ A_8 \parallel 0 \parallel 0 \parallel 0 \parallel A_{13} \parallel A_{12} \parallel A_{11}\ )$

$D_2 = (\ A_{11} \parallel A_9 \parallel 0 \parallel 0 \parallel A_{15} \parallel A_{14} \parallel A_{13} \parallel A_{12}\square\ )$

$D_3 = (\ A_{12}\square\ \parallel 0 \parallel A_{10} \parallel A_9 \parallel A_8 \parallel A_{15} \parallel A_{14} \parallel A_{13}\ )$

$D_4 = (\ A_{13} \parallel 0 \parallel A_{11} \parallel A_{10} \parallel A_9 \parallel 0 \parallel A_{15} \parallel A_{14}\ )$

D.2.4 Curve P-384

The modulus for this curve is $p = 2^{384} - 2^{128} - 2^{96} + 2^{32} - 1$. Every integer A less than p^2 can be written as:

$$A = A_{23} \cdot 2^{736} + A_{22} \cdot 2^{704} + A_{21} \cdot 2^{672} + A_{20} \cdot 2^{640} + A_{19} \cdot 2^{608} + A_{18} \cdot 2^{576} + A_{17} \cdot 2^{544} + A_{16} \cdot 2^{512} +$$
$$A_{15} \cdot 2^{480} + A_{14} \cdot 2^{448} + A_{13} \cdot 2^{416} + A_{12} \cdot 2^{384} + A_{11} \cdot 2^{352} + A_{10} \cdot 2^{320} + A_9 \cdot 2^{288} + A_8 \cdot 2^{256} +$$
$$A_7 \cdot 2^{224} + A_6 \cdot 2^{192} + A_5 \cdot 2^{160} + A_4 \cdot 2^{128} + A_3 \cdot 2^{96} + A_2 \cdot 2^{64} + A_1 \cdot 2^{32} + A_0,$$

where each A_i is a 32-bit integer. As a concatenation of 32-bit words, this can be denoted by

$$A = (A_{23} \parallel A_{22} \parallel \cdots \parallel A_0\ ).$$

The expression for B is:

$$B = T + 2S_1 + S_2 + S_3 + S_4 + S_5 + S_6 - D_1 - D_2 - D_3 \bmod p,$$

where the 384-bit terms are given by:

$T = (A_{11} \parallel A_{10} \parallel A_9 \parallel A_8 \parallel A_7 \parallel A_6 \parallel A_5 \parallel A_4 \parallel A_3 \parallel A_2 \parallel A_1 \parallel A_0\ )$

$S_1 = (\ 0 \parallel 0 \parallel 0 \parallel 0 \parallel 0 \parallel A_{23} \parallel A_{22} \parallel A_{21} \parallel 0 \parallel 0 \parallel 0 \parallel 0\ )$

$S_2 = (A_{23} \parallel A_{22} \parallel A_{21} \parallel A_{20} \parallel A_{19} \parallel A_{18} \parallel A_{17} \parallel A_{16} \parallel A_{15} \parallel A_{14} \parallel A_{13} \parallel A_{12})$

$S_3 = (A_{20} \parallel A_{19} \parallel A_{18} \parallel A_{17} \parallel A_{16} \parallel A_{15} \parallel A_{14} \parallel A_{13} \parallel A_{12} \parallel A_{23} \parallel A_{22} \parallel A_{21})$

$S_4 = (\ A_{19} \parallel A_{18} \parallel A_{17} \parallel A_{16} \parallel A_{15} \parallel A_{14} \parallel A_{13} \parallel A_{12} \parallel A_{20} \parallel 0 \parallel A_{23} \parallel 0\ )$

$S_5 = (\ 0 \parallel 0 \parallel 0 \parallel 0 \parallel A_{23} \parallel A_{22} \parallel A_{21} \parallel A_{20} \parallel 0 \parallel 0 \parallel 0 \parallel 0\ )$

$$S_6 = (\, 0 \,\|\, 0 \,\|\, 0 \,\|\, 0 \,\|\, 0 \,\|\, 0 \,\|\, A_{23} \,\|\, A_{22} \,\|\, A_{21} \,\|\, 0 \,\|\, 0 \,\|\, A_{20}\,)$$

$$D_1 = (\, A_{22} \,\|\, A_{21} \,\|\, A_{20} \,\|\, A_{19} \,\|\, A_{18} \,\|\, A_{17} \,\|\, A_{16} \,\|\, A_{15} \,\|\, A_{14} \,\|\, A_{13} \,\|\, A_{12} \,\|\, A_{23}\,)$$

$$D_2 = (\, 0 \,\|\, 0 \,\|\, 0 \,\|\, 0 \,\|\, 0 \,\|\, 0 \,\|\, 0 \,\|\, A_{23} \,\|\, A_{22} \,\|\, A_{21} \,\|\, A_{20} \,\|\, 0\,)$$

$$D_3 = (\, 0 \,\|\, 0 \,\|\, 0 \,\|\, 0 \,\|\, 0 \,\|\, 0 \,\|\, 0 \,\|\, A_{23} \,\|\, A_{23} \,\|\, 0 \,\|\, 0 \,\|\, 0\,).$$

D.2.5 Curve P-521

The modulus for this curve is $p = 2^{521} - 1$. Every integer A less than p^2 can be written

$$A = A_1 \cdot 2^{521} + A_0,$$

where each A_i is a 521-bit integer. As a concatenation of 521-bit words, this can be denoted by

$$A = (A_1 \,\|\, A_0).$$

The expression for B is:

$$B = (A_0 + A_1) \bmod p.$$

D.3 Normal Bases

The elements of $GF(2^m)$ are expressed in terms of the type T normal *basis*[5] B for $GF(2^m)$, for some T. Each element has a unique representation as a bit string:

$$(\, a_0 \; a_1 \; \ldots \; a_{m-1}\,).$$

The arithmetic operations are performed as follows.

Addition: addition of two elements is implemented by bit-wise addition modulo 2. Thus, for example,

$$(1100111) + (1010010) = (0110101).$$

Squaring: if

$$\alpha = (\, a_0 \; a_1 \; \ldots \; a_{m-1}\,)$$

then

$$\alpha^2 = (a_{m-1} \; a_0 \; a_1 \; \ldots \; a_{m-2}).$$

Multiplication: to perform multiplication, a function $F(\underline{u},\underline{v})$ is constructed on inputs

---

[5] It is assumed in this section that m is odd and T is even, since this is the only case considered in this Standard.

104

$$\underline{u} = (\, u_0 \; u_1 \; \ldots \; u_{m-1} \,) \qquad \text{and} \qquad \underline{v} = (\, v_0 \; v_1 \; \ldots \; v_{m-1} \,)$$

as follows.

1. Set $p \leftarrow Tm + 1$.

2. Let u be an integer having order T modulo p.

3. Compute the sequence $F(1), F(2), \ldots, F(p-1)$ as follows:

   3.1   Set $w \leftarrow 1$.

   3.2   For j from 0 to $T-1$ do

        3.2.1   Set $n \leftarrow w$.

        3.2.2   For $i = 0$ to $m-1$ do

            3.2.2.1   Set $F(n) \leftarrow i$.

            3.2.2.2   Set $n \leftarrow 2n \bmod p$.

        3.2.3   Set $w \leftarrow uw \bmod p$.

4. Output the formula:

$$F(u,v) := \sum_{k=1}^{p-2} u_{F(k+1)} v_{F(p-k)}.$$

This computation need only be performed once per basis.

Given the function F for B, the product

$$(\, c_0 \; c_1 \; \ldots \; c_{m-1} \,) = (\, a_0 \; a_1 \; \ldots \; a_{m-1} \,) \; * \; (\, b_0 \; b_1 \; \ldots \; b_{m-1} \,)$$

is computed as follows:

1. Set $(\, u_0 \; u_1 \; \ldots \; u_{m-1} \,) \leftarrow (\, a_0 \; a_1 \; \ldots \; a_{m-1} \,)$.

2. Set $(\, v_0 \; v_1 \; \ldots \; v_{m-1} \,) \leftarrow (\, b_0 \; b_1 \; \ldots \; b_{m-1} \,)$.

3. For $k = 0$ to $m - 1$ do

   3.1   Compute

$$c_k = F(\underline{u}, \underline{v}).$$

   3.2   Set $u \leftarrow \textbf{LeftShift}\,(u)$ and $v \leftarrow \textbf{LeftShift}\,(v)$, where **LeftShift** denotes the circular left shift operation.

4. Output $c = (\, c_0 \; c_1 \; \ldots \; c_{m-1} \,)$.

Example: For the type 4 normal basis for $GF(2^7)$, $p = 29$ and $u = 12$ or 17. Thus, the values of F are given by:

$$F(1) = 0 \quad F(8) = 3 \quad F(15) = 6 \quad F(22) = 5$$
$$F(2) = 1 \quad F(9) = 3 \quad F(16) = 4 \quad F(23) = 6$$
$$F(3) = 5 \quad F(10) = 2 \quad F(17) = 0 \quad F(24) = 1$$
$$F(4) = 2 \quad F(11) = 4 \quad F(18) = 4 \quad F(25) = 2$$
$$F(5) = 1 \quad F(12) = 0 \quad F(19) = 2 \quad F(26) = 5$$
$$F(6) = 6 \quad F(13) = 4 \quad F(20) = 3 \quad F(27) = 1$$
$$F(7) = 5 \quad F(14) = 6 \quad F(21) = 3 \quad F(28) = 0$$

Therefore,

$$F(\underline{u}, \underline{v}) = u_0 v_1 + u_1 (v_0 + v_2 + v_5 + v_6) + u_2 (v_1 + v_3 + v_4 + v_5) + u_3 (v_2 + v_5) +$$
$$u_4 (v_2 + v_6) + u_5 (v_1 + v_2 + v_3 + v_6) + u_6 (v_1 + v_4 + v_5 + v_6).$$

Thus, if

$$a = (1\ 0\ 1\ 0\ 1\ 1\ 1) \text{ and } b = (1\ 1\ 0\ 0\ 0\ 0\ 1),$$

then

$$c_0 = F((1\ 0\ 1\ 0\ 1\ 1\ 1), (1\ 1\ 0\ 0\ 0\ 0\ 1)) = 1,$$
$$c_1 = F((0\ 1\ 0\ 1\ 1\ 1\ 1), (1\ 0\ 0\ 0\ 0\ 1\ 1)) = 0,$$
$$\vdots$$
$$c_6 = F((1\ 1\ 0\ 1\ 0\ 1\ 1), (1\ 1\ 1\ 0\ 0\ 0\ 0)) = 1,$$

so that $c = ab = (1\ 0\ 1\ 1\ 0\ 0\ 1)$.

D.4   Scalar Multiplication on Koblitz Curves

This section describes a particularly efficient method of computing the scalar multiple nP on the Koblitz curve E_a over $GF(2^m)$.

The operation τ is defined by:

$$\tau(x, y) = (x^2, y^2).$$

When the normal basis representation is used, then the operation τ is implemented by performing right circular shifts on the bit strings representing x and y.

Given m and a, define the following parameters:

- C is some integer greater than 5.

- $\mu = (-1)^{1-a}$.

- For $i = 0$ and $i = 1$, define the sequence $s_i(m)$ by:

$$s_i(0) = 0, \quad s_i(1) = 1 - i,$$

$$s_i(m) = \mu \bullet s_i(m - 1) - 2\,s_i(m - 2) + (-1)^i$$

- Define the sequence $V(m)$

$$V(0) = 2, \quad V(1) = \mu$$

$$V(m) = \mu \bullet v(m - 1) - 2V(m - 2).$$

For the example curves, the quantities $s_i(m)$ and $V(m)$ are as follows.

Curve K-163:

$s_0(163) =$ 2579386439110731650419537

$s_1(163) =$ –7553600644476226375461594

$V(163) =$ –4845466632539410776804317

Curve K-233:

$s_0(233) =$ –2785971174143442976175834964435883

$s_1(233) =$ –44192136247082304936052160908934886

$V(233) =$ –13738154601110823539498729965136779

Curve K-283:

$s_0(283) =$ –6659815321090490411087955360015914694280025

$s_1(283) =$ 11558600549091367751922810725916099139945968

$V(283) =$ 7777244870872830999287791970962823977569917

Curve K-409:

$s_0(409) =$ –183075104560023821378103171987564613785905424875568693384419259

$s_1(409) =$ –889304852613830409719665324184421267962656610099660644481679 0

$V(409)=$ 104572887373156259274476853870483207376387969576875757911738 29

Curve K-571:

$s_0(571) =$ –37373194468764636924293858924761155671472939645961310241234064 20\
 235241916729983261305

$s_1(571) =$ –31918577064464160995838145959489596741319689121485646586105651 17\
 58982848515832612248752

107

$$V(571)= -14838092698169141389961914029705149036454257418049393362329123395\backslash$$
$$34208516828973111459843$$

The following algorithm computes the scalar multiple nP on the Koblitz curve E_a over $GF(2^m)$. The average number of elliptic additions and subtractions is at most $\sim 1 + (m/3)$, and is at most $\sim m/3$ with probability at least $1 - 2^{5-C}$.

1. For $i = 0$ to 1 do

   1.1 $n' \leftarrow \lfloor n/2^{a-C+(m-9)/2} \rfloor$.

   1.2 $g' \leftarrow s_i(m) \cdot n'$.

   1.3 $h' \leftarrow \lfloor g'/2^m \rfloor$.

   1.4 $j' \leftarrow V(m) \cdot h'$.

   1.5 $l' \leftarrow \text{Round}((g'+j')/2^{(m+5)/2})$.

   1.6 $\lambda_i \leftarrow l'/2^C$.

   1.7 $f_i \leftarrow \text{Round}(\lambda_i)$.

   1.8 $\eta_i \leftarrow \lambda_i - f_i$.

   1.9 $h_i \leftarrow 0$.

2. $\eta \leftarrow 2\eta_0 + \mu\eta_1$.

3. If $(\eta \geq 1)$,

   then

      if $(\eta_o - 3\mu\eta_1 < -1)$

         then set $h_1 \leftarrow \mu$

         else set $h_0 \leftarrow 1$.

   else

      if $(\eta_0 + 4\mu\eta_1 \geq 2)$

         then set $h_1 \leftarrow \mu$.

4. If $(\eta < -1)$

      then

      if $(\eta_0 - 3\mu\eta_1 \geq 1)$

         then set $h_1 \leftarrow -\mu$

         else set $h_0 \leftarrow -1$.

else

$$\text{if } (\eta_0 + 4 \mu \eta_1 < -2)$$

$$\text{then set } h_1 \leftarrow - \mu.$$

5. $q_0 \leftarrow f_0 + h_0$.

6. $q_1 \leftarrow f_1 + h_1$.

7. $r_0 \leftarrow n - (s_0 + \mu s_1) q_0 - 2 s_1 q_1$.

8. $r_1 \leftarrow s_1 q_0 - s_0 q_1$.

9. Set $Q \leftarrow O$.

10. $P_0 \leftarrow P$.

11. While $((r_0 \neq 0) \text{ or } (r_1 \neq 0))$

    11.1 If *(r_0 odd)*, then

        11.1.1 set $u \leftarrow 2 - (r_0 - 2 r_1 \bmod 4)$.

        11.1.2 set $r_0 \leftarrow r_0 - u$.

        11.1.3 if $(u = 1)$, then set $Q \leftarrow Q + P_0$.

        11.1.4 if $(u = -1)$, then set $Q \leftarrow Q - P_0$.

    11.2 Set $P_0 \leftarrow \tau P_0$.

    11.3 Set $(r_0 , r_1) \leftarrow (r_1 + \mu r_0 /2, - r_0 /2)$.

        Endwhile

12. Output Q.

D.5 Generation of Pseudo-Random Curves (Prime Case)

Let l be the bit length of p, and define

$$v = \lfloor (l - 1) /160 \rfloor$$

$$w = l - 160v - 1.$$

1. Choose an arbitrary 160-bit string s as the domain parameter seed.

2. Compute $h = \text{SHA-1}(s)$.

3. Let h_0 be the bit string obtained by taking the w rightmost bits of h.

4. Let z be the integer whose binary expansion is given by the 160-bit string s.

5. For i from 1 to v do:

5.1 Define the 160-bit string s_i to be binary expansion of the integer

$$(z + i) \bmod (2^{160}).$$

5.2 Compute $h_i = \text{SHA-1}(s_i)$.

6. Let h be the bit string obtained by the concatenation of h_0, h_1, ... , h_v as follows:

$$h = h_0 \parallel h_1 \parallel \ldots \parallel h_v.$$

7. Let c be the integer whose binary expansion is given by the bit string h.

8. If $((c = 0 \text{ or } 4c + 27 \equiv 0 \pmod{p}))$, then go to Step 1.

9. Choose integers $a, b \in GF(p)$ such that

$$c\, b^2 \equiv a^3 \pmod{p}.$$

(The simplest choice is $a = c$ and $b = c$. However, one may want to choose differently for performance reasons.)

10. Check that the elliptic curve E over $GF(p)$ given by $y^2 = x^3 + ax + b$ has suitable order. If not, go to Step 1.

D.6 Verification of Curve Pseudo-Randomness (Prime Case)

Given the 160-bit domain parameter seed value s, verify that the coefficient b was obtained from s via the cryptographic hash function SHA-1 as follows.

Let l be the bit length of p, and define

$$v = \lfloor (l - 1)/160 \rfloor$$
$$w = l - 160v - 1.$$

1. Compute $h = \text{SHA-1}(s)$.

2. Let h_0 be the bit string obtained by taking the w rightmost bits of h.

3. Let z be the integer whose binary expansion is given by the 160-bit string s.

4. For $i = 1$ to v do

4.1 Define the 160-bit string s_i to be binary expansion of the integer

$$(z + i) \bmod (2^{160}).$$

4.2 Compute $h_i = \text{SHA-1}(s_i)$.

5. Let h be the bit string obtained by the concatenation of h_0, h_1, ... , h_v as follows:

$$h = h_0 \parallel h_1 \parallel \ldots \parallel h_v.$$

6. Let c be the integer whose binary expansion is given by the bit string h.

7. Verify that $b^2\, c \equiv -27 \pmod{p}$.

D.7   Generation of Pseudo-Random Curves (Binary Case)

Let:

$$v = \lfloor (m-1)/B \rfloor$$
$$w = m - Bv.$$

1. Choose an arbitrary 160-bit string s as the domain parameter seed.
2. Compute $h = \text{SHA-1}(s)$.
3. Let h_0 be the bit string obtained by taking the w rightmost bits of h.
4. Let z be the integer whose binary expansion is given by the 160-bit string s.
5. For i from 1 to v do:

    5.1 Define the 160-bit string s_i to be binary expansion of the integer

        $(z+i) \bmod (2^{160})$.

    5.2 Compute $h_i = \text{SHA-1}(s_i)$.

6. Let h be the bit string obtained by the concatenation of h_0, h_1, $\ldots$, h_v as follows:

$$h = h_0 \parallel h_1 \parallel \ldots \parallel h_v.$$

7. Let b be the element of $GF(2^m)$ which binary expansion is given by the bit string h.
8. Choose an element a of $GF(2^m)$.
9. Check that the elliptic curve E over $GF(2^m)$ given by $y^2 + xy = x^3 + ax^2 + b$ has suitable order. If not, go to Step 1.

D.8   Verification of Curve Pseudo-Randomness (Binary Case)

Given the 160-bit domain parameter seed value s, verify that the coefficient b was obtained from s via the cryptographic hash function SHA-1 as follows.

Define

$$v = \lfloor (m-1)/160 \rfloor$$
$$w = m - 160v$$

1. Compute $h = \text{SHA-1}(s)$.
2. Let h_0 be the bit string obtained by taking the w rightmost bits of h.

3. Let z be the integer whose binary expansion is given by the 160-bit string s.

4. For $i = 1$ to v do

   4.1 Define the 160-bit string s_i to be binary expansion of the integer $(z + i) \bmod (2^{160})$.

   4.2 Compute $h_i = $ SHA-1(s_i).

5. Let h be the bit string obtained by the concatenation of h_0, h_1, ... , h_v as follows:

$$h = h_0 \parallel h_1 \parallel \ldots \parallel h_v.$$

6. Let c be the element of $GF(2^m)$ which is represented by the bit string h.

7. Verify that $c = b$.

D.9 Polynomial Basis to Normal Basis Conversion

Suppose that α is an element of the field $GF(2^m)$. Let p be the bit string representing α with respect to a given polynomial basis. It is desired to compute n, the bit string representing α with respect to a given normal basis. This is done via the matrix computation

$$p\,\Gamma = n,$$

where Γ is an m-by-m matrix with entries in $GF(2)$. The matrix Γ, which depends only on the bases, can be computed easily given its second-to-last row. The second-to-last row for each conversion is given the below.

Degree 163:

        3 e173bfaf 3a86434d 883a2918 a489ddbd 69fe84e1

Degree 233:

        0be 19b89595 28bbc490 038f4bc4 da8bdfc1 ca36bb05 853fd0ed
0ae200ce

Degree 283:

 3347f17 521fdabc 62ec1551 acf156fb 0bceb855 f174d4c1 7807511c
9f745382 add53bc3

Degree 409:

 0eb00f2 ea95fd6c 64024e7f 0b68b81f 5ff8a467 acc2b4c3 b9372843
6265c7ff a06d896c ae3a7e31 e295ec30 3eb9f769 de78bef5

Degree 571:

 7940ffa ef996513 4d59dcbf e5bf239b e4fe4b41 05959c5d 4d942ffd
46ea35f3 e3cdb0e1 04a2aa01 cef30a3a 49478011 196bfb43 c55091b6
1174d7c0 8d0cdd61 3bf6748a bad972a4

Given the second-to-last row r of Γ, the rest of the matrix is computed as follows. Let β be the element of $GF(2^m)$ whose representation with respect to the normal basis is r. Then the rows of Γ, from top to bottom, are the bit strings representing the elements

$$\beta^{m-1}, \beta^{m-2}, \ldots, \beta^2, \beta, 1$$

with respect to the normal basis. (Note that the element 1 is represented by the all-1 bit string.)

Alternatively, the matrix is the inverse of the matrix described in Appendix D.10.

More details of these computations can be found in Annex A.7 of the IEEE Standard 1363-2000 standard.

D.10 Normal Basis to Polynomial Basis Conversion

Suppose that α is an element of the field $GF(2^m)$. Let n be the bit string representing α with respect to a given normal basis. It is desired to compute p, the bit string representing α with respect to a given polynomial basis. This is done via the matrix computation

$$n\,\Gamma = p,$$

where Γ is an m-by-m matrix with entries in $GF(2)$. The matrix Γ, which depends only on the bases, can be computed easily given its top row. The top row for each conversion is given below.

Degree 163:

```
    7 15169c10 9c612e39 0d347c74 8342bcd3 b02a0bef
```

Degree 233:

```
  149 9e398ac5 d79e3685 59b35ca4 9bb7305d a6c0390b cf9e2300
253203c9
```

Degree 283:

```
 31e0ed7 91c3282d c5624a72 0818049d 053e8c7a b8663792 bc1d792e
ba9867fc 7b317a99
```

Degree 409:

```
 0dfa06b e206aa97 b7a41fff b9b0c55f 8f048062 fbe8381b 4248adf9
2912ccc8 e3f91a24 e1cfb395 0532b988 971c2304 2e85708d
```

Degree 571:

```
 452186b bf5840a0 bcf8c9f0 2a54efa0 4e813b43 c3d41496 06c4d27b
487bf107 393c8907 f79d9778 beb35ee8 7467d328 8274caeb da6ce05a
eb4ca5cf 3c3044bd 4372232f 2c1a27c4
```

Given the top row r of Γ, the rest of the matrix is computed as follows. Let β be the element of $GF(2^m)$ whose representation with respect to the polynomial basis is r. Then the rows of Γ, from top to bottom, are the bit strings representing the elements

$$\beta, \beta^2, \beta^{2^2}, \ldots, \beta^{2^{m-1}}$$

with respect to the polynomial basis.

Alternatively, the matrix is the inverse of the matrix described in Appendix D.9.

More details of these computations can be found in Annex A.7 of the IEEE Std 1363-2000 standard.

Appendix E: A Proof that $v = r$ in the DSA
(Informative)

The purpose of this appendix is to show that if $M' = M$, $r' = r$ and $s' = s$ in the signature verification, then $v = r'$. Let **Hash** be an approved hash function. The following result is needed.

Lemma: Let p and q be primes such that q divides $(p - 1)$, let h be a positive integer less than p, and let $g = (h^{(p-1)/q} \bmod p)$. Then $(g^q \bmod p) = 1$, and if $(m \bmod q) = (n \bmod q)$, then $(g^m \bmod p) = (g^n \bmod p)$.

Proof:

$$g^q \bmod p = (h^{(p-1)/q} \bmod p)^q \bmod p$$
$$= h^{(p-1)} \bmod p$$
$$= 1$$

by Fermat's Little Theorem. Now let $(m \bmod q) = (n \bmod q)$, i.e., $m = (n + kq)$ for some integer k. Then

$$g^m \bmod p = g^{n+kq} \bmod p$$
$$= (g^n \, g^{kq}) \bmod p$$
$$= ((g^n \bmod p)\,(g^q \bmod p)^k) \bmod p$$
$$= g^n \bmod p,$$

since $(g^q \bmod p) = 1$.

Proof of the main result:

Theorem: If $M' = M$, $r' = r$, and $s' = s$ in the signature verification, then $v = r'$.

Proof:

$$w = (s')^{-1} \bmod q = s^{-1} \bmod q$$
$$u1 = ((\textbf{Hash}(M'))w) \bmod q = ((\textbf{Hash}(M))w) \bmod q$$
$$u2 = ((r')w) \bmod q = (rw) \bmod q.$$

Now $y = (g^x \bmod p)$, so that by the lemma,

$$v = ((g^{u1}\, y^{u2}) \bmod p) \bmod q$$
$$= ((g^{\textbf{Hash}(M)w}\, y^{rw}) \bmod p) \bmod q$$
$$= ((g^{\textbf{Hash}(M)w}\, g^{xrw}) \bmod p) \bmod q$$
$$= ((g^{(\textbf{Hash}(M) + xr)w} \bmod p) \bmod q.$$

Also:

$$s = (k^{-1} \, (\textbf{Hash}(M) + xr)) \bmod q.$$

Hence:

$$w = (k \, (\textbf{Hash}(M) + xr)^{-1}) \bmod q$$

$$(\textbf{Hash}(M) + xr)w \bmod q = k \bmod q.$$

Thus, by the lemma:

$$v = (g^k \bmod p) \bmod q = r$$

Appendix F: Calculating the Required Number of Rounds of Testing Using the Miller-Rabin Probabilistic Primality Test

(Informative)

F.1   The Required Number of Rounds of the Miller-Rabin Primality Tests

The ideas of paper [1] were applied to estimate $p_{k,t}$, the probability that an odd k-bit integer that passes t rounds of Miller-Rabin (M-R) testing is actually composite. The probability $p_{k,t}$ is understood as the ratio of the number of odd composite numbers of a binary length k that can be expected to pass t rounds of M-R testing (with randomly generated bases) to the sum of that value and the number of odd prime integers of binary length k. This is equivalent to assuming that candidates selected for testing will be chosen uniformly at random from the entire set of odd k-bit integers. Following Pomerance, et al., $p_{k,t}$ can be (over) estimated by the ratio of the expected number of odd composite numbers of binary length k that will pass t rounds of M-R testing (with randomly generated bases) to the total number of odd primes of binary length k. From the perspective of a party charged with the responsibility of generating a k-bit prime, the objective is to determine a value of t such that $p_{k,t}$ is no greater than an acceptably small target value p_{target}.

Using [1], it is possible to compute an upper bound for $p_{k,t}$ as a function of k and t. From this, an upper bound can be computed for t as a function of k and p_{target}, the maximum allowed probability of accidentally generating a composite number. The following is an algorithm for computing t:

1. For $t = 1, 2 \ldots \lceil -\log_2(p_{target})/2 \rceil$

    1.1 For $M = 3, 4 \ldots \lfloor 2\sqrt{k-1} - 1 \rfloor$ (1)

           1.1.1   Compute $p_{k,t}$ as in (2).

           1.1.2   If $p_{k,t} \le p_{target}$

                 1.1.2.1   Accept t.

                 1.1.2.2   Stop.

In (1), k is the bit length of the candidate primes and (2) is as follows:

$$p_{k,t} = 2.00743 \cdot \ln(2) \cdot k \cdot 2^{-k} \left[2^{k-2-Mt} + \frac{8(\pi^2 - 6)}{3} 2^{k-2} \sum_{m=3}^{M} 2^{m-(m-1)t} \sum_{j=2}^{m} \frac{1}{2^{\left(j + \frac{(k-1)}{j} \right)}} \right] . \quad (2)$$

Using this expression for t, the following methodologies are used for testing the DSA and RSA candidate primes.

F.2   Generating DSA Primes

For DSA, the maximum possible care must be taken when generating the primes p and q that are used for the domain parameters. The same primes p and q are used by many parties. This means that any weakness that these numbers may possess would affect multiple users. It also means that the primes are not generated very often; typically, an entire system uses the same set of domain parameters for an extended period of time. Therefore, in this case, some additional care is called for.

With this in mind, it may be too optimistic to simply subject candidate primes to t rounds of M-R testing, where the minimal acceptable value for t is determined according to (1) and (2) in Appendix F.1. This might be the case, for example, if there is a reason to doubt that the assumptions made in [1] have been satisfied during the process of selecting candidates for primality testing. One may gain more confidence in the process by performing some additional (different) primality test(s) on the candidates that survive the M-R testing. As another option, one could, of course, perform additional rounds of M-R testing. These considerations lead to the following alternatives: either (A) use the number of rounds of M-R testing determined according to (1) and (2) in Appendix F.1, and follow that with a single Lucas test (as recommended in ANS X9.31), or (B) use a (much) more conservative approach when determining t (e.g., as described below) and subject candidate primes to additional rounds of M-R testing.

One approach for strategy (B) would be to adopt the viewpoint of the majority of system users, who have no part in generating the (supposed) prime, but who must rely upon its primality for their security. Such parties may be concerned that the candidates for M-R testing have been selected in a fashion that deviates significantly from the uniform distribution – which was assumed when determining t according to (1) and (2) in Appendix F.1. In cases where the selection process could be unusually biased in some way, it is important to minimize the probability that a composite number will survive testing. It can be shown that for any k-bit odd composite number (regardless of how it was selected), the probability that it will pass t rounds of M-R testing with randomly chosen bases is less than 4^{-t} (although this is not a particularly tight bound). Selecting t such that $4^{-t} \leq p_{target}$ is equivalent to choosing $t \geq -\log_2(p_{target})/2$. To ensure that a composite number has a probability no greater than p_{target} of surviving the M-R tests, the number of rounds can be set at $t = \lceil -\log_2(p_{target})/2 \rceil$. Even if the method of selecting candidates were so biased that it offered nothing but composite numbers for testing, it is reasonable to expect that it would take at least $1/p_{target}$ attempts (which is greater than 4^{t}) before a composite number would slip through the t-round M-R testing process.

WARNING: As the discussion above illustrates, care must be taken when using the phrase "error probability" in connection with the recommended number of rounds of M-R testing. The probability that a composite number survives t rounds of Miller-Rabin testing is <u>not</u> the same as

118

$p_{k,t}$, which is the probability that a number surviving t rounds of Miller-Rabin testing is composite. Ordinarily, the latter probability is the one that should be of most interest to a party responsible for generating primes, while the former may be more important to a party responsible for validating the primality of a number generated by someone else. However, for sufficiently large k (e.g., $k \geq 51$), it can be shown that $p_{k,t} \leq 4^{-t}$ under the same assumptions concerning the selection of candidates as those made to obtain formula (2) in Appendix F.1 (see [1].) In such cases, $t = \lceil -\log_2(p_{target})/2 \rceil$ rounds of Miller-Rabin testing can be used both in generating and validating primes, with p_{target} serving as an upper bound on both the probability that the generation process yields a composite number and the probability that a composite number would survive an attempt to validate its primality.

Table C.1 in Appendix C.3 identifies the minimum values for t when generating the primes p and q for DSA using either strategy (A) or (B) above. To obtain the t values shown in the column titled "M-R Tests Only", the conservative strategy (B) was followed; those t values are sufficient to validate the primality of p and q. The t values shown in the column titled "M-R Tests when followed by One Lucas Test" result from following strategy (A) using computations (1) and (2) in Appendix F.1.

F.3   Generating Primes for RSA Signatures

When generating primes for the RSA signature algorithm, it is still very important to reduce the probability of errors in the M-R testing procedure. However, since the (probable) primes are used to generate a user's key pair, if a composite number survives the testing process, the consequences of the error may be less dramatic than in the case of generating DSA domain parameters; only one user's transactions are affected, rather than a domain of users. Furthermore, if the p or q value generated for some user is composite, the problem will not be undiscovered for long, since it is almost certain that signatures generated by that user will not be verifiable.

Therefore, when generating the RSA primes p and q, it is sufficient to use the number of rounds derived from (1) and (2) in Appendix F.1 as the minimum number of M-R tests to be performed. However, if the definition of $p_{k,t}$ is not considered to be sufficiently conservative when testing p and q, it is recommended that the t rounds of Miller-Rabin tests be followed by a single Lucas test.

The lengths for p and q that are recommended for use in RSA signature algorithms are 512, 1024 and 1536 bits; recall that $n = pq$, so the corresponding lengths for n are 1024, 2048 and 3072 bits, respectively. As currently specified in SP 800-57, Part 1, these lengths correspond to security strengths of 80, 112 and 128 bits, respectively. Hence, it makes sense to match the number of rounds of Miller-Rabin testing to the target error probability values of 2^{-80}, 2^{-112}, and 2^{-128}. A probability of 2^{-100} is included for all prime lengths, since this probability has often been used in the past and may be acceptable for many applications.

When generating the RSA primes p and q with conditions, it is sufficient to use the value t derived from (1) and (2) as the minimum number of M-R tests to be performed when generating

119

the auxiliary primes p_1, p_2, q_1 and q_2. It is not necessary to use an additional Lucas test on these numbers. In the extremely unlikely event that one of the numbers p_1, p_2, q_1 or q_2 is composite, there is still a high probability that the corresponding RSA prime (p or q) will satisfy the requisite conditions.

The sizes of p_1, p_2, q_1, and q_2 were chosen to ensure that, for an adversary with significant but not overwhelming resources, Lenstra's elliptic curve factoring method [2] (against which there is no protection beyond choosing large p and q) is a more effective factoring algorithm than either the Pollard P–1 method [2], the Williams P+1 method [3] or various cycling methods [2]. For an adversary with overwhelming resources, the best all-purpose factoring algorithm is assumed to be the General Number Field Sieve [2].

Tables C.2 and C.3 in Appendix C.3 specify the minimum number of rounds of M-R testing when generating primes to be used in the construction of RSA signature key pairs.

Appendix G: References

[1] I. Damgard, P. Landrock, and C. Pomerance, C. "Average Case Error Estimates for the Strong Probable Prime Test," Mathematics of Computation, v. 61, No, 203, pp. 177-194, 1993.

[2] A.J Menezes, P.C. Oorschot, and S.A. Vanstone. Handbook of Applied Cryptography. CRC Press, 1996.

[3] H.C. Williams. "A p+1 Method of factoring". *Math. Comp.* 39, 225-234, 1982.

[4] D.E. Knuth, The Art of Computer Programming, Vol. 2, 3rd Ed., Addison-Wesley, 1998, Algorithm P, page 395.

[5] R. Baillie and S.S. Wagstaff Jr., Mathematics of Computation, V. 35 (1980), pages 1391 – 1417.

FIPS PUB 199

FEDERAL INFORMATION PROCESSING STANDARDS PUBLICATION

Standards for Security Categorization of Federal Information and Information Systems

Computer Security Division
Information Technology Laboratory
National Institute of Standards and Technology
Gaithersburg, MD 20899-8900

February 2004

U.S. DEPARTMENT OF COMMERCE
Donald L. Evans, Secretary

TECHNOLOGY ADMINISTRATION
Phillip J. Bond, Under Secretary for Technology

NATIONAL INSTITUTE OF STANDARDS AND TECHNOLOGY
Arden L. Bement, Jr., Director

FOREWORD

The Federal Information Processing Standards Publication Series of the National Institute of Standards and Technology (NIST) is the official series of publications relating to standards and guidelines adopted and promulgated under the provisions of Section 5131 of the Information Technology Management Reform Act of 1996 (Public Law 104-106) and the Federal Information Security Management Act of 2002 (Public Law 107-347). These mandates have given the Secretary of Commerce and NIST important responsibilities for improving the utilization and management of computer and related telecommunications systems in the federal government. The NIST, through its Information Technology Laboratory, provides leadership, technical guidance, and coordination of government efforts in the development of standards and guidelines in these areas.

Comments concerning Federal Information Processing Standards Publications are welcomed and should be addressed to the Director, Information Technology Laboratory, National Institute of Standards and Technology, 100 Bureau Drive, Stop 8900, Gaithersburg, MD 20899-8900.

-- SUSAN ZEVIN, ACTING DIRECTOR
INFORMATION TECHNOLOGY LABORATORY

AUTHORITY

Federal Information Processing Standards Publications (FIPS PUBS) are issued by the National Institute of Standards and Technology (NIST) after approval by the Secretary of Commerce pursuant to Section 5131 of the Information Technology Management Reform Act of 1996 (Public Law 104-106) and the Federal Information Security Management Act of 2002 (Public Law 107-347).

TABLE OF CONTENTS

1   PURPOSE

The E-Government Act of 2002 (Public Law 107-347), passed by the one hundred and seventh Congress and signed into law by the President in December 2002, recognized the importance of information security to the economic and national security interests of the United States. Title III of the E-Government Act, entitled the Federal Information Security Management Act of 2002 (FISMA), tasked NIST with responsibilities for standards and guidelines, including the development of:

- Standards to be used by all federal agencies to categorize all information and information systems collected or maintained by or on behalf of each agency based on the objectives of providing appropriate levels of information security according to a range of risk levels;

- Guidelines recommending the types of information and information systems to be included in each category; and

- Minimum information security requirements (i.e., management, operational, and technical controls), for information and information systems in each such category.

FIPS Publication 199 addresses the first task cited—to develop standards for categorizing information and information systems. Security categorization standards for information and information systems provide a common framework and understanding for expressing security that, for the federal government, promotes: (i) effective management and oversight of information security programs, including the coordination of information security efforts throughout the civilian, national security, emergency preparedness, homeland security, and law enforcement communities; and (ii) consistent reporting to the Office of Management and Budget (OMB) and Congress on the adequacy and effectiveness of information security policies, procedures, and practices. Subsequent NIST standards and guidelines will address the second and third tasks cited.

2   APPLICABILITY

These standards shall apply to: (i) all information within the federal government other than that information that has been determined pursuant to Executive Order 12958, as amended by Executive Order 13292, or any predecessor order, or by the Atomic Energy Act of 1954, as amended, to require protection against unauthorized disclosure and is marked to indicate its classified status; and (ii) all federal information systems other than those information systems designated as national security systems as defined in 44 United States Code Section 3542(b)(2). Agency officials shall use the security categorizations described in FIPS Publication 199 whenever there is a federal requirement to provide such a categorization of information or information systems. Additional security designators may be developed and used at agency discretion. State, local, and tribal governments as well as private sector organizations comprising the critical infrastructure of the United States may consider the use of these standards as appropriate. These standards are effective upon approval by the Secretary of Commerce.

3   CATEGORIZATION OF INFORMATION AND INFORMATION SYSTEMS

This publication establishes security categories for both information[1] and information systems. The security categories are based on the potential impact on an organization should certain events occur which jeopardize the information and information systems needed by the organization to accomplish its assigned mission, protect its assets, fulfill its legal responsibilities, maintain its day-to-day functions, and protect individuals. Security categories are to be used in conjunction with vulnerability and threat information in assessing the risk to an organization.

---

[1] Information is categorized according to its *information type*. An information type is a specific category of information (e.g., privacy, medical, proprietary, financial, investigative, contractor sensitive, security management) defined by an organization or, in some instances, by a specific law, Executive Order, directive, policy, or regulation.

Security Objectives

The FISMA defines three security objectives for information and information systems:

CONFIDENTIALITY

"Preserving authorized restrictions on information access and disclosure, including means for protecting personal privacy and proprietary information…" [44 U.S.C., Sec. 3542]

A loss of *confidentiality* is the unauthorized disclosure of information.

INTEGRITY

"Guarding against improper information modification or destruction, and includes ensuring information non-repudiation and authenticity…" [44 U.S.C., Sec. 3542]

A loss of *integrity* is the unauthorized modification or destruction of information.

AVAILABILITY

"Ensuring timely and reliable access to and use of information…" [44 U.S.C., SEC. 3542]

A loss of *availability* is the disruption of access to or use of information or an information system.

Potential Impact on Organizations and Individuals

FIPS Publication 199 defines three levels of *potential impact* on organizations or individuals should there be a breach of security (i.e., a loss of confidentiality, integrity, or availability). The application of these definitions must take place within the context of each organization and the overall national interest.

The *potential impact* is LOW if—

– The loss of confidentiality, integrity, or availability could be expected to have a **limited** adverse effect on organizational operations, organizational assets, or individuals.[2]

AMPLIFICATION: A limited adverse effect means that, for example, the loss of confidentiality, integrity, or availability might: (i) cause a degradation in mission capability to an extent and duration that the organization is able to perform its primary functions, but the effectiveness of the functions is noticeably reduced; (ii) result in minor damage to organizational assets; (iii) result in minor financial loss; or (iv) result in minor harm to individuals.

The *potential impact* is MODERATE if—

– The loss of confidentiality, integrity, or availability could be expected to have a **serious** adverse effect on organizational operations, organizational assets, or individuals.

AMPLIFICATION: A serious adverse effect means that, for example, the loss of confidentiality, integrity, or availability might: (i) cause a significant degradation in mission capability to an extent and duration that the organization is able to perform its primary functions, but the effectiveness of the functions is significantly reduced; (ii) result in significant damage to organizational assets; (iii) result in significant financial loss; or (iv) result in significant harm to individuals that does not involve loss of life or serious life threatening injuries.

---

[2] Adverse effects on individuals may include, but are not limited to, loss of the privacy to which individuals are entitled under law.

The *potential impact* is **HIGH** if—

− The loss of confidentiality, integrity, or availability could be expected to have a **severe or catastrophic** adverse effect on organizational operations, organizational assets, or individuals.

AMPLIFICATION: A severe or catastrophic adverse effect means that, for example, the loss of confidentiality, integrity, or availability might: (i) cause a severe degradation in or loss of mission capability to an extent and duration that the organization is not able to perform one or more of its primary functions; (ii) result in major damage to organizational assets; (iii) result in major financial loss; or (iv) result in severe or catastrophic harm to individuals involving loss of life or serious life threatening injuries.

Security Categorization Applied to Information Types

The security category of an information type can be associated with both user information and system information[3] and can be applicable to information in either electronic or non-electronic form. It can also be used as input in considering the appropriate security category of an information system (see description of security categories for information systems below). Establishing an appropriate security category of an information type essentially requires determining the *potential impact* for each security objective associated with the particular information type.

The generalized format for expressing the security category, SC, of an information type is:

SC information type = {(**confidentiality**, *impact*), (**integrity**, *impact*), (**availability**, *impact*)},

where the acceptable values for potential impact are LOW, MODERATE, HIGH, or NOT APPLICABLE.[4]

EXAMPLE 1: An organization managing *public information* on its web server determines that there is no potential impact from a loss of confidentiality (i.e., confidentiality requirements are not applicable), a moderate potential impact from a loss of integrity, and a moderate potential impact from a loss of availability. The resulting security category, SC, of this information type is expressed as:

SC public information = {(**confidentiality**, NA), (**integrity**, MODERATE), (**availability**, MODERATE)}.

EXAMPLE 2: A law enforcement organization managing extremely sensitive *investigative information* determines that the potential impact from a loss of confidentiality is high, the potential impact from a loss of integrity is moderate, and the potential impact from a loss of availability is moderate. The resulting security category, SC, of this information type is expressed as:

SC investigative information = {(**confidentiality**, HIGH), (**integrity**, MODERATE), (**availability**, MODERATE)}.

EXAMPLE 3: A financial organization managing routine *administrative information* (not privacy-related information) determines that the potential impact from a loss of confidentiality is low, the potential impact from a loss of integrity is low, and the potential impact from a loss of availability is low. The resulting security category, SC, of this information type is expressed as:

SC administrative information = {(**confidentiality**, LOW), (**integrity**, LOW), (**availability**, LOW)}.

---

[3] System information (e.g., network routing tables, password files, and cryptographic key management information) must be protected at a level commensurate with the most critical or sensitive user information being processed, stored, or transmitted by the information system to ensure confidentiality, integrity, and availability.

[4] The potential impact value of *not applicable* only applies to the security objective of confidentiality.

Security Categorization Applied to Information Systems

Determining the security category of an information system requires slightly more analysis and must consider the security categories of all information types resident on the information system. For an information system, the potential impact values assigned to the respective security objectives (confidentiality, integrity, availability) shall be the highest values (i.e., high water mark) from among those security categories that have been determined for each type of information resident on the information system.[5]

The generalized format for expressing the security category, SC, of an information system is:

SC information system = {(**confidentiality**, *impact*), (**integrity**, *impact*), (**availability**, *impact*)},

where the acceptable values for potential impact are LOW, MODERATE, or HIGH.

Note that the value of *not applicable* cannot be assigned to any security objective in the context of establishing a security category for an information system. This is in recognition that there is a low minimum potential impact (i.e., low water mark) on the loss of confidentiality, integrity, and availability for an information system due to the fundamental requirement to protect the system-level processing functions and information critical to the operation of the information system.

EXAMPLE 4: An information system used for large acquisitions in a contracting organization contains both sensitive, pre-solicitation phase contract information and routine administrative information. The management within the contracting organization determines that: (i) for the sensitive contract information, the potential impact from a loss of confidentiality is moderate, the potential impact from a loss of integrity is moderate, and the potential impact from a loss of availability is low; and (ii) for the routine administrative information (non-privacy-related information), the potential impact from a loss of confidentiality is low, the potential impact from a loss of integrity is low, and the potential impact from a loss of availability is low. The resulting security categories, SC, of these information types are expressed as:

SC contract information = {(**confidentiality**, MODERATE), (**integrity**, MODERATE), (**availability**, LOW)},

and

SC administrative information = {(**confidentiality**, LOW), (**integrity**, LOW), (**availability**, LOW)}.

The resulting security category of the information system is expressed as:

SC acquisition system = {(**confidentiality**, MODERATE), (**integrity**, MODERATE), (**availability**, LOW)},

representing the high water mark or maximum potential impact values for each security objective from the information types resident on the acquisition system.

---

[5] It is recognized that information systems are composed of both programs and information. Programs in execution within an information system (i.e., system processes) facilitate the processing, storage, and transmission of information and are necessary for the organization to conduct its essential mission-related functions and operations. These system processing functions also require protection and could be subject to security categorization as well. However, in the interest of simplification, it is assumed that the security categorization of all information types associated with the information system provide an appropriate *worst case* potential impact for the overall information system—thereby obviating the need to consider the system processes in the security categorization of the information system.

EXAMPLE 5: A power plant contains a SCADA (supervisory control and data acquisition) system controlling the distribution of electric power for a large military installation. The SCADA system contains both real-time sensor data and routine administrative information. The management at the power plant determines that: (i) for the sensor data being acquired by the SCADA system, there is no potential impact from a loss of confidentiality, a high potential impact from a loss of integrity, and a high potential impact from a loss of availability; and (ii) for the administrative information being processed by the system, there is a low potential impact from a loss of confidentiality, a low potential impact from a loss of integrity, and a low potential impact from a loss of availability. The resulting security categories, SC, of these information types are expressed as:

$$SC \text{ sensor data} = \{(\textbf{confidentiality}, \text{NA}), (\textbf{integrity}, \text{HIGH}), (\textbf{availability}, \text{HIGH})\},$$

and

$$SC \text{ administrative information} = \{(\textbf{confidentiality}, \text{LOW}), (\textbf{integrity}, \text{LOW}), (\textbf{availability}, \text{LOW})\}.$$

The resulting security category of the information system is initially expressed as:

$$SC \text{ SCADA system} = \{(\textbf{confidentiality}, \text{LOW}), (\textbf{integrity}, \text{HIGH}), (\textbf{availability}, \text{HIGH})\},$$

representing the high water mark or maximum potential impact values for each security objective from the information types resident on the SCADA system. The management at the power plant chooses to increase the potential impact from a loss of confidentiality from low to moderate reflecting a more realistic view of the potential impact on the information system should there be a security breach due to the unauthorized disclosure of system-level information or processing functions. The final security category of the information system is expressed as:

$$SC \text{ SCADA system} = \{(\textbf{confidentiality}, \text{MODERATE}), (\textbf{integrity}, \text{HIGH}), (\textbf{availability}, \text{HIGH})\}.$$

5

Table 1 summarizes the potential impact definitions for each security objective—confidentiality, integrity, and availability.

	POTENTIAL IMPACT		
Security Objective	**LOW**	**MODERATE**	**HIGH**
Confidentiality Preserving authorized restrictions on information access and disclosure, including means for protecting personal privacy and proprietary information. [44 U.S.C., SEC. 3542]	The unauthorized disclosure of information could be expected to have a **limited** adverse effect on organizational operations, organizational assets, or individuals.	The unauthorized disclosure of information could be expected to have a **serious** adverse effect on organizational operations, organizational assets, or individuals.	The unauthorized disclosure of information could be expected to have a **severe or catastrophic** adverse effect on organizational operations, organizational assets, or individuals.
Integrity Guarding against improper information modification or destruction, and includes ensuring information non-repudiation and authenticity. [44 U.S.C., SEC. 3542]	The unauthorized modification or destruction of information could be expected to have a **limited** adverse effect on organizational operations, organizational assets, or individuals.	The unauthorized modification or destruction of information could be expected to have a **serious** adverse effect on organizational operations, organizational assets, or individuals.	The unauthorized modification or destruction of information could be expected to have a **severe or catastrophic** adverse effect on organizational operations, organizational assets, or individuals.
Availability Ensuring timely and reliable access to and use of information. [44 U.S.C., SEC. 3542]	The disruption of access to or use of information or an information system could be expected to have a **limited** adverse effect on organizational operations, organizational assets, or individuals.	The disruption of access to or use of information or an information system could be expected to have a **serious** adverse effect on organizational operations, organizational assets, or individuals.	The disruption of access to or use of information or an information system could be expected to have a **severe or catastrophic** adverse effect on organizational operations, organizational assets, or individuals.

TABLE 1: POTENTIAL IMPACT DEFINITIONS FOR SECURITY OBJECTIVES

APPENDIX A   TERMS AND DEFINITIONS

AVAILABILITY: Ensuring timely and reliable access to and use of information. [44 U.S.C., SEC. 3542]

CONFIDENTIALITY: Preserving authorized restrictions on information access and disclosure, including means for protecting personal privacy and proprietary information. [44 U.S.C., SEC. 3542]

EXECUTIVE AGENCY: An executive department specified in 5 U.S.C., SEC. 101; a military department specified in 5 U.S.C., SEC. 102; an independent establishment as defined in 5 U.S.C., SEC. 104(1); and a wholly owned Government corporation fully subject to the provisions of 31 U.S.C., CHAPTER 91. [41 U.S.C., SEC. 403]

FEDERAL INFORMATION SYSTEM: An information system used or operated by an executive agency, by a contractor of an executive agency, or by another organization on behalf of an executive agency. [40 U.S.C., SEC. 11331]

INFORMATION: An instance of an information type.

INFORMATION RESOURCES: Information and related resources, such as personnel, equipment, funds, and information technology. [44 U.S.C., SEC. 3502]

INFORMATION SECURITY: The protection of information and information systems from unauthorized access, use, disclosure, disruption, modification, or destruction in order to provide confidentiality, integrity, and availability. [44 U.S.C., SEC. 3542]

INFORMATION SYSTEM: A discrete set of information resources organized for the collection, processing, maintenance, use, sharing, dissemination, or disposition of information. [44 U.S.C., SEC. 3502]

INFORMATION TECHNOLOGY: Any equipment or interconnected system or subsystem of equipment that is used in the automatic acquisition, storage, manipulation, management, movement, control, display, switching, interchange, transmission, or reception of data or information by the executive agency. For purposes of the preceding sentence, equipment is used by an executive agency if the equipment is used by the executive agency directly or is used by a contractor under a contract with the executive agency which: (i) requires the use of such equipment; or (ii) requires the use, to a significant extent, of such equipment in the performance of a service or the furnishing of a product. The term information technology includes computers, ancillary equipment, software, firmware and similar procedures, services (including support services), and related resources. [40 U.S.C., SEC. 1401]

INFORMATION TYPE: A specific category of information (e.g., privacy, medical, proprietary, financial, investigative, contractor sensitive, security management), defined by an organization, or in some instances, by a specific law, Executive Order, directive, policy, or regulation.

INTEGRITY: Guarding against improper information modification or destruction, and includes ensuring information non-repudiation and authenticity. [44 U.S.C., SEC. 3542]

NATIONAL SECURITY SYSTEM: Any information system (including any telecommunications system) used or operated by an agency or by a contractor of an agency, or other organization on behalf of an agency— (i) the function, operation, or use of which involves intelligence activities; involves cryptologic activities related to national security; involves command and control of military forces; involves equipment that is an integral part of a weapon or weapons system; or is critical to the direct fulfillment of military or intelligence missions (excluding a system that is to be used for routine administrative and business applications, for example, payroll, finance, logistics, and personnel management applications); or, (ii) is protected at all times by procedures established for information that have been specifically authorized under criteria established by an Executive Order or an Act of Congress to be kept classified in the interest of national defense or foreign policy. [44 U.S.C., SEC. 3542]

SECURITY CATEGORY: The characterization of information or an information system based on an assessment of the potential impact that a loss of confidentiality, integrity, or availability of such information or information system would have on organizational operations, organizational assets, or individuals.

SECURITY CONTROLS: The management, operational, and technical controls (i.e., safeguards or countermeasures) prescribed for an information system to protect the confidentiality, integrity, and availability of the system and its information.

SECURITY OBJECTIVE: Confidentiality, integrity, or availability.

APPENDIX B   REFERENCES

[1]   Privacy Act of 1974 (Public Law 93-579), September 1975.

[2]   Paperwork Reduction Act of 1995 (Public Law 104-13), May 1995.

[3]   OMB Circular A-130, Transmittal Memorandum #4, *Management of Federal Information Resources*, November 2000.

[4]   Information Technology Management Reform Act of 1996 (Public Law 104-106), August 1996.

[5]   Federal Information Security Management Act of 2002 (Public Law 107-347), December 2002.

FIPS PUB 200

FEDERAL INFORMATION PROCESSING STANDARDS PUBLICATION

Minimum Security Requirements for Federal Information and Information Systems

---

Computer Security Division
Information Technology Laboratory
National Institute of Standards and Technology
Gaithersburg, MD 20899-8930

March 2006

U.S. DEPARTMENT OF COMMERCE
Carlos M. Gutierrez, Secretary

NATIONAL INSTITUTE OF STANDARDS AND TECHNOLOGY
William Jeffrey, Director

FOREWORD

The Federal Information Processing Standards (FIPS) Publication Series of the National Institute of Standards and Technology (NIST) is the official series of publications relating to standards and guidelines adopted and promulgated under the provisions of the Federal Information Security Management Act (FISMA) of 2002. Comments concerning FIPS publications are welcomed and should be addressed to the Director, Information Technology Laboratory, National Institute of Standards and Technology, 100 Bureau Drive, Stop 8900, Gaithersburg, MD 20899-8900.

-- CITA M. FURLANI, ACTING DIRECTOR
INFORMATION TECHNOLOGY LABORATORY

AUTHORITY

Federal Information Processing Standards Publications (FIPS PUBS) are issued by the National Institute of Standards and Technology after approval by the Secretary of Commerce pursuant to Section 5131 of the Information Technology Management Reform Act of 1996 (Public Law 104-106) and the Federal Information Security Management Act of 2002 (Public Law 107-347).

Federal Information Processing Standards 200
March 9, 2006

Announcing the Standard for
Minimum Security Requirements for
Federal Information and Information Systems

Federal Information Processing Standards Publications (FIPS PUBS) are issued by the National Institute of Standards and Technology (NIST) after approval by the Secretary of Commerce pursuant to the Federal Information Security Management Act (FISMA) of 2002.

1. Name of Standard.

FIPS Publication 200: *Minimum Security Requirements for Federal Information and Information Systems*.

2. Category of Standard.

Information Security.

3. Explanation.

The E-Government Act (P.L. 107-347), passed by the one hundred and seventh Congress and signed into law by the President in December 2002, recognized the importance of information security to the economic and national security interests of the United States. Title III of the E-Government Act, entitled the Federal Information Security Management Act (FISMA), emphasizes the need for each federal agency to develop, document, and implement an enterprise-wide program to provide information security for the information and information systems that support the operations and assets of the agency including those provided or managed by another agency, contractor, or other source. FISMA directed the promulgation of federal standards for: (i) the security categorization of federal information and information systems based on the objectives of providing appropriate levels of information security according to a range of risk levels; and (ii) minimum security requirements for information and information systems in each such category. This standard addresses the specification of minimum security requirements for federal information and information systems.

4. Approving Authority.

Secretary of Commerce.

5. Maintenance Agency.

Department of Commerce, NIST, Information Technology Laboratory.

6. Applicability.

This standard is applicable to: (i) all information within the federal government other than that information that has been determined pursuant to Executive Order 12958, as amended by Executive Order 13292, or any predecessor order, or by the Atomic Energy Act of 1954, as amended, to require protection against unauthorized disclosure and is marked to indicate its classified status; and (ii) all federal information systems other than those information systems designated as national security systems as defined in 44 United States Code Section 3542(b)(2). The standard has been broadly developed from a technical perspective to complement similar standards for national security systems. In addition to the agencies of the federal government, state, local, and tribal governments, and private sector organizations that compose the critical infrastructure of the United States are encouraged to consider the use of this standard, as appropriate.

7. Specifications.

FIPS Publication 200, *Minimum Security Requirements for Federal Information and Information Systems*.

8. Implementations.

This standard specifies minimum security requirements for federal information and information systems in seventeen security-related areas. Federal agencies must meet the minimum security requirements as defined herein through the use of the security controls in accordance with NIST Special Publication 800-53, *Recommended Security Controls for Federal Information Systems*, as amended.

9. Effective Date.

This standard is effective immediately. Federal agencies must be in compliance with this standard not later than one year from its effective date.

10. Qualifications.

The application of the security controls defined in NIST Special Publication 800-53 required by this standard represents the current state-of-the-practice safeguards and countermeasures for information systems. The security controls will be reviewed by NIST at least annually and, if necessary, revised and extended to reflect: (i) the experience gained from using the controls; (ii) the changing security requirements within federal agencies; and (iii) the new security technologies that may be available. The minimum security controls defined in the low, moderate, and high security control baselines are also expected to change over time as well, as the level of security and due diligence for mitigating risks within federal agencies increases. The proposed additions, deletions, or modifications to the catalog of security controls and the proposed changes to the security control baselines in NIST Special Publication 800-53 will go through a rigorous, public review process to obtain government and private sector feedback and to build consensus for the changes. Federal agencies will have up to one year from the date of final publication to fully comply with the changes but are encouraged to initiate compliance activities immediately.

11. Waivers.

No provision is provided under FISMA for waivers to FIPS made mandatory by the Secretary of Commerce.

12. Where to Obtain Copies.

This publication is available from the NIST Computer Security Division web site by accessing http://csrc.nist.gov/publications.

TABLE OF CONTENTS

1 PURPOSE

The E-Government Act of 2002 (Public Law 107-347), passed by the one hundred and seventh Congress and signed into law by the President in December 2002, recognized the importance of information security to the economic and national security interests of the United States. Title III of the E-Government Act, entitled the Federal Information Security Management Act (FISMA) of 2002, tasked NIST with the responsibility of developing security standards and guidelines for the federal government including the development of:

- Standards for categorizing information and information systems[1] collected or maintained by or on behalf of each federal agency based on the objectives of providing appropriate levels of information security according to a range of risk levels;

- Guidelines recommending the types of information and information systems to be included in each category; and

- Minimum information security requirements for information and information systems in each such category.

FIPS Publication 199, *Standards for Security Categorization of Federal Information and Information Systems*, approved by the Secretary of Commerce in February 2004, is the first of two mandatory security standards required by the FISMA legislation.[2] FIPS Publication 200, the second of the mandatory security standards, specifies minimum security requirements for information and information systems supporting the executive agencies of the federal government and a risk-based process for selecting the security controls necessary to satisfy the minimum security requirements. This standard will promote the development, implementation, and operation of more secure information systems within the federal government by establishing minimum levels of due diligence for information security and facilitating a more consistent, comparable, and repeatable approach for selecting and specifying security controls for information systems that meet minimum security requirements.

2 INFORMATION SYSTEM IMPACT LEVELS

FIPS Publication 199 requires agencies to categorize their information systems as low-impact, moderate-impact, or high-impact for the security objectives of confidentiality, integrity, and availability. The potential impact values assigned to the respective security objectives are the highest values (i.e., high water mark[3]) from among the security categories that have been determined for each type of information resident on those information systems.[4] The generalized format for expressing the security category (SC) of an information system is:

$$\text{SC}_{\text{information system}} = \{(\textbf{confidentiality}, \textit{impact}), (\textbf{integrity}, \textit{impact}), (\textbf{availability}, \textit{impact})\},$$

where the acceptable values for potential impact are low, moderate, or high.

---

[1] An *information system* is a discrete set of information resources organized for the collection, processing, maintenance, use, sharing, dissemination, or disposition of information. Information resources include information and related resources, such as personnel, equipment, funds, and information technology.

[2] NIST security standards and guidelines referenced in this publication are available at http://csrc.nist.gov.

[3] The *high water mark* concept is employed because there are significant dependencies among the security objectives of confidentiality, integrity, and availability. In most cases, a compromise in one security objective ultimately affects the other security objectives as well.

[4] NIST Special Publication 800-60, *Guide for Mapping Types of Information and Information Systems to Security Categories*, provides implementation guidance on the assignment of security categories to information and information systems.

Since the potential impact values for confidentiality, integrity, and availability may not always be the same for a particular information system, the high water mark concept must be used to determine the overall impact level of the information system. Thus, a *low-impact system* is an information system in which all three of the security objectives are low. A *moderate-impact system* is an information system in which at least one of the security objectives is moderate and no security objective is greater than moderate. And finally, a *high-impact system* is an information system in which at least one security objective is high. The determination of information system impact levels must be accomplished prior to the consideration of minimum security requirements and the selection of appropriate security controls for those information systems.

3   MINIMUM SECURITY REQUIREMENTS

The minimum security requirements cover seventeen security-related areas with regard to protecting the confidentiality, integrity, and availability of federal information systems and the information processed, stored, and transmitted by those systems. The security-related areas include: (i) access control; (ii) awareness and training; (iii) audit and accountability; (iv) certification, accreditation, and security assessments; (v) configuration management; (vi) contingency planning; (vii) identification and authentication; (viii) incident response; (ix) maintenance; (x) media protection; (xi) physical and environmental protection; (xii) planning; (xiii) personnel security; (xiv) risk assessment; (xv) systems and services acquisition; (xvi) system and communications protection; and (xvii) system and information integrity. The seventeen areas represent a broad-based, balanced information security program that addresses the management, operational, and technical aspects of protecting federal information and information systems.

Policies and procedures play an important role in the effective implementation of enterprise-wide information security programs within the federal government and the success of the resulting security measures employed to protect federal information and information systems. Thus, organizations must develop and promulgate formal, documented policies and procedures governing the minimum security requirements set forth in this standard and must ensure their effective implementation.

Specifications for Minimum Security Requirements

Access Control (AC): Organizations must limit information system access to authorized users, processes acting on behalf of authorized users, or devices (including other information systems) and to the types of transactions and functions that authorized users are permitted to exercise.

Awareness and Training (AT): Organizations must: (i) ensure that managers and users of organizational information systems are made aware of the security risks associated with their activities and of the applicable laws, Executive Orders, directives, policies, standards, instructions, regulations, or procedures related to the security of organizational information systems; and (ii) ensure that organizational personnel are adequately trained to carry out their assigned information security-related duties and responsibilities.

Audit and Accountability (AU): Organizations must: (i) create, protect, and retain information system audit records to the extent needed to enable the monitoring, analysis, investigation, and reporting of unlawful, unauthorized, or inappropriate information system activity; and (ii) ensure that the actions of individual information system users can be uniquely traced to those users so they can be held accountable for their actions.

Certification, Accreditation, and Security Assessments (CA): Organizations must: (i) periodically assess the security controls in organizational information systems to determine if the controls are effective in their application; (ii) develop and implement plans of action designed to correct deficiencies and reduce or eliminate vulnerabilities in organizational information systems; (iii) authorize the operation of organizational information systems and any associated information system connections; and (iv) monitor information system security controls on an ongoing basis to ensure the continued effectiveness of the controls.

Configuration Management (CM): Organizations must: (i) establish and maintain baseline configurations and inventories of organizational information systems (including hardware, software, firmware, and documentation) throughout the respective system development life cycles; and (ii) establish and enforce security configuration settings for information technology products employed in organizational information systems.

Contingency Planning (CP): Organizations must establish, maintain, and effectively implement plans for emergency response, backup operations, and post-disaster recovery for organizational information systems to ensure the availability of critical information resources and continuity of operations in emergency situations.

Identification and Authentication (IA): Organizations must identify information system users, processes acting on behalf of users, or devices and authenticate (or verify) the identities of those users, processes, or devices, as a prerequisite to allowing access to organizational information systems.

Incident Response (IR): Organizations must: (i) establish an operational incident handling capability for organizational information systems that includes adequate preparation, detection, analysis, containment, recovery, and user response activities; and (ii) track, document, and report incidents to appropriate organizational officials and/or authorities.

Maintenance (MA): Organizations must: (i) perform periodic and timely maintenance on organizational information systems; and (ii) provide effective controls on the tools, techniques, mechanisms, and personnel used to conduct information system maintenance.

Media Protection (MP): Organizations must: (i) protect information system media, both paper and digital; (ii) limit access to information on information system media to authorized users; and (iii) sanitize or destroy information system media before disposal or release for reuse.

Physical and Environmental Protection (PE): Organizations must: (i) limit physical access to information systems, equipment, and the respective operating environments to authorized individuals; (ii) protect the physical plant and support infrastructure for information systems; (iii) provide supporting utilities for information systems; (iv) protect information systems against environmental hazards; and (v) provide appropriate environmental controls in facilities containing information systems.

Planning (PL): Organizations must develop, document, periodically update, and implement security plans for organizational information systems that describe the security controls in place or planned for the information systems and the rules of behavior for individuals accessing the information systems.

Personnel Security (PS): Organizations must: (i) ensure that individuals occupying positions of responsibility within organizations (including third-party service providers) are trustworthy and meet established security criteria for those positions; (ii) ensure that organizational information and information systems are protected during and after personnel actions such as terminations and transfers; and (iii) employ formal sanctions for personnel failing to comply with organizational security policies and procedures.

Risk Assessment (RA): Organizations must periodically assess the risk to organizational operations (including mission, functions, image, or reputation), organizational assets, and individuals, resulting from the operation of organizational information systems and the associated processing, storage, or transmission of organizational information.

System and Services Acquisition (SA): Organizations must: (i) allocate sufficient resources to adequately protect organizational information systems; (ii) employ system development life cycle processes that incorporate information security considerations; (iii) employ software usage and installation restrictions; and (iv) ensure that third-party providers employ adequate security measures to protect information, applications, and/or services outsourced from the organization.

System and Communications Protection (SC): Organizations must: (i) monitor, control, and protect organizational communications (i.e., information transmitted or received by organizational information systems) at the external boundaries and key internal boundaries of the information systems; and (ii) employ architectural designs, software development techniques, and systems engineering principles that promote effective information security within organizational information systems.

System and Information Integrity (SI): Organizations must: (i) identify, report, and correct information and information system flaws in a timely manner; (ii) provide protection from malicious code at appropriate locations within organizational information systems; and (iii) monitor information system security alerts and advisories and take appropriate actions in response.

4   SECURITY CONTROL SELECTION

Organizations must meet the minimum security requirements in this standard by selecting the appropriate security controls and assurance requirements as described in NIST Special Publication 800-53, *Recommended Security Controls for Federal Information Systems*.[5] The process of selecting the appropriate security controls and assurance requirements for organizational information systems to achieve *adequate security*[6] is a multifaceted, risk-based activity involving management and operational personnel within the organization. Security categorization of federal information and information systems, as required by FIPS Publication 199, is the first step in the risk management process.[7] Subsequent to the security categorization process, organizations must select an appropriate set of security controls for their information systems that satisfy the minimum security requirements set forth in this standard. The selected set of security controls must include one of three, appropriately tailored[8] security control baselines from NIST Special Publication 800-53 that are associated with the designated impact levels of the organizational information systems as determined during the security categorization process.

- For *low-impact* information systems, organizations must, as a minimum, employ appropriately tailored security controls from the low baseline of security controls defined in NIST Special Publication 800-53 and must ensure that the minimum assurance requirements associated with the low baseline are satisfied.

- For *moderate-impact* information systems, organizations must, as a minimum, employ appropriately tailored security controls from the moderate baseline of security controls defined in NIST Special Publication 800-53 and must ensure that the minimum assurance requirements associated with the moderate baseline are satisfied.

- For *high-impact* information systems, organizations must, as a minimum, employ appropriately tailored security controls from the high baseline of security controls defined in NIST Special Publication 800-53 and must ensure that the minimum assurance requirements associated with the high baseline are satisfied.

Organizations must employ all security controls in the respective security control baselines unless specific exceptions are allowed based on the tailoring guidance provided in NIST Special Publication 800-53.

---

[5] Organizations must use the most current version of NIST Special Publication 800-53, as amended, for the security control selection process.

[6] The Office of Management and Budget (OMB) Circular A-130, Appendix III, defines *adequate security* as security commensurate with the risk and the magnitude of harm resulting from the loss, misuse, or unauthorized access to or modification of information.

[7] Security categorization must be accomplished as an enterprise-wide activity with the involvement of senior-level organizational officials including, but not limited to, chief information officers, senior agency information security officers, authorizing officials (a.k.a. accreditation authorities), information system owners, and information owners.

[8] Tailoring guidance for security control baselines is provided in NIST Special Publication 800-53.

To ensure a cost-effective, risk-based approach to achieving adequate security across the organization, security control baseline tailoring activities must be coordinated with and approved by appropriate organizational officials (e.g., chief information officers, senior agency information security officers, authorizing officials, or authorizing officials designated representatives). The resulting set of security controls must be documented in the security plan for the information system.

APPENDIX A   TERMS AND DEFINITIONS

ACCREDITATION: The official management decision given by a senior agency official to authorize operation of an information system and to explicitly accept the risk to agency operations (including mission, functions, image, or reputation), agency assets, or individuals, based on the implementation of an agreed-upon set of security controls.

ADEQUATE SECURITY: Security commensurate with the risk and the magnitude of harm resulting from the loss, misuse, or unauthorized access to or modification of information. [OMB Circular A-130, Appendix III]

AGENCY: Any executive department, military department, government corporation, government controlled corporation, or other establishment in the executive branch of the government (including the Executive Office of the President), or any independent regulatory agency, but does not include: (i) the Government Accountability Office; (ii) the Federal Election Commission; (iii) the governments of the District of Columbia and of the territories and possessions of the United States, and their various subdivisions; or (iv) government-owned contractor-operated facilities, including laboratories engaged in national defense research and production activities. [44 U.S.C., SEC. 3502]

AUTHENTICATION: Verifying the identity of a user, process, or device, often as a prerequisite to allowing access to resources in an information system.

AUTHORIZING OFFICIAL: Official with the authority to formally assume responsibility for operating an information system at an acceptable level of risk to agency operations (including mission, functions, image, or reputation), agency assets, or individuals. *Synonymous with Accreditation Authority.*

AVAILABILITY: Ensuring timely and reliable access to and use of information. [44 U.S.C., SEC. 3542]

CERTIFICATION: A comprehensive assessment of the management, operational, and technical security controls in an information system, made in support of security accreditation, to determine the extent to which the controls are implemented correctly, operating as intended, and producing the desired outcome with respect to meeting the security requirements for the system.

CHIEF INFORMATION OFFICER: Agency official responsible for: (i) providing advice and other assistance to the head of the executive agency and other senior management personnel of the agency to ensure that information technology is acquired and information resources are managed in a manner that is consistent with laws, Executive Orders, directives, policies, regulations, and priorities established by the head of the agency; (ii) developing, maintaining, and facilitating the implementation of a sound and integrated information technology architecture for the agency; and (iii) promoting the effective and efficient design and operation of all major information resources management processes for the agency, including improvements to work processes of the agency. [44 U.S.C., Sec. 5125(b)]

CHIEF INFORMATION SECURITY OFFICER: See Senior Agency Information Security Officer.

CONFIDENTIALITY: Preserving authorized restrictions on information access and disclosure, including means for protecting personal privacy and proprietary information. [44 U.S.C., SEC. 3542]

COUNTERMEASURES: Actions, devices, procedures, techniques, or other measures that reduce the vulnerability of an information system. [CNSS Instruction 4009] *Synonymous with security controls and safeguards.*

ENVIRONMENT: Aggregate of external procedures, conditions, and objects affecting the development, operation, and maintenance of an information system. [CNSS Instruction 4009]

EXECUTIVE AGENCY: An executive department specified in 5 U.S.C., SEC. 101; a military department specified in 5 U.S.C., SEC. 102; an independent establishment as defined in 5 U.S.C., SEC. 104(1); and a wholly-owned Government corporation fully subject to the provisions of 31 U.S.C., CHAPTER 91. [41 U.S.C., SEC. 403]

FEDERAL AGENCY: See Agency.

FEDERAL INFORMATION SYSTEM: An information system used or operated by an executive agency, by a contractor of an executive agency, or by another organization on behalf of an executive agency. [40 U.S.C., SEC. 11331]

HIGH-IMPACT SYSTEM: An information system in which at least one security objective (i.e., confidentiality, integrity, or availability) is assigned a FIPS 199 potential impact value of high.

INCIDENT: An occurrence that actually or potentially jeopardizes the confidentiality, integrity, or availability of an information system or the information the system processes, stores, or transmits or that constitutes a violation or imminent threat of violation of security policies, security procedures, or acceptable use policies.

INFORMATION: An instance of an information type. [FIPS Publication 199]

INFORMATION OWNER: Official with statutory or operational authority for specified information and responsibility for establishing the controls for its generation, collection, processing, dissemination, and disposal. [CNSS Instruction 4009]

INFORMATION RESOURCES: Information and related resources, such as personnel, equipment, funds, and information technology. [44 U.S.C., SEC. 3502]

INFORMATION SECURITY: The protection of information and information systems from unauthorized access, use, disclosure, disruption, modification, or destruction in order to provide confidentiality, integrity, and availability. [44 U.S.C., SEC. 3542]

INFORMATION SYSTEM: A discrete set of information resources organized for the collection, processing, maintenance, use, sharing, dissemination, or disposition of information. [44 U.S.C., SEC. 3502]

INFORMATION SYSTEM OWNER: Official responsible for the overall procurement, development, integration, modification, or operation and maintenance of an information system. [CNSS Instruction 4009 Adapted]

INFORMATION TECHNOLOGY: Any equipment or interconnected system or subsystem of equipment that is used in the automatic acquisition, storage, manipulation, management, movement, control, display, switching, interchange, transmission, or reception of data or information by the executive agency. For purposes of the preceding sentence, equipment is used by an executive agency if the equipment is used by the executive agency directly or is used by a contractor under a contract with the executive agency which: (i) requires the use of such equipment; or (ii) requires the use, to a significant extent, of such equipment in the performance of a service or the furnishing of a product. The term information technology includes computers, ancillary equipment, software, firmware and similar procedures, services (including support services), and related resources. [40 U.S.C., SEC. 1401]

INFORMATION TYPE: A specific category of information (e.g., privacy, medical, proprietary, financial, investigative, contractor sensitive, security management), defined by an organization or, in some instances, by a specific law, Executive Order, directive, policy, or regulation. [FIPS Publication 199]

INTEGRITY: Guarding against improper information modification or destruction, and includes ensuring information non-repudiation and authenticity. [44 U.S.C., SEC. 3542]

LOW-IMPACT SYSTEM: An information system in which all three security objectives (i.e., confidentiality, integrity, and availability) are assigned a FIPS 199 potential impact value of low.

MANAGEMENT CONTROLS: The security controls (i.e., safeguards or countermeasures) for an information system that focus on the management of risk and the management of information system security.

MEDIA: Physical devices or writing surfaces including, but not limited to, magnetic tapes, optical disks, magnetic disks, Large-Scale Integration (LSI) memory chips, printouts (but not including display media) onto which information is recorded, stored, or printed within an information system.

MODERATE-IMPACT SYSTEM: An information system in which at least one security objective (i.e., confidentiality, integrity, or availability) is assigned a FIPS 199 potential impact value of moderate, and no security objective is assigned a FIPS 199 potential impact value of high.

NATIONAL SECURITY INFORMATION: Information that has been determined pursuant to Executive Order 12958 as amended by Executive Order 13292, or any predecessor order, or by the Atomic Energy Act of 1954, as amended, to require protection against unauthorized disclosure and is marked to indicate its classified status.

NATIONAL SECURITY SYSTEM: Any information system (including any telecommunications system) used or operated by an agency or by a contractor of an agency, or other organization on behalf of an agency— (i) the function, operation, or use of which involves intelligence activities; involves cryptologic activities related to national security; involves command and control of military forces; involves equipment that is an integral part of a weapon or weapons system; or is critical to the direct fulfillment of military or intelligence missions (excluding a system that is to be used for routine administrative and business applications, for example, payroll, finance, logistics, and personnel management applications); or (ii) is protected at all times by procedures established for information that have been specifically authorized under criteria established by an Executive Order or an Act of Congress to be kept classified in the interest of national defense or foreign policy. [44 U.S.C., SEC. 3542]

OPERATIONAL CONTROLS: The security controls (i.e., safeguards or countermeasures) for an information system that primarily are implemented and executed by people (as opposed to systems).

ORGANIZATION: A federal agency or, as appropriate, any of its operational elements.

POTENTIAL IMPACT: The loss of confidentiality, integrity, or availability could be expected to have a limited adverse effect, a serious adverse effect, or a severe or catastrophic adverse effect on organizational operations, organizational assets, or individuals. [FIPS Publication 199]

RECORDS: All books, papers, maps, photographs, machine-readable materials, or other documentary materials, regardless of physical form or characteristics, made or received by an agency of the United States Government under Federal law or in connection with the transaction of public business and preserved or appropriate for preservation by that agency or its legitimate successor as evidence of the organization, functions, policies, decisions, procedures, operations or other activities of the Government or because of the informational value of the data in them. [44 U.S.C. SEC. 3301]

RISK: The level of impact on organizational operations (including mission, functions, image, or reputation), organizational assets, or individuals resulting from the operation of an information system given the potential impact of a threat and the likelihood of that threat occurring.

RISK MANAGEMENT: The process of managing risks to organizational operations (including mission, functions, image, or reputation), organizational assets, or individuals resulting from the operation of an information system, and includes: (i) the conduct of a risk assessment; (ii) the implementation of a risk mitigation strategy; and (iii) employment of techniques and procedures for the continuous monitoring of the security state of the information system.

SAFEGUARDS: Protective measures prescribed to meet the security requirements (i.e., confidentiality, integrity, and availability) specified for an information system. Safeguards may include security features, management constraints, personnel security, and security of physical structures, areas, and devices. [CNSS Instruction 4009 Adapted] *Synonymous with security controls and countermeasures.*

SANITIZATION: Process to remove information from media such that information recovery is not possible. It includes removing all labels, markings, and activity logs. [CNSS Instruction 4009 Adapted]

SECURITY CATEGORY: The characterization of information or an information system based on an assessment of the potential impact that a loss of confidentiality, integrity, or availability of such information or information system would have on organizational operations, organizational assets, or individuals. [FIPS Publication 199]

SECURITY CONTROLS: The management, operational, and technical controls (i.e., safeguards or countermeasures) prescribed for an information system to protect the confidentiality, integrity, and availability of the system and its information. [FIPS Publication 199]

SECURITY CONTROL BASELINE: The set of minimum security controls defined for a low-impact, moderate-impact, or high-impact information system.

SECURITY OBJECTIVE: Confidentiality, integrity, or availability. [FIPS Publication 199]

SECURITY PLAN: See System Security Plan.

SECURITY REQUIREMENTS: Requirements levied on an information system that are derived from applicable laws, Executive Orders, directives, policies, standards, instructions, regulations, or procedures, or organizational mission/business case needs to ensure the confidentiality, integrity, and availability of the information being processed, stored, or transmitted.

SENIOR AGENCY INFORMATION SECURITY OFFICER: Official responsible for carrying out the Chief Information Officer responsibilities under FISMA and serving as the Chief Information Officer's primary liaison to the agency's authorizing officials, information system owners, and information system security officers. [44 U.S.C., Sec. 3544]

SYSTEM: See information system.

SYSTEM SECURITY PLAN: Formal document that provides an overview of the security requirements for an information system and describes the security controls in place or planned for meeting those requirements. [NIST Special Publication 800-18, Revision 1]

TECHNICAL CONTROLS: The security controls (i.e., safeguards or countermeasures) for an information system that are primarily implemented and executed by the information system through mechanisms contained in the hardware, software, or firmware components of the system.

THREAT: Any circumstance or event with the potential to adversely impact organizational operations (including mission, functions, image, or reputation), organizational assets, or individuals through an information system via unauthorized access, destruction, disclosure, modification of information, and/or denial of service. Also, the potential for a threat-source to successfully exploit a particular information system vulnerability. [CNSS Instruction 4009 Adapted]

THREAT SOURCE: The intent and method targeted at the intentional exploitation of a vulnerability or a situation and method that may accidentally trigger a vulnerability. *Synonymous with threat agent.*

USER: Individual or (system) process authorized to access an information system. [CNSS Instruction 4009]

VULNERABILITY: Weakness in an information system, system security procedures, internal controls, or implementation that could be exploited or triggered by a threat source. [CNSS Instruction 4009 Adapted]

APPENDIX B   REFERENCES

[1]   Committee for National Security Systems (CNSS) Instruction 4009, *National Information Assurance Glossary*, May 2003.

[2]   E-Government Act of 2002 (Public Law 107-347), December 2002.

[3]   Federal Information Processing Standards Publication 199, *Standards for Security Categorization of Federal Information and Information Systems*, February 2004.

[4]   Federal Information Security Management Act of 2002 (Public Law 107-347, Title III), December 2002.

[5]   Information Technology Management Reform Act of 1996 (Public Law 104-106), August 1996.

[6]   National Institute of Standards and Technology Special Publication 800-18, Revision 1, *Guide for Developing Security Plans for Federal Information Systems*, February 2006.

[7]   National Institute of Standards and Technology Special Publication 800-53, *Recommended Security Controls for Federal Information Systems*, February 2005.

[8]   National Institute of Standards and Technology Special Publication 800-60, *Guide for Mapping Types of Information and Information Systems to Security Categories*, June 2004.

[9]   Office of Management and Budget, Circular A-130, Transmittal Memorandum #4, *Management of Federal Information Resources*, Appendix III, *Security of Federal Automated Information Resources*, November 2000.

APPENDIX C   ACRONYMS

CIO	Chief Information Officer
CNSS	Committee for National Security Systems
FIPS	Federal Information Processing Standards
FISMA	Federal Information Security Management Act
NIST	National Institute of Standards and Technology
OMB	Office of Management and Budget
USC	United States Code